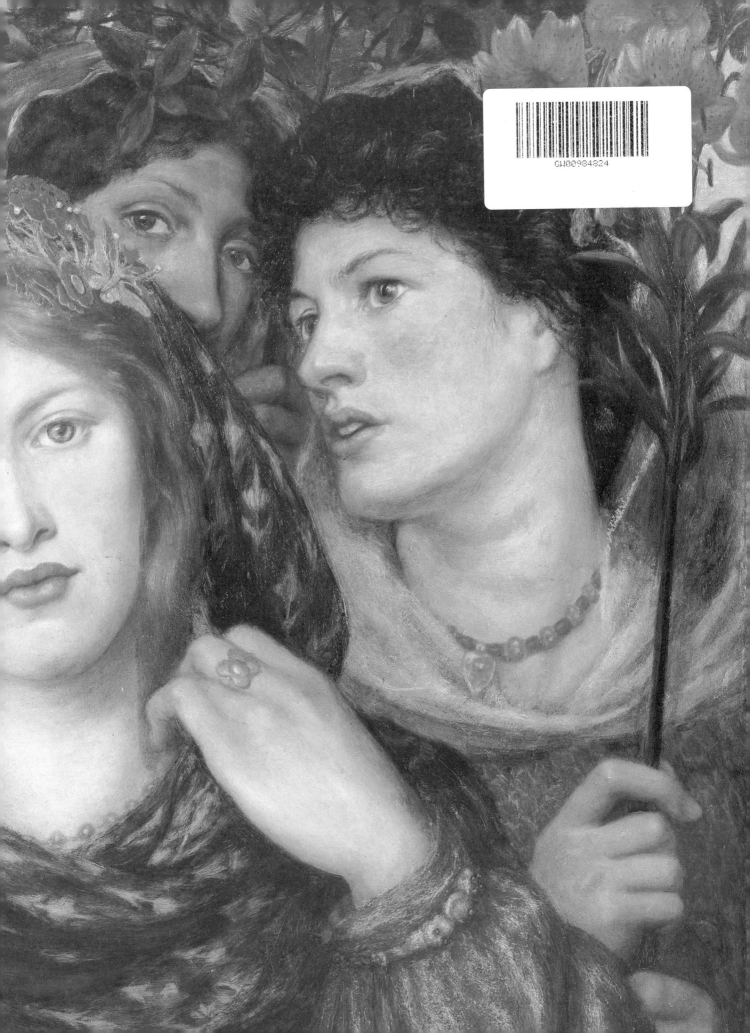

ARTISTS' JEWELLERY

Pre~Raphaelite to Arts and Crafts

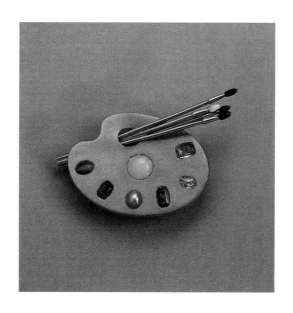

Charlotte Gere and Geoffrey C. Munn

For colour captions see overleaf.

Antique Collectors' Club

ISBN 1 85149 024 8

Published for the Antique Collectors' Club
by the Antique Collectors' Club Ltd.

British Library CIP Data
Gere, Charlotte
Artists' jewellery: from the Pre-
Raphaelites to the Arts & Crafts Movement.
1. British jewellery, 1850-1920
I. Title II. Munn, Geoffrey C.
739.27'0941

Printed in England by
the Antique Collectors' Club Ltd.
Church Street, Woodbridge, Suffolk

Frontispiece, Colour Plate 1. 'Choosing', a portrait of Ellen Terry (1847-1928) by George Frederick Watts, 1864. (The National Portrait Gallery, London.)

As a child bride, Ellen Terry was married to Watts for a brief period, and was divorced by him in 1877. As a famous actress she had wide ranging connections with artists: the ring illustrated in Colour Plate 88 was made for her by John Paul Cooper. Ellen Terry's dress was designed by Holman Hunt and is clearly influenced by Renaissance costume, specifically by the dress worn by Isabella d'Este in the Giulio Romano portrait which hangs at Hampton Court in the Royal Collection. (The same source was used for the dress of the sorceress, Sidonia von Bork, in the painting of 1860 by Burne-Jones.) The artist's granddaughter Angela Thirkell, remembered the dress which still survived during her childhood; she was drawn in pastel wearing the dress by Neville Lytton, c.1905. Another relic of the Pre-Raphaelites to survive is a coral necklace which had adorned the models in paintings by both Burne-Jones and Rossetti and it was given by Angela's sister, Clare, to a niece-in-law as a wedding present (see Angela Thirkell, Portrait of a Lady Novelist, *by Margot Strickland, 1977).*

Title page. A gold brooch (c.1880) in the form of an artist's palette and brushes set with a chrysoberyl cat's eye, a ruby, pearl, sapphire, diamond and an emerald, set centrally with an opal which suggests that the colours represented have been mixed. The brushes which emerge from the palette are tipped with enamel to represent the presence of paint. (Private Collection.)

The Antique Collectors' Club

The Antique Collectors' Club was formed in 1966 and now has a five figure membership spread throughout the world. It publishes the only independently run monthly antiques magazine *Antique Collecting* which caters for those collectors who are interested in widening their knowledge of antiques, both by greater awareness of quality and by discussion of the factors which influence the price that is likely to be asked. The Antique Collectors' Club pioneered the provision of information on prices for collectors and the magazine still leads in the provision of detailed articles on a variety of subjects.

It was in response to the enormous demand for information on "what to pay" that the price guide series was introduced in 1968 with the first edition of *The Price Guide to Antique Furniture* (completely revised, 1978), a book which broke new ground by illustrating the more common types of antique furniture, the sort that collectors could buy in shops and at auctions rather than the rare museum pieces which had previously been used (and still to a large extent are used) to make up the limited amount of illustrations in books published by commercial publishers. Many other price guides have followed, all copiously illustrated, and greatly appreciated by collectors for the valuable information they contain, quite apart from prices. The Antique Collectors' Club also publishes other books on antiques, including horology and art reference works, and a full book list is available.

Club membership, which is open to all collectors, costs £15.95 per annum. Members receive free of charge *Antique Collecting,* the Club's magazine (published every month except August), which contains well-illustrated articles dealing with the practical aspects of collecting not normally dealt with by magazines. Prices, features of value, investment potential, fakes and forgeries are all given prominence in the magazine.

Among other facilities available to members are private buying and selling facilities, the longest list of "For Sales" of any antiques magazine, an annual ceramics conference and the opportunity to meet other collectors at their local antique collectors' clubs. There are over eighty in Britain and more than a dozen overseas. Members may also buy the Club's publications at special pre-publication prices.

As its motto implies, the Club is an amateur organisation designed to help collectors get the most out of their hobby: it is informal and friendly and gives enormous enjoyment to all concerned.

For Collectors — By Collectors — About Collecting

The Antique Collectors' Club, 5 Church Street, Woodbridge, Suffolk

Contents

Foreword

I have been familiar, since early childhood, with the kind of jewellery so well described and illustrated in this splendid book. I am no scholar and must confess that I deeply regret that I did not appreciate the jewellery of this period in my youth, but I find it quite fascinating now.

Although I was born at 18 Melbury Road in the bed in which my grandfather Holman Hunt had died a few years before, I left the house soon after to be brought up by my mother's parents, the Freemans, in Sussex. I have no recollections of my Hunt grandmother, whom I called 'Grand', before the end of the First World War when I was sent to spend the day with her by my maternal grandparents from their London house. She seemed incredibly old and was in fact seventy-two. She was unrecognisable from the portrait commissioned by my great-grandfather George Waugh on her twenty-first birthday, wearing the jewels she had been given. When the picture was exhibited at the Royal Academy in 1873, the critic Tom Taylor condemned the model as 'repulsively ugly'. She and her elder sister Fanny, Hunt's first wife, were quite unlike the sensational 'stunners' made so popular by Rossetti such as May Morris and Annie Miller.

I think it was greatly to her credit that in order to amuse a four year old she had already created my 'museum'. I much approve of this idea and have encouraged my children and grandchildren to create their own museums and scrap-books. I had to sit on her knee in order to examine the contents of a brass-bound, glass cabinet. Some of the objects were rather creepy, but I particularly liked the bunch of spillikins and an exquisitely carved Chinese ivory puzzle. I also remember a silver Indian hobble ring, tasselled strings of coloured beads, some scarabs and the tiny Syrian anklets, dangling with silver bells, and various coloured glass bracelets from Damascus, all worn by my Hunt aunt as a child in *The Triumph of the Innocents.* In fact there were lots of odds and ends of what is now fashionable ethnic jewellery.

I did not actually stay with Grand until I was seven when my artistic education began in earnest. I hated trudging round the V & A and National Gallery and much resented the stares provoked by our eccentric appearance. Until I grew too tall, I was dressed in musty garments from the studio prop-box and Grand looked really weird. However, on Sunday mornings when we went to St. Paul's, and on Sunday afternoons when we were 'at home' from five o'clock to many friends, she looked more presentable, usually wearing a Paisley shawl over a long black dress with at her waist, a large, ornamental buckle. She might wear a diamond dove at her throat, or some other brooch in the form of a winged heart or garland. She usually wore long earrings set with small dark stones and she always wore unusual bracelets — mostly Italian — and exotic rings.

When we went to tea at Kensington Palace with Princess Louise, Grand carried her best black velvet reticule with a jewelled, silver clasp and wore a silk dress and lots of unusual jewellery. The Princess too was very keen on such things being, as Grand said, 'extremely artistic'. On such occasions Grand would attach strange ornaments to the ends of braids which looked like embroidered or tapestry bell-pulls about five inches wide, which reached below her knees. These objects were quite heavy metal and as we walked all the way to the Palace, they swung to and fro and had she not worn many petticoats would have bruised her shins. I much enjoyed visits to the Royal convenience where the paper was Bromo rather than the assorted rough stuff I was obliged to cut to a template 'keeping the print on one side' and thread on to a string to hang on a nail in our own spartan lavabo.

We always retired early, especially in winter, as downstairs the house was freezing. As a great treat, sometimes I would lead the way with a candle and the elderly general servant would stagger up the dark stairs to Grand's bedroom with our supper on a tray.

I slept beside her bed on an extremely uncomfortable chesterfield with no sheets, covered by scratchy rugs from the Middle East. We would light the gas and the coal fire, which was rather exciting and, once the room was warm and full of shadows, we undressed and put on our night clothes. At last Grand would unlock the bureau which held her collection of jewellery. I would perch on a stool in front of a long cheval-glass and try on the treasures which emerged from many small drawers and pigeon-holes. Some things were nestling in satin-lined funny-shaped leather boxes. The necklaces, glittering with coloured stones and pearls set in enamel and gold, and various brooches and pendants looked to me like curios fit only for museums, or to be worn at fancy dress parties and charades. The ornaments with the most sparkling stones were kept under a slide in the well of the desk, including a beautiful diamond and turquoise necklace. Grand told me she would give it to my half-uncle Cyril when he next came on leave because it had been given by Hunt to Fanny his mother; it was entailed on me but he sold it when he was broke. There was a marvellous gold collar hung with cornelian intaglios. This is one of the many pieces that I wish I had today. In the first long drawer there were extraordinary head-dresses, Spanish tortoiseshell combs and many elaborate hair ornaments. I remember one in particular. It was a large spray of feathers, made of thousands of seed pearls on to a carved frame of mother-of-pearl; graduated larger pearls forming the quills. It was impossible to fix these strange things in my curls and my reflection in the mirror was hilarious. These head-dresses were quite unlike the diamond tiara which my other grandmother's maid told me ladies wore at dinner parties in London. I liked Grand's rings although they were far too large when she slipped them on to my childish fingers until my hands were heavy with diamonds, rubies, emeralds and turquoise; there was one of solid jade.

The next long drawer of the bureau held a jumble of oriental gewgaws, elaborate buckles, clasps and belts jangling with Arabian coins, including the one worn in *The Afterglow*. Rummaging among these made by hands black. There were some huge sham pearls which I think the American girl wore as *Bianca, the Patroness of Heavenly Harmony*. All the Waughs, including Grand of course, were much alarmed by this picture painted after Fanny died in Italy.

I also remember tins full of opals and moonstones which my half-uncle Cyril had brought from Ceylon. Some of these Grand gave to me: I had no idea if they were worth a hundred pounds each or a penny. She also gave me a rope of amber and some corals which I wore in my teens. There was a large filigree silver arrow, about eight inches long, set with pale green stones. Grand said that her beloved Holman had designed it because he had chosen as his motto: 'From Truth Unswerving'. Even one of his paintings took years to paint so of course he hadn't had nearly as much time as other artists to design jewellery. The breastplate worn by Christ for *The Light of the World* was very similar to an illustration in the family Bible and I'm sure Hunt must have deisgned and had it made by a jeweller. He was so meticulous, taking immense pains over the design of the elaborate brass lantern, made by the Chelsea ironmonger Mr Hacking, and even embroidering the dress Lizzie Siddall wore for the picture I called *Valentine and Silvia*.

On my seventh birthday, Grand presented me with my silver prayer-book which she had designed and had, she said, actually made herself. It is repoussé work, inset with gems and depicts two peacocks drinking from a fountain, with crescent moons and a sprig of daphne symbolising my Christian names. Double consonants to follow H-H being thought essential, the first choice had been Victoria Violet, the second Iris Irene. I feel happier as Diana Daphne.

I gave the amber necklace to my godmother Enid Morse, because she dressed in what I considered arty-crafty fashion. She was a painter and the daughter of Sidney Morse who had a marvellous collection of antique silver, and paintings by Blake which were bought eventually by Sir Colin Anderson. When I visited Enid, she would open the spinet, the interior of which had been converted into a chest of drawers. It was full of Henry Wilson jewellery, mostly in silver set with semi-precious stones. Wilson, known as Peter to intimates, was her uncle. I dared not confess that I could not imagine ever wearing any of his work. In 1946 I remarried at Holy Trinity, Sloane Street, *the* Arts and Crafts church, well appreciated by John Betjeman. Henry Wilson had designed the reredos and many other features there. No one who came to the wedding had ever heard of him, so I kept quiet.

I admired only my fashionable Freeman aunt's jewellery, especially a Cartier bracelet and ring with diamonds and onyx set in platinum, and of course strings of graduated pearls. In my teens I had quite a lot of jewellery given me by various family friends which I never wore and I would not have been seen dead wearing any of the things in Grand's bureau. I was thrilled with a rolled gold bangle given me by my other grandmother's servants for Christmas. I even wore it at school, and in bed, until it had to be cut off my arm. When I first married, still in my teens, I strove to follow the fashion.

A rather strange lady called Estella Canziani, a friend of Grand's, once gave me a peculiar, unwearable, gold necklace. I was hard up as a young bride and exchanged it with a West End jeweller for a pair of oval Georgian silver-plated entrée dishes which I thought essential for my first dinner party. What a Philistine I was!

Mrs Minshall, who lived at Tower House in Melbury Road, was a friend of my Freeman grandmother's. At the age of five I signed the visitors' book which is owned by her descendants. I was often invited to this strange house but Grand would leave me at the door. They disliked each other as rival eccentrics perhaps. Mrs Minshall always wore fancy dress and weird jewellery maybe designed by Burges, like the amazing house and furniture. One day I hope his dog-collar and other canine jewellery will turn up.

I'm afraid Grand always despaired of my taste, just as she had when I was six and she asked which was my favourite colour and I answered 'pink'. Soon after when asked which I preferred, St. Paul's or the Albert Memorial, I tried to explain that I found it impossible to appreciate buildings, large pictures, Persian rugs and furniture and could only enjoy small objects such as shells, birds' eggs and of course butterflies and flowers. Maybe most children's judgement is thus restricted.

Since my twenties, I have not entirely disregarded ephemeral fashion but still have a horror of being stared at for looking conspicuous or peculiar. My taste and style, not only in dress and jewellery but in my surroundings, have evolved over the years to become much more eclectic. I'm sure this book and exhibition will inspire collectors. Also I hope a great many women of all ages who in the past have rejected such ornaments as outré or old-fashioned, will long to possess and actually wear them and look quite stunning in consequence.

by Diana Holman Hunt

Acknowledgements

The subject of this book has preoccupied the authors for many years. Numbers of people have helped to fill out the dimly discerned pattern of inspiration and patronage behind the distinctive 'artistic' taste that emerged in parallel with fashionable Victorian jewellery in the second half of the nineteenth century. The information which led to discoveries of authorship or surviving pieces emerged piecemeal, often as an unexpected bonus in some related line of enquiry. As the shape of the subject became clearer we made a deliberate search for lost jewels, and the discoveries that resulted were due to energetic assistance from present owners, their families and friends.

We are grateful to Her Majesty the Queen for graciously allowing the reproduction of the paintings in Colour Plates 31, 33 and 44.

To Her Majesty Queen Elizabeth the Queen Mother, we are indebted for gracious permission to reproduce the jewel casket in plate 113.

Their Graces the Duke and Duchess of Devonshire have generously allowed the reproduction of the Devonshire parure in Colour Plate 45. We are grateful to the Duke and Duchess of Marlborough for permission to illustrate the Giuliano pendant in plate 37. The Marquis and Marchioness of Bute have generously consented to the reproduction of the famous marriage jewel designed by William Burges in plate 52.

We are especially fortunate that Miss Diana Holman Hunt has agreed to write the foreword to our book. Memories of the Pre-Raphaelite world which still survived in her youth and enthusiasm for the artistic make this a truly fascinating and valuable piece.

We would like to thank the following people for their special help during the research for this book and particularly for their unfailing generosity in sharing hard-won knowledge: Lady Abdy; Sir Alastair Aird K.C.V.O., Comptroller to H.M. Queen Elizabeth the Queen Mother; Mr. George Allison, Sacrist, Norwich Cathedral; Mr. Victor Arwas; Mrs. Julia Atkins; Mr. Keith Baker of Phillips, Son and Neal, Art Nouveau Department; Miss Vivienne Becker; Mr. Victor Bond of Ashton School, Cork; Mr. Charles Bone, President of the Royal Society of Painters in Watercolours; Mrs. M.G. Booth and Mrs. F. Lawton, who are nieces of Arthur Giuliano; Dr. Judith Bronkhurst; Mrs. Marilyn Bronkhurst; Professor Van Akin Bird; Mrs. Shirley Bury; Miss Annette Carruthers of Cheltenham Art Gallery and Museums; Dr. Chapman of the Society of Antiquaries; Mr. John Cherry of the Department of Medieval and Later Antiquities at the British Museum; Mr. and Mrs. Peter Child; Mr. John Christian; Mr. Malcolm Cole and Mr. Roy Knight of Whitelands College; Miss Philippa Cooke; the late Lady Diana Cooper and Miss Artemis Cooper; Mr. Simon Cottle of the Glasgow Museums and Art Gallery; Mrs. Crick; Mr. John Culme of Sotheby's; Sir Geoffrey de Bellaigue, K.C.V.O., F.S.A., Surveyor of Her Majesty the Queen's Works of Art; Mr. J.S. Dearden, Curator of the Ruskin Galleries; Susan, the late Viscountess de Vesci, and the Viscount and Viscountess de Vesci; Mrs. Jocelyn Diethelm; Miss Frances Dimond, M.V.O., Curator of the Photographic Archives and Royal Archives, Windsor Castle; Mr. A.R. Dufty of The Society of Antiquaries, Kelmscott Manor; Mr. Richard Edgcumbe of the Metalwork Department, Victoria and Albert Museum; Miss Mary Feilden of Christie's Antique Jewellery Department; Miss Mary Fitzgerald and Seamus O'Coigligh of Cork Public Museum; Mrs Margaret Flower; Mr. John Gere; Mr. and Mrs. Stanley Goldfein; Mr. Bruce Hanson of the Brantwood Trust; Dr. Roger Harding of the Geological Museum; Mr. David Hopkinson of the *Mid Derbyshire Times*; Sir Hugo Huntington-Whiteley, Bt., D.L., and Mr. J.M. Huntington-Whiteley; Miss Alison Inglis; Mr. Alan Irvine, R.D.I., A.R.I.B.A., des R.C.A.; Mrs. Dora Jane Janson; Mr. John Jesse and Miss Irina Laski; Mr. William Joll of Agnew and Son; Miss C. Sylvia Ker; the Rev. Malcolm King of All Saints Vicarage, Croxley Green; Mr. and Mrs.

Lawrence; Miss I.M. Lilley; Mr. W.F. Little, the grandson of Federico Giuliano; Miss Mary Lutyens; Mrs. McInnes; Mr. Jeremy Maas and his son Rupert; Dr. Cyndy Manton; Mr. Peter Miall of the National Trust; Sir Ralph Millais; Mrs. Diana Millar; Mrs Caroline Munn; the late Mr. Hans Nadelhoffer; the Lord Neidpath; Mrs. Neill; Mr. and Mrs. Christopher Newall; Mrs. Ralph Oliphant and the late Mrs. Anne Yorke, great granddaughters of Sir Edward Burne-Jones; Mr. Richard Ormond and Mr. David Cordingly of the National Maritime Museum; The Venerable Derek Palmer, The Archdeacon of Rochester; Dr. Nicholas Penny of the Ashmolean Museum, Oxford; Miss Julia Poole and Mr. Robin Chrighton of the Fitzwilliam Museum, Cambridge; Miss Jane Preger and Mr. Ian Shaw of the Royal Institute of British Architects; Miss Prendergast of the National Portrait Gallery; Miss Penelope Proddow; Mrs. Pyne; Miss Rosemary Ransome-Wallis, Curator, Worshipful Company of Goldsmiths; Miss Christine Rew, Keeper of Applied Art at Aberdeen Art Gallery and Museums; the Rt. Hon. Nicholas Ridley, M.P.; Mr. Erminio Rizzoli; The Hon. Mrs. Jane Roberts, Curator of the Print Room at Windsor Castle; Mrs. Althea Robson; Miss Andrea Rose; Miss Judith Rudoe of the Department of Medieval and Later Antiquities at the British Museum; Mrs. Pauline Sargent; Miss Gertrud Seidmann; Mr. Peyton Skipwith of the Fine Art Society; The Hon. Georgina Stonor; Mr. S. Storer; Mrs. Virginia Surtees; Mr. Anthony Symondson; Mr. Hugh Tait of the Department of Medieval and Later Antiquities at the British Museum; Mr. William Tallon, R.V.M., Steward to H.M. Queen Elizabeth the Queen Mother; Miss Tetley-Rowe; Mrs. Elizabeth Tompkin; The Hon. Mrs. Richard Vane; Mr. and Mrs. Van Enter; Miss Rosemary Watt of the Burrell Collection, formerly of the Glasgow Museums and Art Gallery; Mrs. M.A. Weare, Custodian-in-Charge, Ellen Terry Museum; Miss Glennys Wild of the Birmingham City Museum and Art Gallery.

Miss Susan Hare and Mr. David Beasley of the Goldsmiths' Hall Library have been generous with their valuable time and knowledge over many years. Mrs. Diana Scarisbrick has been typically generous with her knowledge and time, with particular reference to those jewels designed by Charles Ricketts.

At Wartski, Mrs. June Trager, Mr. Stephen Dale and Mr. Robert Parsons have always offered their fullest support and encouragement during the preparation of this book. Miss Katherine Purcell has offered daily help with our project and has made the final manuscript fit to go to press. Mr. Kenneth Snowman's intimate knowledge of the jeweller's art has consistently been at our disposal and he has generously hosted an exhibition at Wartski to coincide with the publication of this book.

Our publishers the Antique Collectors' Club have been especially tolerant of the authors' foibles and alterations to the original text. Mrs. Jill Champion, as editor, has overseen the production of the book from beginning to end and her contributions have been invaluable.

Note: Unless otherwise stated all objects are made of gold and are illustrated actual size.

Overleaf: Colour Plate 2. A group of gem-set and enamelled gold jewellery by Carlo Giuliano (1831-1895) and his two sons Carlo and Arthur who ran the business from 1895 until 1914. Giuliano's shop at 115 Piccadilly was a favourite resort of the Pre-Raphaelites and their circle. (Wartski and Private Collections.)

CHAPTER I
Art and Fashion

During the second half of the nineteenth century a great creative energy was focused on the decorative and applied arts, giving birth to art movements in which, for the first time since the Renaissance, quite minor crafts such as metalwork and pottery became the most important vehicle for the artistic intentions of some of the major figures involved. The work of the jeweller/designer René Lalique is regarded as more important in the context of the Art Nouveau movement in France than the paintings of, say, Alphonse Mucha, who though he had been trained as a history painter in the traditional 'Salon' taste of the period, found his most effective style in decorative art. A number of painters, sculptors and architects who would formerly have felt no wish to be involved in the conventional world of decorative design, dominated as it was by the debilitating reliance on historical revivals for inspiration, turned their attention to the design of jewellery, silverwork, furniture, glasswork and pottery, with the most beneficial results.

The number of artists who turned to designing jewellery and metalwork was greater than in any other field, and was almost equalled by the number of trained jewellers whose work in this period was original enough to give them the same status as that enjoyed by a successfully exhibiting painter or sculptor. This had not been true of more than a handful of jewellers before the 1850s and 1860s — Froment-Meurice had an enormous reputation amongst his contemporaries and was known as 'the Cellini of the nineteenth century', and the Castellani family were highly regarded as technical experts and innovators, but they were famous as jewellers, not artists — and it was only in the later atmosphere, where jewellery came to be seen as a fine art, largely unconnected with fashions in dress, that the most outstandingly original work was done.

The long list of European artists and architects who made metalwork and jewellery designs includes such well known names as D.G. Rossetti, William Burges, Alfred Gilbert, Edward Burne-Jones, Charles Ricketts, C.R. Mackintosh and Henry Wilson in Britain; Philippe Wolfers (who trained as a sculptor) and Henri van de Velde in Belgium; Hector Guimard, Alphonse Mucha, Eugène Grasset and Georges de Feure (the last two were both important Symbolist painters) in France; Josef Hoffmann, Koloman Moser and Otto Czeschka in Austria; Mogens Ballin and Thorvald Bindesbøll in Scandinavia; W.L. von Cranach in Germany; and, in the United States, L.C. Tiffany. Among those who were either trained as jewellers, or who had a more general artistic training but were primarily known for their work as jewellers, and who can claim the right to be judged by the same standards as the artists listed above, were the Frenchmen Lalique, Lucien Gaillard, Henri Vever, Georges Fouquet and his son Jean, Eugène Feuillâtre, Edward Colonna, Charles Boutet de Monvel, Raymond Templier and Jean Després in France; the British designers C.R. Ashbee, Nelson and Edith Dawson, Alexander Fisher, Archibald Knox, John Paul Cooper, Mr. and Mrs. Arthur Gaskin, H.G. Murphy, Edward Spencer, Edgar Simpson and Harold Stabler; Georg Jensen in Denmark; and Peter Carl and Agathon Fabergé in Russia. All these

people attained high artistic status during their lifetimes with their work widely exhibited and reproduced in the growing number of periodicals devoted to the decorative arts. These designers fall into national groups from the point of view of style, the Frenchmen for the most part working in a flowing and sinuous Art Nouveau style, the Germans and Austrians in a more linear and geometric style; of the two major Belgian designers, the work of Wolfers is more French in taste, while that of van de Velde is more Germanic (much of the German work at the turn of the century was in any case inspired by van de Velde, who spent a considerable period of his working life in Berlin); with the exception of Gilbert and Ricketts, most of the later English designers tended to work in the Craft Revival style inspired by the teachings of John Ruskin and William Morris. The Glasgow School designers led by C.R. Mackintosh were a law unto themselves; their metalwork designs, which were influential out of all

Colour Plate 4.
A chrysanthemum brooch in gold platinum set with brilliant diamonds and Mississippi pearls, by Tiffany, New York, c.1905. A hemisphere of white enamel conceals the pins which secure the pearls to the flower head. (Wartski, London.)

proportion to their small number, are closest in conception to the ideas of the Javanese-born Dutch artist Jan Toorop, who stands out as an exotic figure amongst the mainly rather severe and restrained Dutch Nieuwe Kunst artists.

The result of this artistic focus on the decorative arts was the emergence of a recognisable 'artistic' style, which for the first time in the history of fashion made a mark on the clothes and decorative surroundings of a section of high society outside the tightly knit clique of artists centred on the 'aesthetes', as they came to be called. The 'aesthetic' style was adopted by many people who were attracted to the work of these painters and designers, and who sought to achieve for themselves an ambience similar to that created from the often random accumulations of art objects and curiosities.

The 'Bohemians' in Paris in the 1830s had established a stereotype of artistic costume, velvet jacket over a full soft shirt with a large collar embellished by

Plate 1. A gold brooch in the form of stylised wistaria set with Mississippi pearls, by Henri Vever, Paris, c.1900. (Hessisches Landsmuseum, Darmstadt.) It is interesting to compare the use of American freshwater pearls in this brooch with the Tiffany chrysanthemum in Colour Plate 4.

Plate 2. A gold painted plaster maquette for a pendant by Sir Alfred Gilbert, R.A. (1854-1934). By integrating the sinuous female form with the design of the pendant, Gilbert displays unequivocally the sculptor's mastery of this type of figural jewellery design. The model was found among the contents of Gilbert's studio when he died. The maquette was presented to Birmingham City Art Gallery but is now lost, and is presumed destroyed.

a large black silk bow tie. Variations on this theme marked artistic male fashion throughout the nineteenth century. The complementary female version had two principal sources, medieval costume and classical draperies; interpretations of these styles were often the subject of derision and must have had a very variable rate of success, attracting a good deal of mockery, notably from *Punch* through the drawings by George du Maurier (see plate 28). Cult fashion seems to thrive on mockery, however, and the aesthetic movement gathered strength and more and more adherents as the century progressed.

The proliferation of periodicals partly or entirely devoted to decorative work is an indication of the importance of this branch of artistic activity at the turn of the century. Their influence, particularly in a vast country like America where in many remote places no other contact with modern decorative art theory and practice was available, was considerable, and there is evidence that the illustrations were used as source material by manufacturers, in the same way as the engraved patterns designed for the use of jewellers, which were widely circulated during the seventeenth and eighteenth centuries, had been used earlier. In England the *Journal of Design* and the *Art Journal* had been in existence since the late 1840s; in 1884 A.H. Mackmurdo and Selwyn Image produced the first issue of *The Hobby Horse,* the magazine of the Century Guild which had been founded by them two years earlier. In the same year the *Revue de l'Art Décoratif* first appeared in Paris. In 1893 *The Studio* started publication; it is still issued and with the special numbers and the annual *Year Book of Decorative Design,* the back numbers remain one of the most valuable sources of information on the subject of decorative art for the whole period from the end of the nineteenth century to the present day. Two years later followed Julius Meier-Graefe's magazine, *Pan.* The next few years saw the first appearance of *Jugend* in Munich (1896), *Art et Décoration* in Paris (1897), three more magazines in Germany, *Kunst und Dekoration, Kunt und Kunsthandwerk* (1898) and *Dekorative Kunst* (1897), and yet another in Paris, *L'Art Décoratif* (1897). In 1899 the first volume of Julius Hoffmann's photographic record of contemporary decorative work, *Der Moderne Stil,* was published in Stuttgart. By the turn of the century the apparatus existed throughout Europe for reporting activity on the artistic front in the most minute detail. In America there were a similar number of art magazines including *The Knight Errant,* which was rather like the Century Guild's *Hobby Horse; The Studio,* which had been in existence since about 1880, long before the magazine of the same name appeared in England; *Modern Art; The Art Student,* which contained straightforward instruction in techniques; *Arts and Crafts,* which was published by the Art Workers' Guild of Philadelphia; and *The Craftsman,* which was edited by Gustav Stickley, a friend and admirer of Morris. In 1898 *Mir Isskusstva* (or *The World of Art*) was produced by Diaghilev, who spared no efforts, through this magazine and through special exhibitions, to introduce the European public to contemporary Russian art. A number of specialist magazines, like *Le Japon Artistique,* published monthly by Siegfried Bing (proprietor of the Galeries de l'Art Nouveau), or *La Plante et ses applications*

Plate 3. A necklace of twisted silver wire set with a cabochon amethyst by Sir Alfred Gilbert, R.A. (Private Collection.)

Alfred Gilbert is arguably one of the most gifted sculptors of the nineteenth and early twentieth centuries. His interest in metalwork went beyond the confines of traditional sculpture and its conventional materials. His most famous work, Eros in Piccadilly Circus, London, is made of aluminium and the silver gilt epergne, presented to Queen Victoria as a Jubilee gift from the officers of the Army (1887-90), is decorated with bronze, ivory, wire, and crystal. He was also a prolific designer of jewellery, some pieces of which are in the tradition of the Renaissance whilst others are extremely individual (see plates 2 and 4). This particular example was made by Gilbert for his niece Dorothy Quirk who was staying with Gilbert at Maida Vale, c.1897, when she and her cousin Mary, Gilbert's elder daughter, were going to a ball. In a few minutes the artist had twisted some wire into two necklaces, one set with an amethyst shown here, the other with a pearl.

ornementales, designed by Grasset, which also appeared monthly, and even more important, the trade magazines like *Die Perle* and *The Watchmaker and Jeweller*, were simply milked wholesale for usable designs by the large scale commercial and mass-production jewellers, whose number was by this period very considerable, and who were turning out quantities of fashionable trinkets in the latest style.

This predominant interest in decorative art was sustained throughout the closing years of the nineteenth century and well into the twentieth, only diminishing after the outbreak of the First World War. The early volumes of *The Studio* devote almost as much space to reports of either the Arts and Crafts

Colour Plate 5. A French Art Nouveau carved and tinted horn comb in the form of cherry blossoms and buds, the stamens decorated with black enamel and set with rose diamonds; probably by Gaillard. This jewel seems likely to have been made for export, since it is unsigned and is contained within another retailer's box. (Wartski, London.)

Colour Plate 6. A gold and silver necklace designed by Edward Spencer and John Bonner and made by the Artificers Guild. Known as the 'Ariadne' necklace, it takes the form of a succession of sailing galleys linked by silver and diamond leaves of ivy, fig and ilex, the clasp decorated with waves and flanked by reliefs of archaic cities, the centre with a diamond crown in a seven pointed star among collet set stones. The pendant represents Ariadne embowered in vines in a sea of blue enamel. The lid satin of its original fitted case reads: 'Montague Fordham Ltd., 9 Maddox St. London W.' (Birmingham City Museum and Art Gallery.)

Presidential badge.

Plate 4. Presidential badge and chain (see right) for the Royal Institute of Painters in Watercolours, of silver gilt, pearls, rock-crystal and other gemstones, made by Sir Alfred Gilbert, R.A. The pendant was made between 1891 and 1897 as a gift to the Institute after Gilbert's election to their membership. A figure symbolising 'Watercolour' stands on a nautilus shell and holds up a hand glass (the mirror of nature) and a pearl (the pearl of art); the design culminates in the crown of 'art achieved'. Gilbert believed that to embellish a design was to improve it; in this piece he has played with the symbolic elements until the sculptural quality has been lost in a thicket of wrought and twisted wirework, a foretaste of the way in which the jewellery was to develop in the later years.

When the badge was finally handed over to the Institute, it was submitted to the Queen for her approval and the President, Sir James D. Linton, received the following reply: 'Sir, The Lord Chamberlain has received the Queen's command to inform you that Her Majesty has been graciously pleased to permit that you and the future Presidents of the Royal Institute of Painters in Watercolours shall wear the Collar and Badge which have been submitted to her, and which are being herewith returned to you when attending Her Majesty's Levées, and on such other occasions as may be considered fitting. I am, Sir, your obedient servant S. Ponsonby Fane.'

Society exhibitions or the decorative work at the Salons in Paris as they do to painting. As early as 1902, however, an article appeared in the *Art Journal* taking a deeply critical view of the technical ability (or lack of it) displayed by the jewellery exhibits, many by students or semi-amateurs, which were shown at the Glasgow Exhibition in that year. In view of the fact that jewellery of this type had only been widely available since the first Arts and Crafts Exhibition Society show in 1886, it can be seen that its initial impact had worn off remarkably quickly. The critical tone of this review, and of others that followed it, seem to have done little to discourage the large output of craft jewellery or to improve the technical standards, which remained far below those maintained by most commercial firms. Thorstein Veblen had already remarked in 1899, in *The Theory of the Leisure Class:* '... the generic feature of the physiognomy of machine-made goods as compared with the hand-wrought article is their greater perfection in workmanship in greater accuracy in the detail execution of the design. Hence it comes about that the visible imperfections of the hand-wrought goods, being honorific, are accounted marks of superiority in point of beauty, or serviceability, or both. Hence has arisen that exaltation of the defective, of which John Ruskin and William Morris were such eager spokesmen in their time; and on this ground their propaganda of crudity and wasted effort has been taken up and carried forward since their time.'

After the turn of the century Arts and Crafts exhibitions were held all over the country; some of them were set up ostensibly to provide a showcase for local artists and students, but they often opened their doors to any craft worker who cared to exhibit his (or her) work. Craft workers who earned their entire living by the practice of their craft were forced to avail themselves of this kind of opportunity for exhibiting and selling their work, because the large shows mounted by the Arts and Crafts Society only took place at three-yearly intervals, and with few exceptions Guilds and individual craftsmen were in no

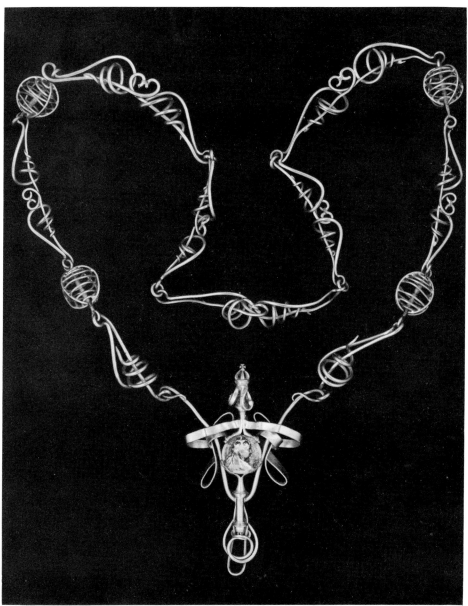

Presidential chain

position financially to maintain showrooms. Exhibitions were also held under the auspices of so-called 'guilds', like the Clarion Guild, which was financed by the newspaper of that name, or the regional ones whose members did not apparently have to undertake to work solely for their guild (which is after all an essential requirement of real guild membership, as proposed by Ruskin in the rules set out for his St. George's Guild). This wide exposure through exhibitions of work which was often essentially trivial in conception and inept in execution, and though perfectly acceptable as the stock of an unpretentious shop, could not measure up to the standards required of an 'exhibit', was bound to attract increasingly critical comment. The same was true of the widely exposed French and Belgian work which, while being more spectacular in conception and usually more technically competent in execution, suffered from stereotyping of designs almost as much as the English craft jewellery, with the added disadvantage that much of the work was virtually unwearable or (in

Colour Plate 7. A tiara of elderberries in purple tinted horn and moonstones, by Frederick James Partridge (1877-1942), contained within its original silk covered case decorated with lilies of the valley. (Private Collection.)

Made for Liberty & Co., this is a naturalistic jewel in materials and techniques more often associated with Parisian jewellers at the turn of the century.

Colour Plate 9. Left: a gold ring as a memorial to Sir Edwin Landseer (1802-1873) decorated with gold letters reading 'LANDSEER' against a dark blue champlevé enamel ground. The ring has the makers' mark of William and Sampson George, goldworkers of 50 King Square, Goswell Road and an 18ct. gold quality mark. It presumably dates from just after 1873. (The Royal Academy of Arts.)

This jewel, once in the possession of the artist, W.P. Frith, was presented to the Academy by Mrs Walter Frith in 1942. Frith's daughter, who later became Mrs Panton, met Landseer when she was about nine years old. 'I was enraptured. He was small and compact and wore a beautiful shirt with a frill in which was placed a glittering diamond brooch or pin. I know not which. . .He was curled and scented and exquisitely turned out. . .' (Mrs Panton, Leaves from a Life, *1908, pp.93-94). (See also* The Victorian Art World in Photographs *by Jeremy Maas, 1984).*

Right: a twisted gilt wirework ring by Sir Alfred Gilbert (1854-1934). (The Royal Academy of Arts.)

Gilbert's extraordinarily free and abstract jewels in this manner are quite unique and seem to belong more to the craft tradition of the late twentieth century.

Colour Plate 8. A gold mounted necklace/tiara set with diamonds in the form of cyclamen flowers and leaves, by Carl Fabergé (1846-1920). (Wartski, London.)
    A sophisticated and traditional interpretation of the organic themes associated with Art Nouveau.

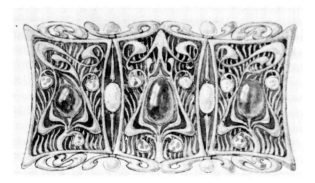

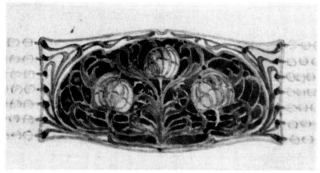

Plate 5. Drawings by Edward Colonna (b.1862), for Maison de l'Art Nouveau. These are plaques des colliers which were to be made of enamelled gold, precious stones and pearls and are elegant interpretations of Art Nouveau themes.

the case of the silver and other metalwork) unusable. The stock displayed by Bing at his Galeries de l'Art Nouveau was offered as an 'exhibition' though by no means all the things he showed were unique items.

A great deal of prominence was given both at L'Art Nouveau and at Julius Meier-Graefe's Maison Moderne to the names of individual designers, with the result that a large number of small and relatively insignificant pieces of commercial 'Art Nouveau' jewellery can be confidently attributed to designers about whom virtually nothing is known except their names and the fact that they were employed by Bing or Meier-Graefe, or one of the commerical firms like Arnould or Murrle, Bennett who also named their designers. Until recently so little was known about Colonna who was one of Bing's star designers that even his correct Christian name was a matter for dispute. Research on the part of Martin Eidelberg unearthed his correct name and his birthplace, and a number of facts about his career. This may not be possible with more than a handful of the known names of turn-of-the-century designers, nor would it always be worth doing. The case of Colonna was a different matter as he was a fine artist who had a wide influence on styles in furniture and jewellery both in France and in the United States where he lived.

A number of English and American commercial firms also made a practice of naming their designers; William Hutton employed Kate Harris, and Murrle, Bennett and Co. give the names of their designers as F. Rico and R. Win. On the other hand, Liberty's of Regent Street, whose experiments in interesting the public in artistic silverwork and jewellery were most successful,

Plate 6. Designs in watercolour for pendants and a necklace by Edward Colonna, incorporating 'wing' and 'dog-tooth' pearls from the Mississippi Valley. (Newark Public Library, Newark, New Jersey.)

Born in Cologne, Germany, Colonna went to Brussels to train as an architect. In 1882, however, he left for America to work as a designer with Associated Artists, the firm founded by L.C. Tiffany in 1879. This connection is especially interesting when considering the design of the accompanying necklace since the use of American freshwater pearls is very reminiscent of the jewellery made by Tiffany in the late nineteenth and early twentieth centuries. (See The Book of the Pearl *by George Frederick Kunz and Charles Hugh Stevenson, New York, 1908; also compare with the brooch in Colour Plate 4). After living in New York, Colonna moved to Ohio where he issued his revolutionary design book on Art Nouveau style entitled* Essays on Broom Corn. *In 1898 Colonna returned to Europe to work for Siegfried Bing and produced jewellery and furniture designs for the Maison de l'Art Nouveau. In 1905 he returned to America, after Bing's shop had closed, and there continued his work. His designs had considerable influence on the Craft Revival in the United States.*

Colour Plate 10. An openwork silver necklace in the form of forget-me-not leaves and flowers decorated with enamel and set with pearls and blue opals, by Arthur Gaskin (1862-1928) and Georgie Gaskin (1866-1934). (Victor Arwas Collection.)

The Gaskins were book illustrators and designers as well as jewellers and were close associates of the Pre-Raphaelite circle which included Sir Edward Burne-Jones and Dante Gabriel Rossetti.

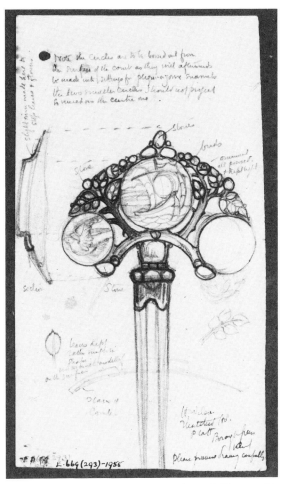

Plate 7. Drawing for Henry Wilson's comb illustrated in Colour Plate 11. (The Victoria and Albert Museum.)

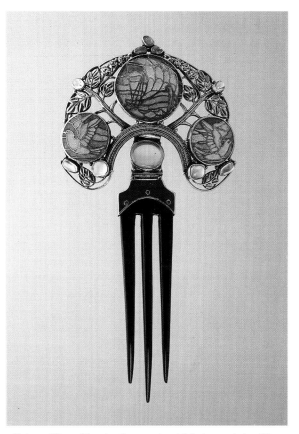

Colour Plate 11. A silver and gold hair comb by Henry Wilson set with cabochon emeralds and moonstones. The three circular medallions of doves and a ship in full sail are in plique à jour enamel. (The Hull Grundy Gift to the Glasgow Art Gallery and Museum.)

Colour Plate 12. Comb with silver and enamelled mount, by Henry Wilson. (Glasgow Art Gallery and Museum.)

Plate 8. Designs for pins by Charles Ricketts in the Art Nouveau style incorporating ears of wheat and acorns. (The British Museum.) Charles Ricketts was considerably impressed by the work of René Lalique (1860-1945), which he saw at Agnew's in 1905. These designs, although lighter in mood than those of Lalique, show this influence on his work.

both commercially and aesthetically, maintained almost complete silence on the subject of their designers. This is all the more surprising since they employed some of the best known and highly regarded of the Craft Revival designers, like Jessie M. King, Fred Partridge, Oliver Baker and Archibald Knox. There are a number of possible reasons for this. For one thing, Liberty's retained the right to make considerable alterations to the designs before using them, both for convenience at the production stage and to conform to the known preferences of their customers, who were, after all, playing safe in going to a well-known shop rather than to the individual craftsman. They would most likely have required a somewhat modified version of the more daringly abstract designs. As well as making modifications to the commissioned designs, Liberty's also appear to have adapted designs taken from various publications, notably *The Studio* special number, *Modern Design in Jewellery and Fans* (1901/2), possibly without permission or acknowledgement. C.R. Ashbee is known to have felt indignant at the extent to which Liberty's borrowed Guild of Handicraft ideas, adding insult to injury by undercutting the prices which the Guild had to charge. Ashbee believed, incorrectly, that Liberty had put £10,000 into the 'Cymric' silver venture, a sum undreamed of in craft circles.

Forcing on to the public the idea that all pieces of experimental jewellery or silverwork should be considered as works of art in their own right, without reference either to their function or to current fashion, was bound in the end to work against the 'artistic' style. The formal design framework in which either the Craft Revival or Art Nouveau or Jugendstil was expressed inhibited stylistic development to a degree which was inappropriate to objects of purely artistic interest. The designers had ignored fashion at their peril, but had in the process learnt a valuable lesson. From the time of the First World War, or even a bit earlier, experimental work in jewellery design was to be far more closely integrated with fashion in dress than it had been since the birth of the 'aesthetic' movement in the 1870s and 1880s.

Lily's Dress Necklace

J Ruskin.
1876

It was in this climate of disillusion with 'art for art's sake' that the movement for the improvement of design in industry, in abeyance for over half a century, was to flourish through the efforts of the members of the Deutsche Werkbund, the Bauhaus and the Design and Industries Association. It was they who produced the most worthwhile decorative art during the years 1918-39. At this point anyone with even a superficial knowledge of official policies towards the decorative and applied arts during the nineteenth century must sense the ghostly presences of Prince Albert and Sir Henry Cole brooding over these new developments.

The early development of mechanisation in industry in the late eighteenth and early nineteenth centuries was greeted with great enthusiasm, and a large amount of research was devoted to the use of machinery in all kinds of manufacturing processes, encouraged in England by the Royal Society of Arts, which awarded prizes to inventors as well as artists, and in France before the Revolution by the explicit support of the reigning monarch. Throughout the second half of the nineteenth century the Royal Society of Arts seems to have kept alive a small amount of artistic interest in industrial art against the general trend of indifference or distaste; some of the papers read at the Society even during the Craft Revival period still dealt realistically with problems posed by mechanisation and mass-production.

A large part of the blame for the total indifference shown by the aesthetic coterie, from the early 1860s until after the turn of the century, to Prince

Plate 9. 'Lily's Dress Necklace' by John Ruskin. Pencil and watercolour, dated 1876. (The Ruskin Galleries, Bembridge School, The Isle of Wight.) Lily was the infant daughter of Ruskin's beloved cousin Joan, who was married to the artist Arthur Severn.

Plate 10. A repoussé gold reliquary made to contain a lock of William Morris's hair. (The Victoria and Albert Museum.)

The gold panel, decorated with roses and inscribed 'William Morris 1834-1896', was designed by Robert Catterson Smith and bears London hallmarks for 1897-7 which are partly illegible (?CJ). A plaque on the reverse is inscribed with the following lines by F.S. Ellis, Morris's friend and publisher:

> *'For folk unborn this shrine doth hold*
> *Thy silvered lock, Oh! heart of gold*
> *Should times' hand mar it, yet thy mind*
> *Shall live, in deathless words enshrined.'*

Robert Catterson Smith (b.1853) was part of the immediate circle of William Morris until he moved to Birmingham where he became head of the Vittoria Street School for Silversmiths and Jewellers, and then head of the Vittoria Street School of Art. This reliquary was bequeathed by Morris's daughter May in 1939.

Albert's ideas for the improvement of design in industry, can be laid squarely on the shoulders of two men — John Ruskin and William Morris. 'Men were not intended to work with the accuracy of tools, to be precise and perfect in all their actions. If you will have that precision out of them, and make their fingers measure degrees like cog-wheels, and their arms strike curves like compasses, you must inhumanize them... there might be more freedom in England, though her feudal lords' lightest words were worth men's lives, and though the blood of the vexed husbandman dropped into the furrows of his fields, than there is while the animation of her multitudes is set fuel to feed the factory smoke, and the strength of them is given daily to be wasted into the fineness of a web, or racked into the exactness of a line.' So wrote Ruskin in

Colour Plate 16. A necklace of enamelled gold, pearls and garnets; an enamelled gold pendant in the Egyptian taste, set centrally with an ancient Egyptian carving of a cat in lapis-lazuli, hung with a nephrite drop. Both the necklace and pendant are by James Cromar Watt. (Victor Arwas Collection.)

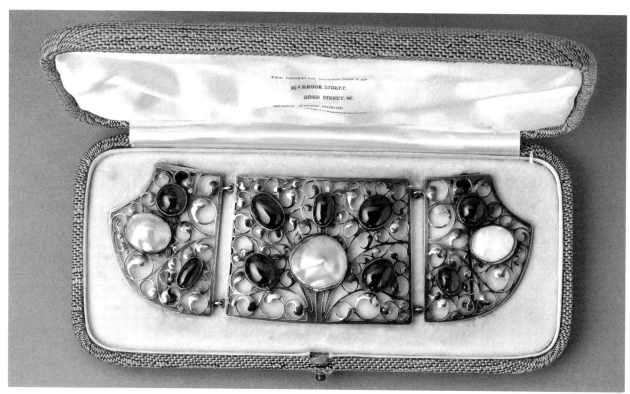

Colour Plate 17. A corsage ornament in silver and gold, set with garnets and pearls, by the Guild of Handicraft, probably designed by Charles Robert Ashbee (1863-1942). (John Jesse.)

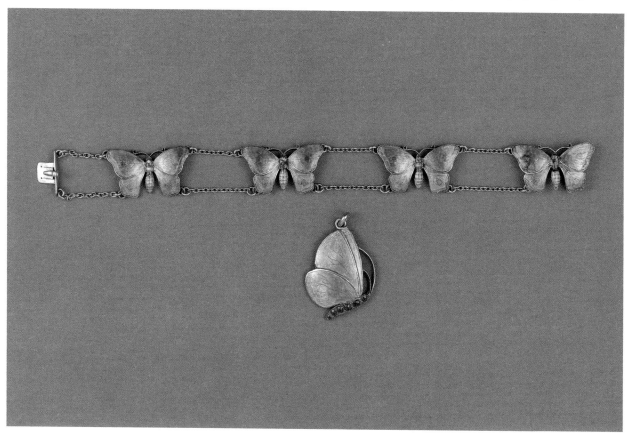

Colour Plate 18. A pendant in silver, set with a ruby and decorated with blue enamel, and a bracelet of similar inspiration, by Child and Child, c.1900. (Wartski, London.)

The second group of work was shown soon afterwards, in September of 1899, when a number of pieces bearing the Liberty mark and sent to the exhibition by them were shown at the Arts and Crafts Exhibition held at the New Gallery. It is significant not only that this group was made in Birmingham, but that the designers, where they have been identified, turn out to be connected either as pupils or teachers with the Birmingham School of Art in Margaret Street or with the Vittoria Street School for Jewellers and Silversmiths. It has been suggested (in a lecture entitled 'The Liberty Metalwork Venture' given by Shirley Bury at the Victoria and Albert Museum on 18th September 1975) that the reason for this is that the Birmingham silversmithing firm of W.H. Haseler had hit upon an idea remarkably similar to that of Arthur Liberty himself, and had collected pieces for a new and rather adventurous range of silverwork from the Birmingham designers. In offering this collection to various firms Haseler had the good luck to approach Liberty at the very moment when his interest in such work was at its height; in other words when he was just beginning to see the potential of this venture into specially commissioned work, and before he had secured the services as a designer of Archibald Knox, whose enormously prolific imagination must gradually have made the services of any number of other designers unnecessary.

Among the Birmingham artists who designed for Liberty at this date or later were Bernard Cuzner and Alfred H. Jones (who also, with Jessie Jones, made the Oliver Baker pieces in the collection shown in September 1899), both students at the Vittoria Street School. Arthur Gaskin, who was teaching at the Birmingham School of Art 1899, and who succeeded R. Catterson Smith as Head of the Vittoria Street School in 1902, may also have had some involvement with Liberty as some of the Liberty jewellery is remarkably close in detail to his own work. This may, however, be the result of 'pirating'. The most distinguished designs were provided by Oliver Baker, the Birmingham painter, etcher and antiquary, who was probably among the first to be approached by Haseler, his brother-in-law. The magnificent silver box designed by Archibald Knox c.1900, now in the Museum of Modern Art in New York, was made by Harry C. Craythorne who made designs for waist clasps, and who also became the principal designer to the firm in the 'twenties when the pioneering activities of Liberty's in this field had considerably diminished, and the commissioning from a band of designers in the forefront of current artistic developments had been abandoned.

The contribution of all these artists, interesting and arresting though the designs are, pales into insignificance in the face of the enormous body of intensely original work produced by Archibald Knox. Born on the Isle of Man, Knox later studied at the School of Art in Douglas, where he subsequently taught. He came to London and is said by one expert on his career to have worked for Christopher Dresser. If this is true it would explain the origin of some of the more startlingly unconventional aspects of his designs, which seem in many cases to be logical developments of themes already explored by Dresser (examples cited by Shirley Bury in the lecture mentioned previously seem to make a clear case for Dresser having had a profound influence on Knox). This professional contact with Dresser would also have provided Knox with access to either Arthur Liberty or John Llewellyn, as Dresser's son worked at one time for Liberty's. Another theory, held by Adrian Tilbroke, is that he worked for M.H. Baillie-Scott, the architect. These theories are not mutually exclusive, and this diversity of experience would explain Knox's capacity to make such a profusion of designs without becoming banal, at least during the earlier period of his employment by Liberty's. Knox seems to have started his work for Liberty at the end of 1899, and his influence is apparent in the work of Rex Silver from an early date. While the work of designers like Knox and Oliver Baker bears the unmistakable stamp of their individual artistic personalities, much of the jewellery and silverwork in the 'Cymric' range is influenced by the designs produced by C.R. Ashbee for the Guild of Handicraft (even Knox's beautiful stemmed and footed cup and cover has many similarities to an Ashbee design of a comparable piece), and the way in which the Liberty pieces were manufactured, partly by machine but with hand-finishing, made the cost very low, enabling Liberty's to undercut the handmade Guild of Handicraft pieces by a significant amount. Ashbee was very bitter about this competition (he and his wife believed that Liberty had spent £10,000 establishing the 'Cymric', a sum wildly in excess of the amount actually invested), which was to be one of the reasons for the failure of the Guild in 1907. Even more embittering than this artistic poaching was the fact that one of Ashbee's own Guildsmen worked for Liberty: the enamellist Fleetwood Varley produced his characteristic landscape enamels for the decoration of the lids of pewter cigarette boxes in the 'Tudric' range.

Liberty's were by no means the only English firm to venture into the Arts and Crafts field, it is the scale of the operation in their case which is unusual. Few of the firms who imitated the idea in principle bothered to establish a team of designers even remotely comparable with that assembled by Arthur Liberty and John Llewellyn.

The Birmingham silversmithing firm of William Hutton and Sons, which had been founded in 1800, exhibited pieces in the Art Nouveau taste at the Centennial Exposition in Paris in 1900 which are credited to the designer Kate Harris. They also produced silver for Mappin and Webb in 1903 which is very close in style to work by still anonymous designers for Liberty dating from the same period. Hutton's were one of the few English firms to produce work, in the form of silver waist clasps in the more sculptural Art Nouveau style, close to the work of the French designers and the German Georg Gurschner. The London firm of silversmiths, William Comyns (founded in 1848), also specialised at this period in waist clasps and buckles in an Art Nouveau style based on natural ornament. A large number of their designs were registered with the Design Registry at the Patent Office, which is surely some indication

Plate 18. A necklace of silver and gold and green hardstone cabochon by Edgar Simpson (working 1896-1910). (The Fine Art Society.)
Simpson was a pupil of Nelson Dawson and worked with him at the Artificers' Guild from its foundation in 1901.

of the seriousness with which the design department worked, but no individual designer has so far been identified as having worked for them.

Another London firm, Murrle, Bennett & Co., of 13 Charterhouse Street, name two of their designers as F. Rico and R. Win, and they are careful to claim in their advertisement that the jewellery designs are their property as well as being manufactured by them. Without this assurance the interested collector might be forgiven for thinking that some of the pieces bearing the Murrle, Bennett mark were copies from Liberty designs of the same date, or from the stock of the large Pforzheim jewellery firm of Theodor Fahrner. Identical pieces exist which are marked in one case with the M.B. & Co. monogram and in the other with the T.F monogram; some pieces are marked with both monograms and the German quality mark, 925, for silver. The existence in Pforzheim of the enormous jewellery production firm of Seliger Bennett seems to point clearly to a connection with the German town, but neither of the mysterious designers named in the advertisement has a particularly German name, and much of the jewellery, especially the goldsmiths' work, appears to be English. The style of work is almost equally divided between a self-consciously Arts and Crafts taste, with heavily hammered silverwork, and fake rivets and visible nail-heads as decoration, and a more linear Jugendstil, inspired by the work of the Wiener Werkstätte, or the German designers like Otto Prutscher and Patriz Huber. A few of the pieces are set with English-style

CHAPTER III

From Romanticism to Aestheticism

A.W.N. Pugin, Owen Jones, William Morris, Christopher Dresser, E.W. Godwin, William Burges and Charles Eastlake, are the names which appear and reappear in the chronology of nineteenth century decorative art, and whose influence contributed so decisively to the development of the art movements of the *fin de siècle*. After half a century of critical oblivion they are now well known, resurrected some years ago from the obscurity into which their once great reputations fell after their deaths, their work is appreciated and much studied and discussed by the growing band of enthusiasts for the period. They are the artistic heroes of the Victorian age, the designers and architects who shaped the environment of a prosperous and stable society, who were the formative influence on the work of the artists involved with the Craft Revival movement, who in their turn inspired the Continental designers, notably the Austrians who freely acknowledged their debt to the Glasgow Four (C.R. Mackintosh, the Macdonald sisters and J.H. MacNair), C.R. Ashbee and Frank Brangwyn. The jewellery designed by J.H. MacNair and exhibited at St. George's Hall, Liverpool in 1901 has not yet come to light. It was described in the *Architectural Review,* vol. 9. 1901 pp.39-40 (see Roger Billcliffe, 'J.H. MacNair in Glasgow and Liverpool', *Annual Report and Bulletin,* vol. I, 1970-1, Walker Art Gallery, Liverpool). Less well recognised is the importance, to the development of the French Art Nouveau style in particular, of the Romantic painters and the Pre-Raphaelites with their interest in nature and archaic forms, which dates back to the early years of the nineteenth century.

The Romantic taste for naturalistic silverwork and jewellery stems from the widespread curiosity about botany and horticulture fostered in the late eighteenth and early nineteenth centuries by the activities of the plant collectors who travelled widely, particularly in the East, in search of specimens. Accustomed as we are nowadays to the rich variety of hardy and semi-hardy garden plants available at very small cost to any interested gardener, it is hard to remember that some of the well-established favourites among these plants were introduced into this country barely a century ago.

In 1853 Ruskin gave a series of lectures on 'Natural Ornament' recommending the use of plant forms in decoration, leaving a legacy that can be seen in the embellishment of modest red-brick houses built in the 1870s and 1880s all over the country. The lectures were written in Scotland on the fateful trip when he and his wife Effie were accompanied by the young painter John Everett Millais. Ruskin wrote to his father from Glenfinlas: 'Millais is chattering at such a rate — designing costumes — helmets with crests of animals, and necklaces of flowers' (see plate 20). Millais' drawings were of Effie, decked in a profusion of decorative ornaments, necklaces of spread-winged birds, hair-ornaments of chestnut leaves — her hair was a bright chestnut colour — and flowers, lizard bracelets encircling the whole of her forearm, fuchsia earrings and a squirrel stomacher, all of which are an uncannily accurate pre-vision of the French Art Nouveau jewellery designed half a century later.

Plate 20. Effie Ruskin, born Euphemia Chalmers Gray, (1828-1898), by John Everett Millais.
(Private Collection.)
    Effie married John Ruskin on 10 April 1848, but by 1852 it was clear that the marriage could
not work. Effie suspected that Ruskin's father was trying to compromise her with with Millais who
was a frequent visitor to their house in Herne Hill. None the less Millais was asked to accompany
the Ruskins on holiday in Perthshire. It was during this time that Millais and Effie established
some sort of relationship and it was Millais' habit to sketch the unhappy Mrs Ruskin on every
possible occasion. Many of these drawings show her with the 'natural ornaments' that so interested
Ruskin, who was writing a series of lectures on the subject. In this drawing she wears tiaras, head
ornaments and necklaces in the form of birds, animals and flowers which anticipate the work of the
French Art Nouveau jewellers. By 1855 Effie Ruskin had divorced her first husband and married
Millais.

    Ruskin's advocacy of natural ornament bore fruit in unexpected places, for
example a private view at the Royal Academy in 1881: 'I never saw so many
shabby or insane dresses and so few pretty women in my life,' wrote Vernon
Lee. 'I was quite astounded, coming out, to see so many grand carriages. The
dresses didn't look at all on a par with them. There were some most crazy
looking creatures: one with crinkled gauze all tied close about her and visibly
no underclothing (and a gold laurel wreath); another with ivy leaves tied by
each other's stalks, on short red hair; another with trimming and necklace of

Plate 21. A watercolour of a spray of orange blossom (almost certainly a design for a brooch of this form) by Queen Victoria. (The Royal Library at Windsor.)

This watercolour is taken from a scrapbook assembled by G. Whitford who worked for Messrs. Garrard from 1857 to 1891. Queen Victoria received a set of jewellery from her husband, Prince Albert, in 1845, made in the form of fruiting orange blossom in enamelled gold and porcelain. The jewellery recreated, in a more permanent form, the orange blossom wreath worn for her marriage with the gold fruits symbolising the children of her marriage. This exquisitely observed drawing may have provided the model for the various different pieces, in the form of a wreath, brooch and earrings.

Plate 22. An enamelled gold brooch in the form of a spray of orange blossom, the flowers are of white porcelain, c.1845. (The Hull-Grundy Gift to the British Museum.)

The jewel is kept within its original fitted case from Hunt and Roskell (lately Storr, Mortimer and Hunt) Jewellers and Goldsmiths to the Queen and Royal Family, 156 New Bond Street, London. It is undoubtedly closely related to the set of jewellery, also with porcelain flowers, given to Queen Victoria by Prince Albert in 1845. Queen Victoria, in a letter dated 1846, said it was designed by her husband, but the watercolour by the Queen herself in the Royal Library at Windsor suggests that she was involved in some degree (see plate 21). The commission for the Royal jewel went to Garrards who had succeeded Rundell and Bridge as Royal jewellers in 1843. It may be that this brooch and Queen Victoria's parure were made in the same workshops. Orange blossom jewels were often given at weddings as a symbol of purity and chastity.

Colour Plate 19. 'The Bridesmaid' by John Everett Millais. Oil on panel, initialled and dated 1851. (Ashmolean Museum, Oxford.)

   One of the first Pre-Raphaelite paintings to deploy abundant red-coloured hair so dramatically, this picture foreshadows the obsession with coiling, enveloping hair which marks the late work of D.G. Rossetti and it has been identified as an embryonic example of the Art Nouveau style. Superstition has it that a bridesmaid who passes a piece of the wedding cake through the ring nine times will have a vision of her future lover. The orange blossom she wears is a symbol of chastity and was much favoured as a wreath for a bride; the orange fruit on the plate is possibly an emblem of fruitfulness to come.

Plate 23. A gold tiara by Carlo and Arthur Giuliano made between 1895 and 1912, the leaves naturalistically enamelled in shades of green, the berries represented by cabochon chrysoberyls. (The Hull-Grundy Gift to the British Museum.)
For the use of ivy as a symbol of 'friendship in adversity' and as a natural ornament see plate 25. Clinging ivy has a number of symbolic meanings associated with constancy and lifelong love. Giuliano might also have had in mind the delicate gold wreaths of antiquity. Examples from the Castellani collection, which Carlo Giuliano (d.1895) would probably have known from his youthful association with the firm, had been in the British Museum since 1872.

Plate 24. 'Ivy', a Herkomer gravure by Sir Hubert von Herkomer, R.A. (1849-1914), published 1897. (Bushey Museum Trust.)

marigolds and parsley fern on thread, a lot of insane slashings and stomachings.' (*Vernon Lee's Letters,* ed. I. Cooper Willis, 1937, p.73).

Certain flowers have such a 'period' flavour that it is fairly safe to date pieces featuring them to the years when they were popular, for example, the sweet pea is peculiarly Edwardian, the chrysanthemum and sunflower are typical of the aesthetic taste of the 'seventies and 'eighties, and the orchid and the iris are, in both colour and form, pure Art Nouveau. Apart from the flowers which are typical of the taste of the period, and which appear frequently in jewellery design, many of the more abstract forms are based on plants and insects or other natural objects such as shells. Much of the rationalisation of the natural forms used in jewellery design at the turn of the century is based on ideas formulated for silver, metal work, glass and pottery by Christopher Dresser. Dresser was a botanist by training, his chief interest being in the structure of plants, and he was also deeply interested in mathematical theory. His ideas, published in a number of treatises on design from 1862 (*The Art of Decorative*

Design), show him to be well in advance of his contemporaries in the field of decorative art, some of his more advanced designs anticipating by nearly half a century the forms of Bauhaus silverwork which were themselves considered very advanced in the 'twenties. Traces of Dresser's influence can be found in commercial jewellery design throughout the last quarter of the nineteenth century, but public taste continued to favour the type of botanical jewellery which had first become fashionable in the 1840s. The tradition of botanical design established in the early years of the century was so strong that it is possible to find exact parallels between the naturalistic silver designs of the Romantic period — i.e. the chambersticks and sugar basins in the form of bluebells and other wild flowers — and the chased silver buckles and clasps produced by firms like William Comyns and William Hutton, as well as a number of other lesser-known Birmingham manufacturers, at the turn of the century.

The use of natural forms as a basis for ornament in all kinds of decorative work was a crucial aspect of the teaching of most of the influential figures in the nineteenth century; from Pugin (whose *Floriated Ornament,* a pattern book of Gothic ornament based on natural forms, appeared in 1849), through Dresser and Ruskin (*Prosperpina,* which appeared at intervals between 1874 and 1886, contains intensely evocative descriptions of plants and their habit of growth) to Mucha and Grasset who each published a series of pattern books on the application of plant forms to modern decorative designs. Pugin wrote in *Floriated Ornament*: 'It is absurd...to talk of Gothic foliage. The foliage is natural, and it is the adaptation and disposition of it which stamps the style. The great difference between ancient and modern artists is their adaptation of nature for decorative purposes...a modern painter would endeavour to give a fictitious idea of relief...instead of a well-defined, clear, and beautiful enrichment, in harmony with the construction...an irregular and confused effect is produced...Nature supplied the mediaeval artists with all their forms and ideas; the same inexhaustible source is open to us...if we go to the fountain head, we shall produce a multitude of beautiful designs treated in the same spirit as the old, but new in form.' Pugin reveals in this passage his preoccupation with two of the major stumbling-blocks which stood in the way of the development of a coherent nineteenth century style, and which were to

Colour Plate 20. A gold pendant in the French Empire style in the form of a tied laurel wreath framing a green glass cameo which simulates malachite, c.1890. It was part of the collection of Edith Holman Hunt. This is an unusually sophisticated Revivalist jewel from Child and Child which on initial inspection seems to date from the early nineteenth century, but it is signed with the firm's monogram of two 'C's and a sunflower and cannot date from before 1880. It is known that Child and Child was a firm popular with the artistic community in London in the late nineteenth century and a jewel of this nature is entirely in tune with Holman Hunt's meticulous attitude towards historical accuracy in his paintings. (Mrs. Elizabeth Tompkin.)

A silver gilt and gold mounted tortoiseshell comb by Child and Child in the form of a spray of ivy leaves and berries. The leaves are naturalistically enamelled in shades of green and the berries represented by garnets in rub round settings. It is signed with the monogram of two 'C's and a sunflower. (The Fitzwilliam Museum, Cambridge.)

The meaning of flowers was a near obsession in artistic circles in Victorian England. Floral jewellery was immensely popular and nearly always had greater symbolic meaning than is now recognised. Ivy is a symbol of eternity and by extension eternal love. The ladies of the Pre-Raphaelite circle liked to decorate themselves with real flowers and this comb echoes the theme (see plates 24 and 25).

A silver and gold mounted watch by Child and Child in the form of closed wings which open to reveal the dial. On the underneath of the watch covers, which are similarly decorated, is found the legend 'Tempus Fugit Semper Amici CVW. 1904'. The watch hangs from a similarly decorated brooch in the form of a bird with a pearl drop hanging from its beak. The dial is signed 'Child and Child London' and the brooch bears the familiar monogram of two 'C's and a marigold. (The Rt. Hon. The Viscount de Vesci.)

The firm of Child and Child was patronised by Sir Edward Burne-Jones and it is now generally believed that the series of jewels, of which this watch is part, was inspired by his designs.

Colour Plate 21. 'Fiametta' by John Atkinson Grimshaw, 1883. (The Cartwright Hall, Bradford.)

Atkinson Grimshaw is best known for his night scenes of the town and docks of Liverpool but he also painted a number of romantic and classical subjects as well as interior and garden scenes in his own home, Knostrop Old Hall, Leeds. 'Fiametta' was the beloved mistres of the poet Boccaccio, and features in the 'Decameron'. Her relationship to Boccaccio could be likened to that of Dante and Beatrice or Laura and Petrarch. She is shown here in a wreath of ivy, a symbol of 'friendship in adversity'. It has been suggested that the wreath may also be an allusion to the identity of the sitter, probably Grimshaw's mistress, Agnes Leaf, who died of consumption at the age of twenty-eight.

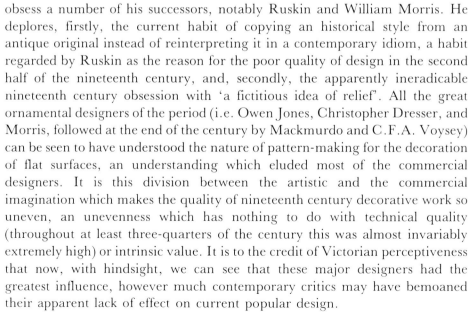

Plate 26. A 'silver' mounted bag designed by William Morris and worked by his wife, Janey. May Morris bequeathed it to the Victoria and Albert Museum when she died in 1938. (The Victoria and Albert Museum.)

Plate 27. A detail of the portrait of John Everett Millais (1829-1896), by C.R. Leslie, which shows the artist wearing the golden goose stick-pin which he designed and had made up by Hunt and Roskell. (National Portrait Gallery, London.)

obsess a number of his successors, notably Ruskin and William Morris. He deplores, firstly, the current habit of copying an historical style from an antique original instead of reinterpreting it in a contemporary idiom, a habit regarded by Ruskin as the reason for the poor quality of design in the second half of the nineteenth century, and, secondly, the apparently ineradicable nineteenth century obsession with 'a fictitious idea of relief'. All the great ornamental designers of the period (i.e. Owen Jones, Christopher Dresser, and Morris, followed at the end of the century by Mackmurdo and C.F.A. Voysey) can be seen to have understood the nature of pattern-making for the decoration of flat surfaces, an understanding which eluded most of the commercial designers. It is this division between the artistic and the commercial imagination which makes the quality of nineteenth century decorative work so uneven, an unevenness which has nothing to do with technical quality (throughout at least three-quarters of the century this was almost invariably extremely high) or intrinsic value. It is to the credit of Victorian perceptiveness that now, with hindsight, we can see that these major designers had the greatest influence, however much contemporary critics may have bemoaned their apparent lack of effect on current popular design.

Pugin's interest in Gothic ornament extended far beyond the simple application of natural forms to his neo-Gothic designs, and the revival of interest in medieval and Renaissance art was ascribed to his influence by G.A. Sala, writing in *Notes and Sketches of the Paris Exhibition* (1868). Pugin's celebrated set of 'marriage' jewellery was designed for his third wife in 1848; it was subsequently shown at the Great Exhibition of 1851 (see plate 48). The full-page illustration of all the pieces was widely used as inspiration for the design of Gothic-style jewellery in the following years. The full set of jewellery exhibited consists of two chains with cruciform pendants, rings, earrings, a headband, a bracelet and two brooches, one of which is in the shape of an 'M' signifying 'Maria' or the Virgin Mary, like the Founder's Jewel of William of Wykeham at New College which Castellani was to copy and make in many versions some years later. With this enamelled jewellery set with polished cabochon stones and bordered with pearls Pugin initiated half a century of historical revival style, and the choice of ornaments of this type rather than the baroque engraved and tortured forms of high Victorian taste, was thereafter to mark a patron of artistic sensibility. Like Pugin, the French goldsmith and jeweller F.D. Froment-Meurice, working in imitation of the German-born jeweller and silversmith Charles Wagner, began designing jewellery in a style based on Gothic architectural details at the end of the 1840s.

Wagner came to Paris from Berlin in about 1830, and introduced the neo-Gothic and Renaissance styles already popular in Germany. His example was eagerly followed by F.D. Froment-Meurice whose designs for jewellery in the 1850s are entirely in tune with the 'style troubadour' prevalent in French decorative design at that date. The 1850s saw a great programme of cathedral and church restoration in France initiated by the architect Viollet-le-Duc; his publication on Gothic architecture, extensively illustrated with details of sculptural ornament, provided a widely influential pattern book. Both Froment-Meurice and his workshop assistant Jules Wièse were obviously inspired by this source as well as by early metalwork and jewellery. It is possible to trace the influence of this early medievalism through the work of William Burges, the paintings of the Pre-Raphaelites, the writings of Ruskin and the decorative work of William Morris to the jewellery of the Craft Revival designers, notably Henry Wilson, J. Paul Cooper and Edward Spencer. Froment-Meurice, again under the influence of Wagner, was also responsible for the revival of interest in the jewellery of the Italian Renaissance, a style which quickly became popular in France and England and remained so until the very end of the nineteenth century. As a device for producing work of 'artistic' quality the copying of old work has one great disadvantage. In a period of intense collecting interest in this style and date of jewellery some — even perhaps many — Victorian neo-Renaissance pieces have become confused with the genuine article. The case of the notorious Aachen goldsmith and restorer Reinhold Vasters is to the point, but his own intentions are still not entirely clear. The book of his drawings, which is now at the Victoria and Albert Museum, was bought in 1909 from Vasters' sale by the dealer Murray Marks who submitted it for comment to Edward Strange, Keeper of the

Plate 28. Drawing of a young girl passing a silk scarf through a wedding ring in the hope of seeing her future husband, by Dante Gabriel Rossetti. (Sotheby's, London.) The model for this charming drawing was Rossetti's model and wife, Elizabeth Siddall. Considering her sad life with the artist and her premature death by an overdose of drugs, the meaning of the drawing has a special poignancy.

1880.

NINCOMPOOPIANA.—THE MUTUAL ADMIRATION SOCIETY.

Our Gallant Colonel (who is not a Member thereof, to Mrs. Cimabue Brown, who is). "AND WHO'S THIS YOUNG HERO THEY'RE ALL SWARMING OVER NOW?"

Mrs. Cimabue Brown. "JELLABY POSTLETHWAITE, THE GREAT POET, YOU KNOW, WHO SAT FOR MAUDLE'S 'DEAD NARCISSUS'! HE HAS JUST DEDICATED HIS *LATTER-DAY SAPPHICS* TO ME. IS NOT HE *BEAUTIFUL?*"

Our Gallant Colonel. "WHY, WHAT'S THERE *BEAUTIFUL* ABOUT HIM?"

Mrs. Cimabue Brown. "OH, LOOK AT HIS GRAND HEAD AND POETIC FACE, WITH THOSE FLOWERLIKE EYES, AND THAT EXQUISITE SAD SMILE! LOOK AT HIS SLENDER WILLOWY FRAME, AS YIELDING AND FRAGILE AS A WOMAN'S! THAT'S YOUNG MAUDLE, STANDING JUST BEHIND HIM—THE GREAT PAINTER, YOU KNOW. HE HAS JUST PAINTED ME AS 'HÉLOÏSE,' AND MY HUSBAND AS 'ABÉLARD.' IS NOT HE *DIVINE?*" *[The Colonel hooks it.*

[N.B.—Postlethwaite and Maudle are quite unknown to fame.

Plate 29. Drawn by George du Maurier for Punch, *1880. It is interesting to note how faithfully the figure second from the left reflects Vernon Lee's description of the Royal Academy visitor in 1881 (see p.51). The artist was evasive about his sources for these character sketches, implying that they were derived purely from his imagination, but this note from Beatrix Potter's* Diary *is illuminating: 'Papa and Mamma went to a Ball at the Millais' a week or two since. There was an extraordinary mixture of actors, rich jews, nobility, literary, etc. Du Maurier had been to the Ball the week before, and Carrie Millais said they thought they had seen him taking sketches on the sly. Oscar Wilde was there. I thought he was a long lanky melancholy man, but he is fat and merry. His only peculiarity was a black choker instead of a shirt-collar, and his hair is a mop. He was not wearing a lily in his button hole, but to make up for it, his wife had her front covered in great water-lilies.' (Sat. 12 July, 1884.)*

It is surely no coincidence that one of du Maurier's most mocking images of 'aesthetic' taste shows a woman in a dress liberally decorated with 'great water-liles'. Vernon Lee's description is complemented, even surpassed in astonished distaste by Mrs Henry Adams' letter of two years' earlier: 'Wednesday evening reception at the Royal Academy, where every art rag-bag seems to have been ransacked to adorn the women. They look like illustrations to Christiana Rossetti's Goblin Market — *fat figures in pea-green; lean symphonies in chewing-gum colour; all in a minor key'. (6 July, 1879, p.151).*

Colour Plate 22. A parure of gold jewellery in the form of laurel leaves and berries in the classical taste, by Carlo Giuliano, c.1863. This sort of jewellery was a particular favourite in 'Aesthetic' society and a comparable tiara is depicted in the cartoon above.

Department of Engraving, Illustration and Design at the Victoria and Albert Museum; he noted that the drawings were 'executed with remarkable skill as designs for goldsmith's work, many pieces of which, I understand, have been placed on the market as old work'. (Quoted by Shirley Bury in the catalogue *Princely Magnificence* 1980/81 p.137.) The same confusion was to occur with Watherston's 'Art' jewellery. In May 1906 an advertising promotion by the firm drew attention to 'The Place of Jewellery in Art' and offered jewels cast from antique and Renaissance originals, among them versions of the sixteenth century German gimmel or puzzle rings similar to Martin Luther's ring. A number of examples of these rings in various collections around the world may well therefore be of London manufacture and date from c.1906!

The fanciful Renaissance style jewels by Alphonse Fouquet, which bear little relation technically or stylistically to their sixteenth century prototypes, were made at the end of the 'seventies. Boucheron and Hippolyte Tetéger were making diamond-set jewellery in a flamboyant *style François I* in the 'eighties and 'nineties, and Louis Rault and Jules Brateau, both highly accomplished *ciseleurs* and sculptors who had earlier worked for Boucheron, were producing ambitious neo-Renaissance objects at the turn of the century. Maurice Rheims (in *L'Objet 1900*, published 1964) describes the gold and ivory coffer made by Brateau at the very end of the century as being a *'pièce exemplaire où l'influence italienne se mêle harmonieusement à l'esprit "Art Nouveau"'*. He also says a little lower down the page that Brateau, while taking his inspiration from the art of the past (i.e. the Italian Renaissance), was, like many artists of his time, working in the Art Nouveau style without knowing it. This comment could also apply to Alfred Gilbert and Charles Ricketts, both of whose jewellery designs show this dual influence, but Gilbert utterly repudiated any connection that might be foisted on him with the decadent decorative style practised on the Continent, and it might possibly be more accurate to say that many of the Art Nouveau designers were producing neo-Renaissance objects without knowing it. It is significant that such neo-Renaissance jewellery as was produced in England is very much more restrained than the later French work, being based on Holbeinesque prototypes mainly taken from early portraits.

Credit for evolving the Victorian Holbeinesque style must be given to C.F. Hancock who in 1856 was commissioned by the 6th Duke of Devonshire to

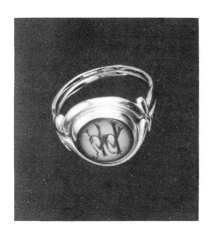

Plate 30. A gold signet ring set with a round red and white layered sardonyx by Hunt and Roskell. The stone is engraved with a monogram of 'WHH'. (Mrs. Elizabeth Tompkin.)

Before they each married William Holman Hunt and John Everett Millais had an exceptionally close friendship, in which they seemed entirely dependent upon one another. When in 1854 Hunt resolved to go to Syria to paint, Millais was distraught and honestly believed that Hunt might not survive the journey. He wrote to him:

'In truth I don't think I should have the strength to say goodbye — scarcely a night passes but what I cry like an infant over the thought that I may not see you again — I wish I had something to remember you by, and I desire that you should go to Hunt and Roskell and get yourself a signet ring which you must always wear. . .get a good one and have your initials engraved thereon. . .'

This is the ring and Hunt wore it until the day he died.

make an immensely elaborate set of jewellery, or 'parure', for the Countess of Granville, the wife of his nephew, to wear in Moscow at the coronation of the Tsar Alexander II (see Colour Plate 45). The complete parure consists of seven pieces, a diadem, a coronet, a comb with an ornamental mount, a bandeau, necklace, stomacher and bracelet, all in enamelled gold set with 320 diamonds and eighty-eight engraved engraved gems from the collection of the Dukes of Devonshire. The architect Sir Joseph Paxton, at that date in the employ of the Duke, recommended Hancock and the jeweller commissioned H. Armstead the sculptor to design the parure. The ornamental setting, it was alleged, was taken from the Tudor setting of one of the engraved gems, a portrait cameo of Queen Elizabeth I set in the cover of a miniature case enclosing portraits of the Queen and the Earl of Leicester. The type of setting is certainly Tudor and repeats almost exactly the border of alternating enamelled flowers and gems set in gold collets which encircle an onyx cameo of a negress in the sixteenth century marriage pendant known as the 'Gresley' jewel. The jewel itself was in the Gresley family until the late nineteenth century but it is also depicted in a portrait of Catherine Walsingham (cousin of Sir Francis Walsingham, Secretary of State to Queen Elizabeth) who married Sir Thomas Gresley. Miniatures enclosed in a case behind the cameo depict Sir Francis Walsingham and Catherine and are traditionally attributed to Nicholas Hilliard. Although many of the miniature cases and portrait cameo settings of the Tudor period do resemble the setting of the Gresley jewel in general, none seems to have precisely the four-lobed flower-head adopted by Armstead for the Devonshire parure. The parure was to set a design precedent that was endlessly imitated. By 1862 Howell and James had ready copies set with a large cabochon garnet to show at the International Exhibition, as did Hancocks themselves. Examples survive from these two firms as well as from Robert Phillips of Cockspur Street, Giuliano and John Brogden, and versions were made into the 1880s.

Mrs Haweis, while deploring the state of fashionable taste in jewellery in *The Art of Beauty* (1878), was prepared to admit as exceptions to the general rule Robert Phillips and Carlo Giuliano, a taste that was shared, it would seem, by the American visitor, Mrs. Henry Adams: 'The daily temptations of London are enormous...[for instance] Giuliano, Phillips', she wrote in a letter of

Plate 32. An Archaeological style gold brooch set with a shell cameo of an amorino. Probably English, c.1860. Engraved on the reverse: 'Fanny' and 'Holman to Edith I.M. 20 Dec. 1866'. (Mrs Elizabeth Tompkin.)
This brooch was worn habitually by both Fanny and Edith Holman Hunt throughout their lives. As a result the face of the cameo is quite disfigured by wear. (See plate 34 and Colour Plate 23).

Plate 33. A photograph of Fanny Holman Hunt, taken just before her marriage in December 1865, in the form of a carte-de-visite, albumen print by Elliott and Fry. (Jeremy Maas.)
   This is the photograph on which Hunt based his portrait of Fanny (plate 34) which he finished after her death. In it the shell cameo brooch is clearly visible once again.

Plate 34. Fanny Holman Hunt (detail) by William Holman Hunt. Oil on canvas. (Toledo Museum of Art, Ohio.) (Photograph: Sotheby, Parke, Bernet and Co.)
   Fanny Waugh (1833-66) married Hunt in 1865 and only eight months after the ceremony they set out for the Middle East. When they reached Florence, she gave birth to a son who was called Cyril Benone (meaning 'son of sorrow' in Hebrew). Fanny died a few weeks afterwards on 20 December 1866. It seems likely that the shell cameo in the Archaeological style gold mount she is wearing in the portrait was given to her by Hunt (see plate 32). After Fanny died he gave the cameo to Edith Waugh as a memento of her sister.

Colour Plate 23. Edith Holman Hunt (The Birthday) by William Holman Hunt. Oil on canvas. (Private Collection.)

Edith Waugh (1846-1931) married her dead sister's husband, despite powerful family and public criticism, in Neuchâtel, Switzerland, in November 1875, where under Swiss law their marriage was legal.

This portrait was painted to celebrate Edith's twenty-first birthday in 1867, she holds rock crystal beads in her hands, a fan, a gold watch, a bouquet and an Archaeological style bracelet set with micro mosaic which may very well have been made by Castellani. About her neck she wears a necklace of coral beads and pinned below her collar is the cameo brooch which Holman Hunt gave her in memory of Fanny.

1879. 'Tell Ned [her brother] Giuliano, Phillips' head workman, who has set up for himself, has a Ceylon cat's eye charmingly set; his prices much lower than Phillips',' she had written a week earlier. Giuliano was to achieve a reputation which made it quite unnecessary for him to undercut the prices of his rivals, but it may have been this aspect which initially led such patrons as Burne-Jones, Charles Ricketts, Poynter, Holman Hunt and Morris to use his services.

Phillips was certain to find favour with Mrs. Haweis because of his use of paintings as a source of inspiration. The National Portrait Exhibition in 1866 has focused attention on the richness of ornament in Tudor portraits, and the pendant jewel worn by the young Princess Elizabeth in a portrait attributed to Holbein was used by Phillips as the source for a jewel of which he made many versions (see Colour Plate 44). In the same exhibition was the portrait by Master John of Lady Jane Grey which provided William Burges with the form for his marriage jewel for Gwendolen Mary Howard, Marchioness of Bute, in 1872 (see plates 50 and 51). The cross he designed, it is thought for his own use, however, is an exercise in Puginesque neo-Gothic of fine workmanship in heavy gold (see Colour Plate 42).

Although much of the neo-Gothic and neo-Renaissance metalwork produced during the nineteenth century was inspired by innovators like Pugin and Froment-Meurice, it was seen for the first time by a very large public at the great International Exhibitions held in Europe at intervals during the mid-nineteenth century. The copiously illustrated catalogues of these exhibitions certainly served as pattern books in the same way as the art magazines of the period, but the influence of Romantic literature and painting was almost equally strong. The literary works of Sir Walter Scott were regarded with a reverence normally reserved for holy writ as most cultivated Victorians had read every one of his novels; the French were equally impressed with the romantic qualities of the world of Victor Hugo. F.D. Froment-Meurice has been called *'le Victor Hugo de l'orfèvrerie'*, and the neo-Gothic and Renaissance jewellery design of the period is the embodiment of the romanticism of contemporary literature.

The medievalising cult of the neo-Gothic designers like Pugin and Burges was reinforced by the example of the Pre-Raphaelite painters and such later adherents of the original group as Morris and Burne-Jones, whose influence on late nineteenth century decorative art, both in England and on the Continent, was of incalculable importance. The founding of Morris and Company in 1861 (as Morris, Marshall, Faulkner & Co., just in time to exhibit for the first time, in company with the Japanese and the Roman goldsmith Castellani, at the 1862 Exhibition, which could thus claim, on these grounds alone, to be the origin of the Art Nouveau movement in Europe and America) provided the example which was to inspire a number of other apparently uncommercial ventures, and to remove the monopoly in supplying the public from the mass-manufacturers whose taste was already being called into

Plate 35. 'The Children's Holiday: Portrait of the Fairbairn Family' by William Holman Hunt. Oil on canvas. (Torre Abbey, Torbay.)

This is a group portrait of the family of Holman Hunt's friend, Sir Thomas Fairbairn, Bt., who was a consistent and loyal patron of the artist and at one time he owned 'The Awakening Conscience' and 'The Scapegoat' by Hunt. Fairbairn was also chairman of the Manchester Art Treasures Exhibition and, for his work, he was presented with a silver and enamel trowel made by Robert Phillips, in 1856. This presentation may have led Fairbairn to go to Phillips to buy the jewellery his wife wears in the family portrait. Made of gold in the Archaeological style the demi-parure is set with corals and heightened with blue enamel. An identical suite of jewellery had been shown by Phillips at the 1862 exhibition and had won a medal. An interest in jewellery seems to be developing between the two small girls in the foreground who have made an attractive necklace from the waxy red wild rose hips.

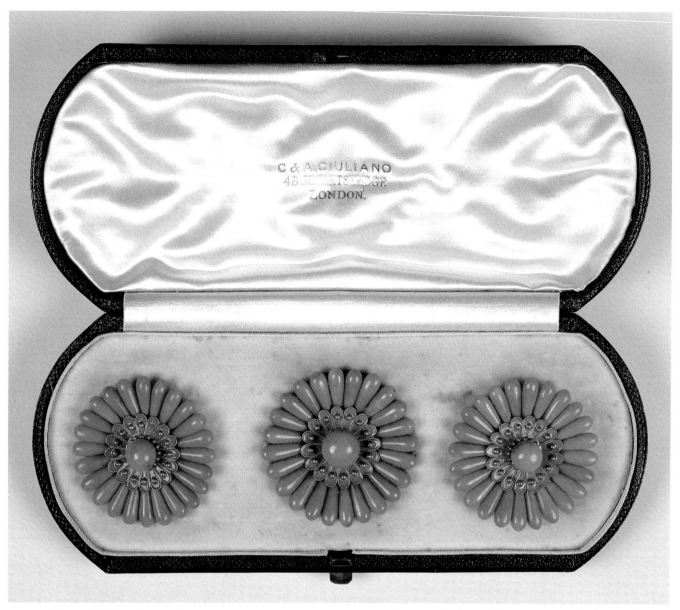

Colour Plate 24. A pair of hair ornaments and brooch en suite *by Giuliano, in the form of flower heads made of coral, from the collection of Edith Holman Hunt. The gold centres are applied with pale green enamel and set centrally with a coral bead. The ornaments are not marked, but the brooch is signed 'CG'. The jewels are contained within a fitted leather case by Kitts, the lid satin of which bears the '48 Knightsbridge' address of Carlo and Arthur Giuliano. Since the brooch is signed 'CG' it cannot have been made later than 1895. (Mrs Elizabeth Tompkin.)*

There is an obvious discrepancy between the date of this brooch and its case, which must have been made between 1912 and 1914. These jewels are owned by the adopted daughter of Gladys Holman Hunt, Mrs Elizabeth Tompkin. She has suggested that the brooch may have been acquired by William Holman Hunt for his wife Edith and that the combs may have been adapted, or commissioned between 1912 and 1914 to match the brooch.

Colour Plate 25. A parure of jewellery by Carlo Giuliano comprising a necklace, bracelet, comb and brooch. The openwork gold is decorated with black and white enamel and is set with opals, green zircons and diamonds. The necklace is equipped with rings so that it may be stitched to the collar of a dress as well as being worn next to the skin. Also, there is some evidence that the necklace is earlier than the other jewels and that they were made to match it. The whole parure is contained in an unusually fine and distinctive gold tooled red morocco leather case. (Photograph by Wartski, London.)

This parure has no precise provenance, but it has close stylistic parallels with those jewels made for Constantine Ionides and the Gibbs family of Bristol, both of whom were devoted enthusiasts of Giuliano's work.

Plate 36. Penelope and Aglaia, the daughters of Constantine Ionides. The photographer is unknown, but the print presumably dates from about 1880. (Private Collection.)

At the collars of their satin blouses, the girls wear enamelled gold brooches by Giuliano. The languorous mood which this photograph evokes, together with the rich effects of the various textiles, calls to mind the photographic work of Dante Gabriel Rossetti. Ionides was a considerable patron and friend of the artist and even asked him to design a monogram for his silk handkerchiefs.

question by an increasingly critical and influential section of the consumer population. In certain aspects the decorative revival which took place during the second half of the nineteenth century can be seen as an ultimately doomed rearguard action fought against the advance of mass-production, a view which is backed up by the failure of the Art Furniture Alliance, Christopher Dresser's unsuccessful attempt to bring aestheticism into mass production. Mrs. Haweis gave the pioneer artist/designers little credit for their efforts when she wrote in 1878: 'Yet it is greatly to be deplored that living artists should do so little to popularise good art, and bring it within the reach of the many who cannot buy pictures but who can buy a bracelet or a tea service'. (*The Art of Beauty,* p.106.)

The art of Japan was of as much importance as the Gothic revival as a source of inspiration to the jewellery designers of the *fin de siècle.* The cult of Japan was an important aspect of the Aesthetic movement, the decorative art movement which has been called the 'prelude to Art Nouveau' (by Elizabeth Aslin, as a sub-title to *The Aesthetic Movement,* 1969), and it is significant that a number of the most important artistic figures whose aestheticism was to make the evolution of the European Art Nouveau movement possible were collectors of Japanese prints, porcelain and other decorative art objects. Many interior decorating schemes, and even actual pieces of furniture, were designed with the intention that they should incorporate collections of Japanese blue and white porcelain (and incidentally look incomplete without them) but the only specifically 'chinamania' jewellery, as distinct from the Japanese style pieces copied more or less unaltered from Japanese originals, is in the form of plate-shaped earrings and brooches in gold enamelled with the famous 'willow-pattern', patented in the 1870s. The Japanese influence on jewellery design came from the prints which were the first Japanese art objects to be widely collected, and from decorative objects in metalwork and enamel, porcelain and ivory. The romantic and possibly apocryphal story of the Japanese prints which were found amongst the wrapping papers on a package sent to France in the late 1850s is often cited as the origin of the cult of Japanese art in Europe, but the fact that an exhibition of Japanese applied art was held in London as early as 1854 is frequently overlooked. By 1858, as the result of prolonged negotiations which had been going on since 1853, the American Commodore Perry had managed to wrest limited trading rights from the still somewhat reluctant Japanese authorities, who were not entirely convinced of the wisdom of ending a segregation from Europe which had lasted for two centuries. Although the 1854 exhibition apparently made little impression at the time it is possible that it paved the way for the immediate impact which the Japanese exhibit shown at the 1862 International Exhibition in London had on the decorative art of the period (see Colour Plates 47, 48 and 50). As early as 1866 Edward Poynter had begun work on the design of the famous grill-room at the South Kensington (now Victoria and Albert) Museum showing very strongly the influence of Japanese taste. The grill itself, with its ovens and hot cupboards in the combination of iron, steel and brass which was to be used effectively for 'Japanese' metalwork fittings by a number of designers, is decorated with 'pies' and diapering in the Japanese manner. The magnificent blue and white tiles in this early decorative scheme have Japanese elements already blended with other 'aesthetic' motifs in anticipation of the effects which were aimed at, according to du Maurier, by his despised Kensingtonian aesthetes whom he ridiculed in his *Punch* cartoons (see plate 29).

After the closing of the 1862 Exhibition a number of the Japanese exhibits were disposed of through the Oriental department of Farmer and Rogers' 'Great Cloak and Shawl Emporium', the manager of the department at that time (from 1863) being the young Arthur Lasenby Liberty. After twelve years as Oriental Manager for Farmer and Rogers Liberty opened his own small shop in Regent Street in 1875. From the first Liberty stocked the finest Oriental art objects, as well as a number of goods which were more curious than decorative, such as the 'Tokio' tooth powder. Edward Godwin, writing in *The Architect* in 1876, described Liberty's premises as being 'literally crammed with objects of oriental manufacture'; thus it provided the most exciting treasure house for the distinguished artistic clientele of the shop, William Morris, Ruskin, D.G. Rossetti, Burne-Jones, Whistler, Norman Shaw and Godwin himself being among the frequent customers of the store.

The enthusiasm in Europe for Japanese decorative objects was satisfied from quite an early date by pieces made by the Japanese for the European market. These are presumably the pieces described in Liberty's catalogue of *Eastern Art Manufacturers* as 'Anglo-Japanese', and are made in what was believed by the Japanese craftsmen to be 'European' taste. Very little cloisonné enamel was used by the Japanese in pieces for home consumption. Most of the exported work was much too highly coloured for Japanese taste, and virtually the only

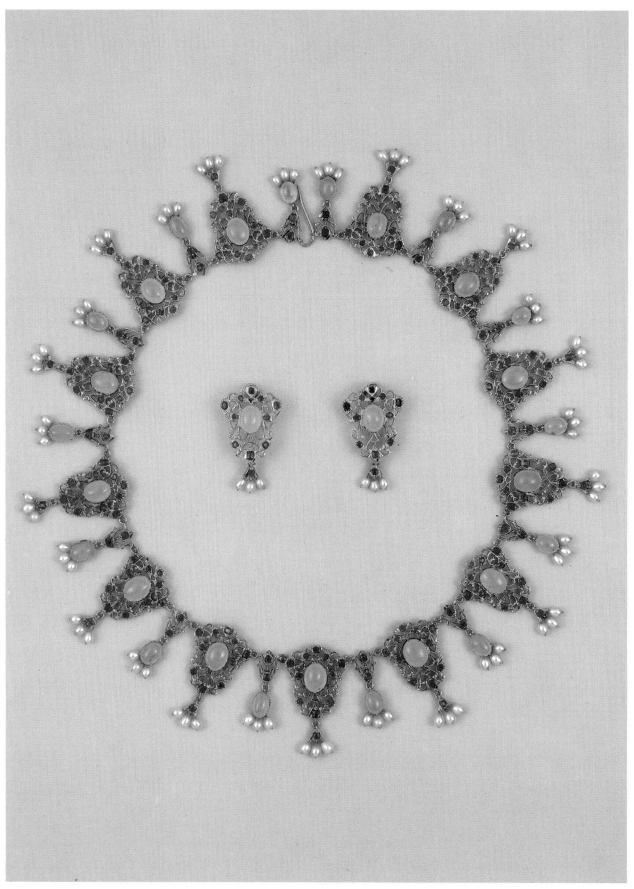

72

pieces bought by the Japanese themselves were for their newly fashionable 'European' rooms, of which certain rich Japanese liked to have one or two in their houses. Mrs. Henry Adams wrote from Paris in 1879: 'Tell Bill Bigelow [Japanese scholar, expert and collector] we went to his "Bing" and were much interested in his Japanese things. I succumbed to a small piece of Japanese silver, a matchbox, which I wear as a pendant from my chatelaine. Tiffany's are good, but this is better...it's a seed vessel of some kind, and the calix opens on a hinge as cover.' (*The Letters of Mrs. Henry Adams*, 1887, p.183). Tiffany's first exhibited jewellery and silverwork in the Japanese style and using adaptations of Japanese techniques at the 1876 Philadelphia Centennial Exposition; in 1878 at the Paris Exposition they were awarded a gold medal and their Japanese style work was particularly commended in the jury reports. Although the firm was founded in 1841, jewellery was only manufactured from about 1848. At the turn of the century the image of Tiffany's was to be transformed by the involvement of C.L. Tiffany's son Louis Comfort Tiffany, an artist of considerable accomplishments.

Most of the small pieces of Japanese metalwork made by the sword furniture makers, unemployed at their traditional trade since the banning of the Samurai sword in the 'sixties, were designed specifically for export, and the enormous influence of these on European metalwork design is Japanese at two removes, in that they are based on designs taken from obsolete functional objects further modified to conform with alien taste. The idea of European taste in Japan was, in any case, gleaned from the decorative pieces made especially for the Oriental market, and was certainly as false as the European idea of Oriental taste which came only from 'Anglo-Japanese' art.

It is curious, in view of the great sophistication of their decorative art both technically and artistically, to recollect that at the time of the International Exhibition in 1862 the Japanese were regarded as barely civilised. C.L. Eastlake writing in *Hints on Household Taste* in 1867 speaks of them as 'half-civilised' and brackets them with a people he describes as the 'rude barbarians of Feejee'. Sir William Hardman, the Victorian observer and recorder, affected to believe that the Japanese visitors to the opening of the 1862 Exhibition smelled, and describes these distinguished and intelligent representatives of the country whose party included two Ambassadors as 'a rum lot'. A note by the editor of Hardman's letters records the information that in London the Japanese were regarded as 'a new variety of curious savage'

Colour Plate 26. A necklace and earrings of openwork gold, set with chrysoprase and rubies, by Giuliano. No marks. (Private Collection.)

This suite is from the collection of Constantine Ionides whose family were well known amongst the artistic community in London in the nineteenth century, and were faithful customers of Carlo Giuliano and his sons Carlo and Arthur. Although it may not be immediately obvious this suite of jewellery is inspired by Indian work, another parure by Giuliano in the same genre is known, and its aesthetic ancestry is quite unmistakable. Although this jewellery is unsigned and is without its original box it is recorded as being by Giuliano in the Ionides jewellery inventory.

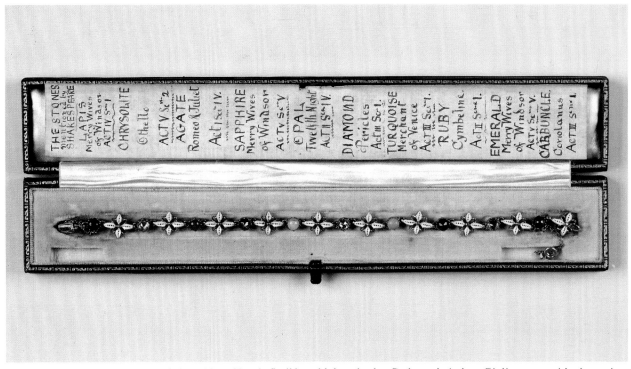

Colour Plate 27. A flexible gold bracelet by Carlo and Arthur Giuliano set with the various gemstones mentioned in the plays of William Shakespeare. Each stone is separated by a gold quatrefoil with opaque white and black enamelling. It is signed 'C and A.G.' and is contained within its original box together with a hand written annotation of the meaning of each stone. (Ulf Breede, Cologne.)

(see *A Mid-Victorian Pepys,* by S.M. Ellis, 1923). Hardman's views on the manners of the Japanese were so well known by his family when he displeased his three-year-old daughter by reprimanding her for her behaviour at table she retorted by calling him a 'Japanese ambassador' (Ellis, p.123). Whatever the initial impression created by the Japanese themselves on the English and the French (the same party of Japanese who visited London in 1862 had first visited Paris where they were regarded as 'objects of curiosity rather than admiration', Ellis, p.119), the fact remains that the influence of Japanese art was to be of profound importance to the development of decorative art at the turn of the century, and the most cursory examination of the art journals and magazines of the period reveals the continuing interest in all aspects of Japanese art which endured until well after the First World War. Impassioned arguments about the exact composition of the alloys used in Japanese metalwork were a commonplace in *The Studio* during the early years of the present century and the founding of the Japan Society of London bears witness to the serious collecting interest which was shown in Japanese art. Japanese art amateurs in the jewellery world included Henry Vever, the French jeweller and author of *La Bijouterie Française au XIXᵉ Siècle,* Edward C. Moore, director and chief designer for C.L. Tiffany, Siegfried Bing, owner of La Maison de l'Art Nouveau and editor of *Le Japon Artistique,* the Glasgow architect and jewellery designer J. Cromar Watt (see Colour Plates 15 and 16), and A.C.D. Jahn, jeweller and headmaster of the Wolverhampton School of Art.

Henri Vever's important position in the world of Japanese art collecting is well known to the London art world and to modern collectors through the sales

Colour Plate 28. *A hexagonal enamelled gold locket by Carlo and Arthur Giuliano made as a charm for the month of April. The jewel is decorated with daisies, almond blossoms, and milkwort being the attributes of the month and is set with a star sapphire. The reverse of the jewel is set with a green sapphire and is enamelled in the Indian manner of shades of green, red and white. (Private Collection.)*

Made for Constantine Ionides to give to his daughter, Lallie, on her birthday. Ionides was the centre of a large and influential Greek family and he was known amongst his relations as 'Zeus' or 'The Thunderer'. He lived at 8 Holland Villas and was a patron of Rossetti.

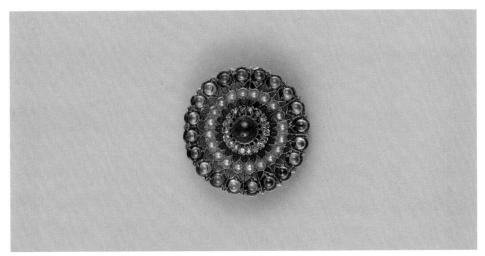

Colour Plate 29. *An openwork gold brooch by Carlo Giuliano set with cabochon green zircons, seed pearls, and rose diamonds. Provenance: Constantine Ionides. (Wartski, London.)*

Plate 37. A gold cruciform pendant by Carlo and Arthur Giuliano decorated with black and white enamel and set with four coloured cabochons. The pendant hangs from an enamelled gold candy-twist chain interspersed with pearls. A note in Queen Alexandra's own hand within the box reads 'For my dear little godchild Alexandra Cadogan from Alexandra'. (By kind permission of His Grace The Duke of Marlborough. Kept in the Second State Room of Blenheim Palace.)

of his Japanese prints and works of art. No less than three full sessions were needed to dispose of the Henri Vever Collection of Fine Japanese Works of Art (two at the end of the 1972 and one in July, 1973) which included examples of the finest metalwork in the form of tsubas and other sword furniture. It was through Vever's enthusiasm that the monthly meetings instituted by Bing for the large Parisian circle of collectors of Japanese art were kept going well after the turn of the century. The meetings of these enthusiastic *amateurs* are described by Coquelin, the theatrical impresario, in his memoirs. It is all the more curious, in view of Vever's passionate interest in Japanese art, that so little of its influence either technical or artistic should appear in the products of the Vever jewellery firm.

Christopher Dresser early recognised the characteristic of Japanese metalworking which distinguished it from European work, and wrote of the Japanese as 'the only perfect metalworkers which the world has yet produced, for they are the only people who do not think of the material, and regard the effect produced as of far greater moment than the material employed.' Dresser's continual propaganda in favour of artistic rather than materialistic criteria for jewellery and metalwork did much to pave the way for the eventual acceptance of the craft ethic.

Plate 38. A photograph of Queen Victoria's daughter, H.R.H. Princess Louise, Marchioness of Lorne. She wears a candy-twist chain and pendant set with faceted stone which appears to be by Giuliano. (The Royal Archives, Windsor Castle.)

The Princess was an enthusiastic patron of contemporary jewellers and some pieces from her collection were shown at the 'Loan Exhibition of Ancient and Modern Jewellery and Personal Ornaments' which was held at the South Kensington Museum in 1872.

Plate 39. A gold and enamel pendant by Carlo Giuliano in the form of a cross decorated with black and white enamel, the terminals are set with a sapphire, a pale ruby, a green sapphire and a star sapphire. A diamond is set at the intersection of the four arms. The candy twist chain from which the jewel hangs is made up of black and white and translucent red enamelled baton shaped links, separated with pearls. It was made betweeen 1874 and 1895. (Sotheby's.)

This jewel was once the property of H.R.H. Princess Louise, the elder daughter of King Edward VII, who was known as the Princess Royal. She was married to the Duke of Fife in 1889 and died in 1931.

One aspect of the Aesthetic movement which certainly contributed to such limited commercial success as the Craft Revival jewellery enjoyed at the turn of the century was its espousal by two of the leading Aesthetic publicists of the campaign for the reform of contemporary female dress. Both Mrs. Haweis,

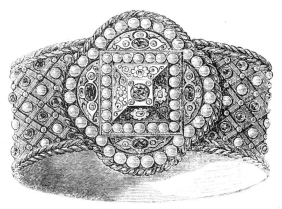

Bracelet given to Princess Helena
by the Maharajah Dhuleep Singh.
Illustrated London News

Colour Plate 31. A gold brooch decorated with white enamel and set with pearls, emeralds and rose diamonds. This jewel was once the detachable centre of a bracelet given by the Maharajah Duleep Singh to Princess Helena (1846-1923). It is photographed against an extract from The Illustrated London News *(see* Jewelry *edited by Harold H. Hart, New York 1978). The shape of the jewel seems to be influenced by Italian medieval themes but the use of enamel and gemstones echoes the exotic origins of the giver. Presumably the jewel was given to the Princess when she married Prince Christian of Schleswig-Holstein in 1866.*

Colour Plate 30. 'The Maharajah Duleep Singh' by Franz Xaver Winterhalter (1805-1873), 1854. Oil on canvas. (Reproduced by Gracious Permission of Her Majesty the Queen.)
 The Maharajah was a close friend of Queen Victoria from the age of sixteen. Their relationship was not invariably happy and carefree, but disagreements between them were ultimately reconciled before his death in 1893.

whose book *The Art of Beauty* deals in considerable detail with artistic dress even to the extent of suggesting the most suitable colour for hair, and Oscar Wilde, whose wife is believed to have suffered from considerable embarrassment at having to appear in public in clothes of her husband's (eccentric) design, were ardent believers in the necessity for dress reform. Anna, Comtesse de Brémont wrote in her study of Oscar Wilde: 'The next thing that arrested my gaze was a young woman arrayed in an exquisite Greek costume of cowslip yellow and apple-leaf green. Her hair, a thick mass of ruddy brown, was wonderfully set off by bands of yellow ribbon, supporting the knot of hair low on the nape of the neck, and crossing the wavy masses above the brow. The whole arrangement was exceedingly becoming to the youthful, almost boyish face with its clear colouring and full, dark eyes. There was an air of shy self-consciousness and restraint about the wearer of that fantastic yet lovely costume that gave me the impression of what is called stage fright, and I jumped to the conclusion that she was a young actress dressed up for a recital, and somewhat nervous before all the Society folk present. Imagine my surprise when she was introduced to me as my hostess.' (*Oscar Wilde and His Mother*, 1911, pp.88-9). Robert Sherrard, Wilde's first biographer, remembered Mrs. Wilde's wedding costume: 'The bride's rich creamy satin dress was of a delicate cowslip tint; the bodice cut somewhat low in front, was finished with a high Medici collar; the ample sleeves were puffed; the skirt, made plain, was gathered by a silver girdle of beautiful workmanship, the gift of Mr. Oscar

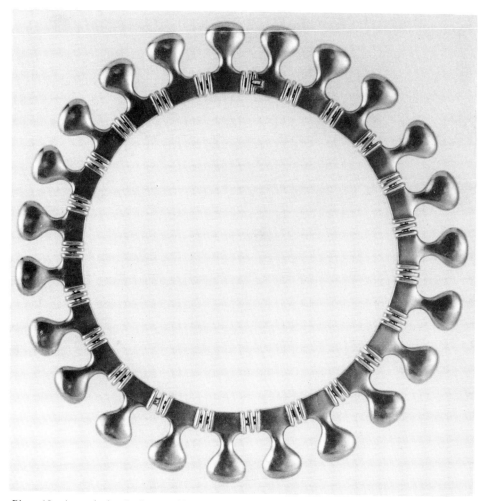

Plate 40. *An articulated silver necklace by Carlo Giuliano, signed with his initials. (Wartski, London.)*

It seems likely that this is one of a series commissioned by Queen Victoria since an identical jewel was given by her to Jenny Lind (1820-1887) the famous soprano called 'The Swedish Nightingale', (see Margaret Flower, Victorian Jewellery, *1952, plate 174.) Another is seen in the portrait of Princess Louise, opposite. The source for this jewel remains obscure; it may be that ancient Scandinavian jewellery had been seen as appropriate to Jenny Lind's origins. Certainly the work recalls that of Georg Jensen. Jenny Lind sang to Queen Victoria on many occasions, sometimes in private.*

Wilde; the veil of saffron-coloured Indian silk gauze was embroidered with pearls and worn in Marie Stuart fashion; a thick wreath of myrtle leaves crowned her frizzed hair; the dress was ornamented with clusters of myrtle leaves; the large bouquet had as much green in it as white'. (*The Life of Oscar Wilde*, 1906, pp.255-6).

Conventional fashionable dress of the period was the exact opposite of rational in any sense, possibly its least rational aspect being the financial outlay involved rather than any consideration of aesthetics or convenience. The elaborate draping, pleating and layering of the dresses fashionable from the mid-'seventies until the turn of the century involved the use of yards of stiff material, some of which was chemically treated with loading to give it the necessary body to hold the shape, not to mention the expensive trimmings of lace, braid and beads. The Rational Dress Association was understandably

Plate 41. H.R.H. Princess Louise, Marchioness of Lorne. A watercolour by Blanche Lindsay (wife of Sir Coutts Lindsay, founder of the Grosvenor Gallery). (Christopher Newall.)
The Princess is shown wearing a version, or perhaps one and the same necklace, as that illustrated opposite. See also plate 38 where the Princess is seen wearing another Giuliano jewel.

Colour Plate 32. A necklace in silver gilt and green hardstone beads, designed by Sir Edward Poynter (1836-1919) and made by Carlo Giuliano (1831-1895) for Poynter's watercolour entitled 'Helen' (see opposite).

The gold jewellery of Helen of Troy which had been discoverd by Heinrich Schliemann in 1873 was well known to Giuliano who had tested the purity of the alloy and minutely described each piece for the famous archaeologist. However, Poynter did not think the jewellery heroic enough for his purposes and decided to ask Giuliano to make up the necklace illustrated above to furnish his model. Minor adaptations to form and colour have taken place during the working of the portrait. The necklace and earrings of agate and gold beads by Carlo Giuliano, also shown above, echo the design of that worn by Poynter's 'Helen'. Although unlikely to have been made for the artist's use they are clearly based on his design. (Wartski, London.)

Colour Plate 33. 'Helen', by Sir Edward Poynter, 1887. Watercolour and gold paint on paper. (Reproduced by Gracious Permission of Her Majesty the Queen.)
  The jewellery worn by the model is a classical fantasy created by the artist and the tiara, still untraced, may owe its origins to the Parisian jewellers of the Second Empire.

concerned mainly with the restriction of movement which these fashions imposed on the women who wore them, and one reads in this connection about the divided skirts and shorter lengths of dress which permitted at least some show of sporting activity. A women's magazine, curiously named *The Owlet Papers,* in 1861 remarked the following: 'Surely it is unworthy of an intellectual being to be attired in a manner which precludes the possibility of almost every rational enjoyment: how is it possible to walk in comfort if the dress is either so long as to sweep the street, or, as the case is at present, so wide as to take up immeasurable space?' One of the features which most distinguished 'aesthetic' dress from the high fashion alternative was the multiplicity of soft gathers allowing a degree of freedom unimagined since the Empire period. The source for the shape is in occupational costume, for example the agricultural worker's smock.

By no means all the comment was favourable with regard to this mode of dress: 'We saw six or eight of them Wednesday night at the Royal Academy reception,' wrote Mrs. Henry Adams in 1873, 'such funny people! Mrs Alma Tadema, the Belgian artist's wife, who is an English woman, looked like a lymphatic tigress draped in yellow Japanese embroidered silk, bracelets at the top of her arms, hair the colour of tiger lilies and that fiery flower hanging in bunches from it. She waved up and down the room like a serpent and we trotted round after her'. (*Letters,* p.130). Lady Alma Tadema's bracelets must surely have been in the 'archaeological' style. Her interest in antique jewellery is attested by the very beautiful seventeenth century enamelled necklace with a centrepiece in the form of a bow which is now in the Victoria and Albert Museum. Aesthetic fashion is very elusive. The aesthetic connection with the Rational Dress Movement was peripheral to say the least, and really amounts to a common belief in the unaesthetic appearance of the tightly corseted female figure. It is doubtful whether the concern for health which motivated Mrs. Bloomer and Herr Jaeger interested the wearers of artistic dresses to any great extent, but the other crucial aspect of Rational Dress propaganda which was very important to them was that the freedom of movement permitted to a woman who wore the loose flowing dresses favoured by the aesthetes liberated the wearer from a useless immobile life spent immured in the drawing-room. Arthur Lasenby Liberty, with his characteristic quick and shrewd appraisal of the situation, saw the commercial possibilities of artistic dress, suitably modified to protect his customers from the embarrassment which Mrs. Wilde endured. As far as can be judged. from the line drawings in the Liberty catalogues the artistic teagowns sold by the firm in the 'eighties were still designed with the main lines of fashionable Parisian dresses kept firmly in mind. Liberty's chief contribution to aesthetic fashion was in the form of the soft Oriental fabrics and lengths of embroidery stocked by his shop which could be used to make artistic dresses of the wearer's own devising. Madame Forma, a dressmaker with premises in Bond Street who was patronised by Mrs. Nelson Dawson among others, made these artistic dresses in straight uncluttered lines, trimmed with wide bands of embroidery, and it was not beyond the capacity of any reasonably competent seamstress to make her own. Attention to the small details of dress also singled out the artistic dresser from the fashionable; for instance the Duchess of Rutland, who was an accomplished portraitist, considered white vulgar and insisted that all her lace dress trimmings be tinted either pink or pale-brown, the latter effect being achieved by immersion in cold tea.

It is inconceivable that, without this cult of the aesthetic in dress, the jewellery produced by the Craft Revival designers could have enjoyed even such limited recognition as it did. In the enormous elaboration of the conventional fashionable dress of the period the modest silver, mother-of-pearl and moonstone pendants produced in the craft workshops would have been completely lost. In the *Handbook of Costume in the Nineteenth Century* (Faber, 1959) C. Willet Cunnington records that in 1884 a magazine was asking its readers if cats, dogs, mice and monkeys were really suitable dress trimmings! The most fashionable jewellery of the period was in the form of minutely realistic insects, even flies were worn without distaste. Fashionable dress in the 'nineties, with the immense sleeves contrasted with the tightly corseted waist, was in its own way as restricting of movement as the crinoline, and fashionable jewellery had still to compete with the elaborate and often garish trimmings which had been regarded as an essential part of the costume for more than three decades. The turn of the century saw no diminution of the luxury and elaboration of fashionable dress, and the period 1900-10 saw the introduction of a further extravagance in the popularity of lavish hand embroidery for evening dresses. Abundant trimmings of real lace and the essential long white gloves added further to the expense of evening dresses and it is impossible to imagine such a toilette without the precious jewellery, preferably of diamonds, which is its natural complement. Seen in the context of the world of fashion, the success of the Craft Revival designers in interesting even a limited number of committed aesthetes in their aims is truly remarkable.

Colour Plate 34. An enamelled gold pendant by Giuliano centering on a composite opal cameo of an angel seen against a seascape, almost certainly carved by Wilhelm Schmidt (1845-1938). The gem is protected by a glass and is contained within an architectural setting, enamelled translucent red and opaque black and white, and set with brilliant cut diamonds. The jewel hangs from a black and white enamelled candy-twist chain interspersed with pearls. (Poynter Family Collection.)

This pendant was designed by Sir Edward Poynter for his wife Agnes. She was one of the celebrated daughters of the Rev. G.B. Macdonald. Her sister was Lady Burne-Jones and it may be that it was she who recommended that Giuliano should be given this commission.

Colour Plate 35. A matching brooch to the pendant designed by Sir Edward Poynter in Colour Plate 34. This time the jewel frames a opal cameo of a girl, also attributable to Schmidt (see 'Wilhelm Schmidt' by Gertrud Siedmann, Apollo, *Vol. CXXVIII, No. 317, July 1988). Poynter seems to have based the subject matter of this gem on one of his oil paintings called 'High Noon', dated 1889, which is illustrated in A.G. Temple's* The Art of Painting in The Queen's Reign, *London, 1897, p.191. This jewel is also by Giuliano. (The Poynter Family Collection.)*

Plate 42. Clara Bell (née Poynter) for whom the Indian style necklace by Giuliano in Colour Plate 36 was made. She was the sister of the painter Sir Edward Poynter, PRA, RWS (1836-1919) who was also a customer of Giuliano's (see Colour Plate 32). Poynter was the brother-in-law of Sir Edward Burne-Jones who also commissioned several pieces of jewellery from Giuliano. (Private Collection.)

Colour Plate 36. A seven row Oriental pearl necklace and pendant by Carlo and Arthur Giuliano in Indian style, strung from black and white champlevé enamelled mounts, set with brilliant cut diamonds taken at the battle of Seringapatam. The openwork gold pendant is set with a central cushion shaped brilliant cut diamond also from Seringapatam, in a neo-Renaissance style collet setting, and is similarly decorated with painted black and white enamel. The necklace mounts are secured by fine 'loop in loop' gold safety chains. It is signed in five places 'C and AG'.

The original fitted case for the jewel bears the initials 'ECB' for Clara Bell, for whom the jewel was made. Clara Bell was the sister of Sir Edward Poynter and the jewel was commissioned from Giuliano between 1895 and 1912 by her son C.F. Bell, keeper of Fine Arts at the Ashmolean Museum. The diamonds were booty resulting from the victory at Seringapatam in 1799 taken by General Robert Bell, Clara Bell's grandfather-in-law. The General, then Major Bell, of the Madras Artillery, led the attack into the assault on the breech and was shown in the painting 'The Storming of Seringapatam' by Sir Robert Ker Porter, reproduced in stipple engraving with accompanying key by J. Vendramini, and published in 1802. (Private Collection.)

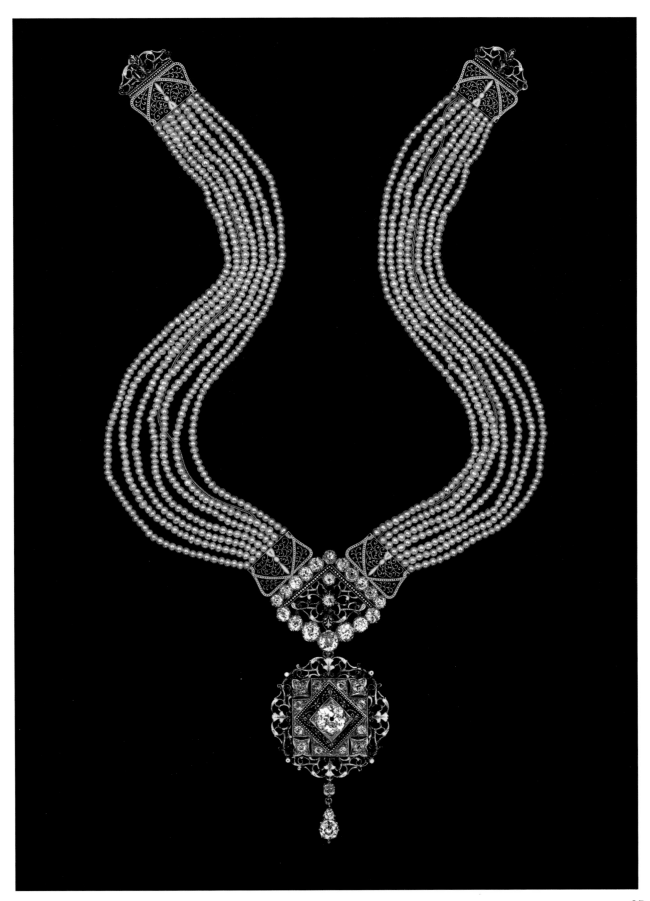

Plate 43. A pendant in Lombardic style by Carlo Giuliano, decorated with enamel and set with a sapphire, four emeralds and four pearls. (The Fine Art Society, London.)

Plate 44. A pencil portrait of Ellen Terry by George Frederick Watts, OM, RA, from the collection of Dame Ellen Terry. (The Fine Art Society, London.)
This drawing was presented to Ellen Terry by her former husband in 1878, about a year after their divorce. It was taken from a photograph showing her in the costume of her Ophelia of 1878-9 at the Lyceum. The brooch she wears in the portrait is based on an Italian early medieval type much favoured by the Revivalist jewellers Castellani. and Giuliano (see plate 43).

Plate 46. An unusually large Scottish silver brooch set with a cairngorn, c.1880. The stone is held by trefoil settings on silver wire buttresses which are in turn supported on pierced and engraved neo-Gothic archways. (The National Trust, Smallhythe Place, Kent.)
This jewel was worn by Ellen Terry when she played Lady Macbeth and can be seen in the portrait of the actress by John Singer Sargent (see plate 45).

Plate 45. A portrait of Ellen Terry as Lady Macbeth, by John Singer Sargent. (The National Portrait Gallery, London.)
   Dame Alice Ellen Terry (1847-1928) played Lady Macbeth in Henry Irving's new production of Shakespeare's famous tragedy which opened at the Lyceum Theatre in London on 29 December 1888. Sargent was in the audience at the first performance and persuaded Terry to allow this portrait to be painted. The vivid green dress embroidered with gold thread was designed by Mrs. Comyns Carr and made by Mrs. Nettleship and was much praised for its barbaric qualities. Similar care has been taken in choosing the jewellery to suggest a 'raw boned daughter of the North' (The Times, 31 December 1888). As well as two heavy belts made of rectangular and oval hammered plaques the actress wears dress ornaments on her shoulders and a large silver brooch set with a cairngorm at her neck (see plate 46). The splendidly primitive crown she holds above her head is Duncan's.

89

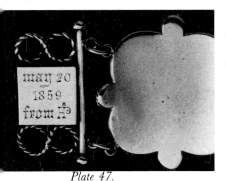

Plate 47.

Colour Plate 37. A gold bracelet decorated with enamel in the medieval taste set with carbuncles, pearls and turquoises. Made by J. Hardman and Co., 1859 (dated inscription on the reverse). The clasp is enamelled with the gothic letters 'AP' dated 'May 20 1859 from HP' on the reverse (see plate 47). (Private Collection.)

The monogram on the reverse probably refers to John Harman Powell who did purchase a 'Gold Bracelet Richly enamelled and set with jewels' for £16.10.0d. on 30 July, 1859. The monogram AP surely stands for Anne Powell (1810-1890) his wife, who was the daughter of Augustus W.N. Pugin.

The three quatrefoil links compare in decoration with those which form the necklace in the set of marriage jewellery (now in the Victoria and Albert Museum), made by Hardman for Pugin and exhibited at the Great Exhibition of 1851 (see Birmingham Gold and Silver 1773-1973, cat. no. C73).

Bracelets

Full size

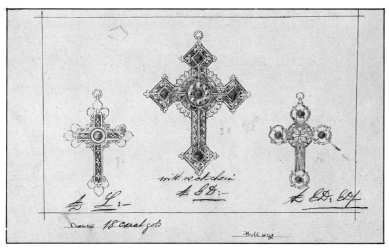

Colour Plate 39. Designs for three 18ct. gold crosses in medieval style from the record book of Hardman and Co. (Birmingham City Museum and Art Gallery.)

Colour Plate 40. A gold brooch by John Hardman and Co. of Birmingham, decorated in the medieval taste with champlevé enamel in the form of a vase of Madonna lilies. The six lobes of the jewel are engraved with fleur-de-lis and set with clusters of three pearls. The borders are defined with filigree and gold granules; the reverse has a glazed compartment for a souvenir. (Private Collection.)

The brooch is photographed against the illustrated warehouse book of Hardman and Co. (now owned by the Birmingham City Museum and Art Gallery) dated 15th February 1883 which shows the preliminary design. The customer's name was Roskell. Jewels of this nature by Hardman are extremely rare and were made for a small group of English Catholic families. Like that illustrated in plate 15 the brooch seems to have some close association with the jewellery designs of William Burges.

Colour Plate 38. Design in watercolour on paper. The drawing for the bracelet in Colour Plate 37 and another bracelet in the medieval style from the daybooks of J. Hardman and Co. (The City Museum and Art Gallery, Birmingham.)

Plate 48. The marriage jewellery designed for his third wife by Augustus Welby Northmore Pugin, shown at the Great Exhibition of 1851, from an illustration in The Industrial Arts of The XIXth Century, *by Matthew Digby Wyatt. Vol. II, Plate LXXXII. Made by Hardman and Co., the pieces are decorated with enamel, and set with pearls, diamonds and carbuncles.*

The jewellery was originally intended for Pugin's fiancée Helen Lumsden but their engagement was terminated in 1848. Pugin soon began courting Jane Knill and owing to the strange and fortuitous similarity between the two family crests there was no necessity to have the parure altered. Pugin wrote to Helen: 'I have thirty or forty people working different ways. There are five at your jewellery in Birmingham: of course I cannot pretend to vie in intrinsic value with thousands of people; but no woman, not excepting the Queen, will have better ornaments as regards taste, than you will.'

However, as a pioneer in the Revivalist movement, Pugin was not happy with the way the jewellery was being made. Letters between Hardman and Pugin (in a private collection) testify to his dissatisfaction: 'I think the half pearls execrable... only show me half pearls in the ancient jewellery'. In another letter Pugin stated: 'all the old examples show the pearls standing out fastened by gold wires... it is no use employing these men of confirmed bad habits... we must begin with a lad of uncorrupted person etc.' The correct way of setting pearls and minute cabochon gemstones on gold rods was later to be employed in jewels for the Marchioness of Bute designed by William Burges and by Castellani and Giuliano who had both studied in detail the workmanship of the medieval and classical goldsmiths' work. In 1851, in a mood of disillusionment Pugin said: 'I have passed my life in thinking fine things, designing fine things, and realizing very poor ones.' (For a full discussion by Shirley Bury of 'Pugin's Marriage Jewellery' see The Victoria and Albert Museum Yearbook, *1, 1969).*

Plate 49. A six lobed gold brooch set with garnets in the medieval style. The centre of the brooch is set with an enamel plaque of a woman in Gothic style dress holding the dove of peace. The letters 'PAX' are arranged in a haphazard way on the enamelled ground. (The Birmingham City Museum and Art Gallery.)

This jewel comes from a group, now in the Birmingham City Museum and Art Gallery which can be attributed to Hardman and Co., (see Birmingham Gold and Silver 1773-1973, *cat. nos. C30-C60, Birmingham City Museum and Art Gallery, 1973). They had made the parure of marriage jewellery designed by Augustus Pugin which was presented to his wife Jane Knill when they married on 10 August 1848 (see plate 48). This was a continuing association which had begun with the Medieval Metalworkers venture set up in 1838 by Hardman's, to supply church furnishings in the Gothic style. At the time of Pugin's death, his son-in-law, John Harman Powell, took over the role of designer to Hardman's, but there is also a demonstrable connection with designs for jewellery by William Burges, who may have been partly responsible for the development of this medievalising vein in Hardman's work.*

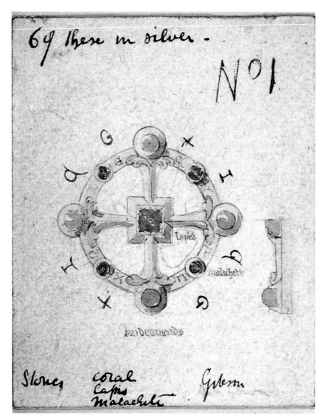

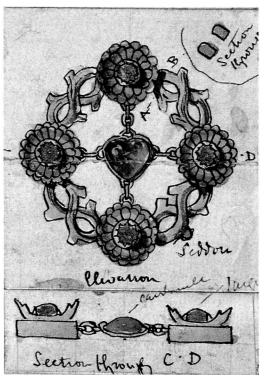

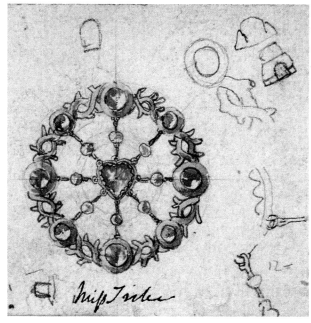

Colour Plate 41. Designs for jewels by William Burges including commissions from Mrs. Gibson, wife of the vicar responsible for the church at Selsey decorated by Morris and Burne-Jones, Seddon (presumably J.R. Seddon, the architect, partner of John Pritchard of Llandaff, a friend of Burges), and Gambier Parry, the antiquarian and collector, whose collection of ancient jewellery included a medieval reliquary pendant with which Burges's design may have been associated. These pieces are all still untraced. (The Victoria and Albert Museum.) Continued on p. 98.

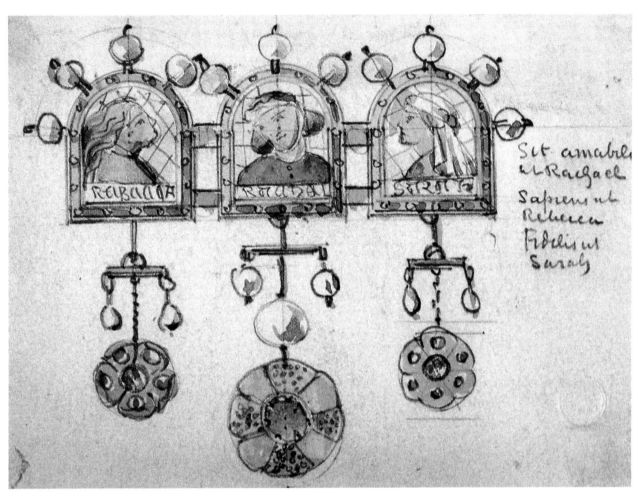

Sit amabl[e]
ut Rachael
Sapiens ut
Rebecca
Fidelis ut
Sarah

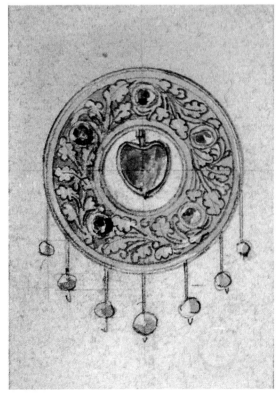

Plate 50. A detail of a portrait of Lady Jane Dudley (later Grey), by Master John, c.1545. (The National Portrait Gallery, London.)

This painting was lent to the Manchester Art Treasures Exhibition (no.16) in 1857 and to the South Kensington Exhibition of Tudor and Stuart portraits (no.131) in 1866, though in the latter exhibition it was labelled as 'Queen Katherine Parr' and attributed to Hans Holbein. The brooch which Lady Jane wears in this portrait seems a likely source of inspiration for the Gothic style brooch designed by Burges for the marriage of the Marquis of Bute (John Patrick Crichton-Stuart) to Miss Gwendolen Mary Ann Howard which took place on 16 April 1872. However the jewel was not completed until a year later (see plates 51 and 52) The same jewel appears in the fanciful portrait of Queen Katherine Parr devised by Richard Burchett for the decoration of the Prince's Chamber at the House of Lords, in 1856, a year before the Manchester Exhibition and ten years before the portrait exhibition. The painting was cited as a source by Burchett, and therefore although it was in the private collections, first of the Earl of Denbigh, and then Mr Richard Booth, it must have been known to the artist.

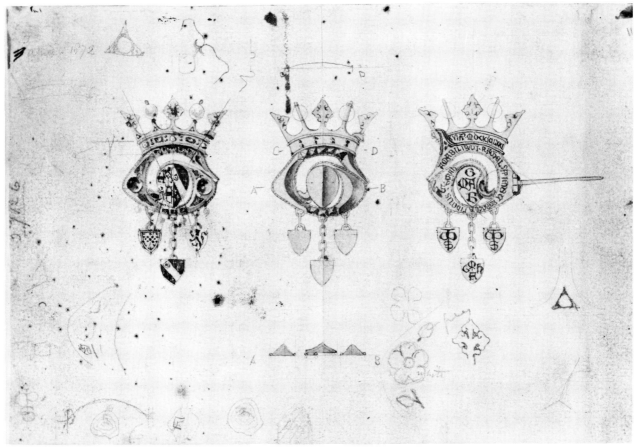

Plate 51. Part of the design for the Gothic style Bute jewel by William Burges, dated 3 April 1872. (The Most Hon. The Marquis of Bute.)

Plate 52. A gold brooch in the form of a Gothic 'G', in enamelled gold, set with faceted and cabochon gemstones and pearls, designed by William Burges in 1871-2. It was given by the famous architect and designer to Lady Bute in September 1872. On the reverse of the jewel the bride's initials are to be seen on the central pendant shield and in the centre of the jewel, where her name has changed to Bute. (The Most Hon. the Marquis of Bute.)

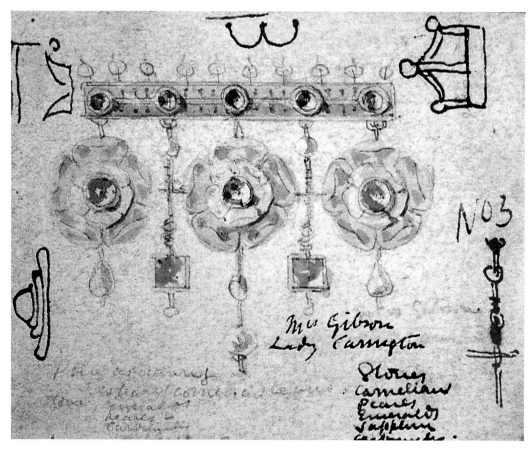

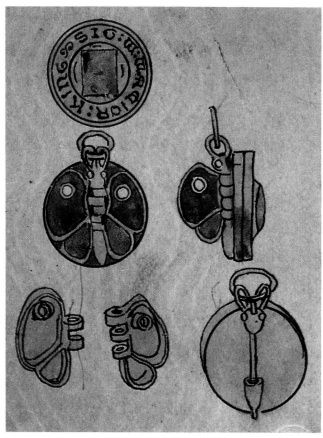

Colour Plate 41 continued. For caption see p.94.

98

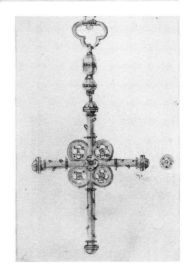

Colour Plate 42. A gold pectoral cross and chain in a Gothic style designed by William Burges, probably for his own use. The arms of the cross end in quatrefoils which are set with emeralds and sapphires and their intersection is set with a central ruby. The cross is pierced with the Latin inscription in Lombardic script 'Per Crucem Ad Lucem' (Through the cross to light). This jewel was made c.1860. (The Hull-Grundy Gift to the British Museum.)

The intended recipient of this cross still eludes research in Burges's records. It has been suggested that it may have been made for his own use for ceremonies connected with the Rosicrucians. Burges, like his patron Lord Bute, had a taste for dressing in medieval costume, and he would not have needed to have had an elaborate excuse for wearing this jewelled cross and chain. The architect and designer, E.W. Godwin, was a great admirer of Burges; eventually he gathered enough courage to seek the acquaintance of his fellow Gothic enthusiast: 'I introduced myself; he was hospitable, poured wine into a silver goblet of his own design, and placed bread upon the table.' Eventually Burges's rooms were to be filled with ornaments and utensils 'of his own design', all in everyday use, although many were of precious materials and very fragile.

Plate 53. Designs for three pectoral crosses by William Burges from one of his sketchbooks (shown reduced). Amongst them is the design for the gold cross now in the Hull-Grundy Gift to the British Museum (Colour Plate 42). (The Victoria and Albert Museum.)

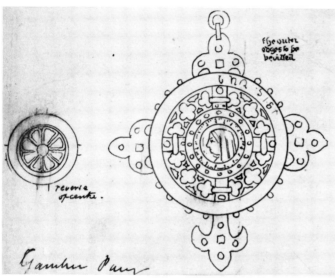

Plate 54. Designs for jewels in the medieval taste by William Burges, presumably intended for Thomas Gambier Parry, a noted connoisseur of Italian primitive paintings. (The Victoria and Albert Museum.)

Plate 55. A gold brooch in the Gothic style, of diamonds, rubies and enamelled gold, ordered from Mackay, Cunningham and Company, Crown Goldsmiths to the Queen, 62 Princes Street, Edinburgh, in February 1872. The reverse of the jewel has a glazed compartment for a souvenir. The jewel was given to the bridesmaids at the marriage of Lord and Lady Bute (see plates 51 and 52). (Private Collection.)

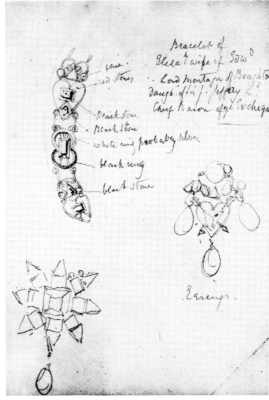

Plate 57. Drawing by Sir Charles Cockerell showing jewellery taken from a Tudor portrait with careful annotations of the colours of the jewels. It seems quite possible that the intention was to have these ornaments reproduced. (British Architectural Library, Royal Institute of British Architects.)

Plate 56. A photograph of H.R.H. Princess Louise, Marchioness of Lorne, dressed as Mary Queen of Scots.

The Scottish Queen was a popular Renaissance heroine in the nineteenth century and interest in her life had never been stronger. From Princess Louise's costume, it is obvious that she had sought advice in order that her costume and particularly her jewellery should look authentic. From a pearl necklace she wears a lozenge shaped cruciform pendant hung with three pearl drops, which is a direct pastiche of a diamond set jewel which once belonged to Elizabeth I when she was a princess. The diamond set jewel can be seen in a portrait by an unknown artist now in the Royal Collection (Colour Plate 44). Robert Phillips made something of a speciality of these pastiches and it may be that Princess Louise's example was made by him (see Colour Plate 43). The Princess was certainly a customer of Phillips; her husband The Marquis of Lorne commissioned a tiara in the form of the leaves and buds of the bog myrtle, emblem of the Campbell clan, to be given to her on their marriage on 21 March 1871. (See the catalogue of the 'Loan Exhibition of Ancient and Modern Jewellery and Personal Ornaments' which was held at the South Kensington Museum in 1872). The rosary which the Princess wears and the crucifix in her left hand are simply references to the Catholicism of Mary Queen of Scots.

Colour Plate 43. An openwork gold cruciform pendant by Robert Phillips of Cockspur Street decorated with black enamel in simulation of diamonds. At the centre are four oval cabochon sapphires and from the jewel hang three pearl drops. Signed with a monogram of two 'P's, c.1869. (The Hull-Grundy Gift to the British Museum.)

This is one of the pastiches of the jewel worn by the Princess Elizabeth in the anonymous portrait now in the Royal Collection (see Colour Plate 44).

Colour Plate 44. A portrait of the Princess Elizabeth, c.1546. Artist unknown, once attributed to Holbein. In this portrait the Princess wears numerous dress ornaments set with gem stones in gold collets which are separated with lavish quantities of pearls. At her neck she wears a pendant set with two stones of amuletic significance. Pinned to her corsage is a cruciform jewel hung with three pearl drops and set with black diamonds of rectangular pyramidal form. The portrait was lent from the Royal Collection to the Manchester Art Treasures Exhibition of 1857 (no. 67) and to the National Exhibition of Portraits in 1866 (no. 79). (Reproduced by Gracious Permission of Her Majesty the Queen.)

This is the source of inspiration for the jewels shown in Plate 56 and Colour Plate 43. One thousand portraits from the Tudor and Stuart period were shown at South Kensington and provided a feast of models for jewellery in the historicist taste so much favoured by fashion at this date. As well as the pendant cited above, Phillips used as a model the cruciform pendant in the form of a Greek gem-set cross worn by the subject of an anonymous portrait identified as Queen Katherine of Aragon (no. 131). A version of this pendant was made for Phillips by Giuliano (see G. Munn, Castellani and Giuliano, Revivalist Jewellers of the 19th Century, *London 1984, plate 189). 'Anne Boleyn' (no. 97) wears an oval pendant in enamelled gold, set with a cabochon stone in a style already in use by 1866. Interest in the English Renaissance dates from much earlier in the nineteenth century and clearly many of these portraits were already known to artists and designers.*

102

Colour Plate 45. The 'Devonshire Parure', from a chromolithographic plate dated 1863 (J.B. Waring, Masterpieces of Industrial Art and Sculpture at the International Exhibition of 1862, *1863, plate 203). The parure consists of seven ornaments 'en suite': coronet, diadem, bandeau, comb, necklace, stomacher and bracelet of enamelled gold set with diamonds and eighty-eight cameos and intaglios from the collection of the Dukes of Devonshire, (see 'Classic Gems in an English Masterpiece, the Devonshire Parure', by Diana Scarisbrick,* Country Life, *7 June 1979, pp.1796-8).*

Sir Joseph Paxton was responsible for commissioning from C.F. Hancock the setting of these engraved gems to provide a suite of ornaments for Countess Granville to wear when she accompanied her husband who had been designated to represent Queen Victoria as Ambassador Extraordinary at the coronation festivities for Tsar Alexander II in 1856. In her biography of Paxton (her grandfather), Violet Markham records: 'Naturally the Duke awaited news of the party with keen interest — interest not diminished by the fact that the Devonshire gems, lent to the Ambassadress for the occasion, were mislaid en route. However, they were retrieved in due course, but the incident threw their owner into a fever of anxiety'. (Paxton and the Bachelor Duke, *1935, p.294).*

The following passage comes from an account in The Illustrated London News: *'The English Ambassador and Lady Granville's State ball, which was given on the night of the 22nd ult., was very brilliant and very successful. . . The ball-room which had been extemporised for the occasion [by Paxton], caused considerable surprise among the Muscovites, familiar as they are with brilliant shows.'*

The Devonshire parure achieves unity in spite of a bewildering eclectic choice of forms, ranging from the necklace in the Pompeiian style, through to the neo-Gothic pinnacled open circlet or diadem reminiscent of currently fashionable taste. Both the Empress Eugenie and Princesse Mathilde are depicted wearing diadems of similar form; the emerald and diamond example belonging to the Empress was made by Eugène Fontenay in 1858.

Although mainly consisting of sombre-coloured gems and enamelled gold (Hancock suggested the addition of the diamonds in order to lighten the design) the parure is of a splendour unsurpassed since the princely commissions of the sixteenth century. Shirley Bury has suggested that the actual design of the pieces and their settings was provided by the sculptor/silversmith Henry Hugh Armstead, who was at that date working with Hancock's on commissions for ceremonial silver and trophies. Armstead is perhaps best known as the sculptor of some of the figures for the Albert Memorial, and the oak relief panels of incidents from British history in the House of Lords, but he was also chief designer for the jewellers Hunt and Roskell, and worked for the Royal Mint on the design of the coins of the realm.

The design of the enamelled settings for the gems is allegedly based on the contemporary setting of the cameo of Queen Elizabeth I which has, in the reverse, a case containing miniatures of the Queen and the Earl of Leicester. There is a surviving precedent for the particular pattern of four-lobed flowerlets which alternate with the diamonds in their square cut collets on the broader settings. This is the 'Gresley' marriage jewel, which is ornamented with exactly the same four-lobed flowerlet in translucent enamel and, incidentally, has two miniatures encased within the setting.

The Gresley jewel was lent in 1857 to the Manchester Art Treasures Exhibition as a complement to the portrait of its first owner, Catherine Gresley, who was shown wearing it. In 1862 the jewel was also lent to the vast South Kensington Loan Exhibition of thousands of treasures of metalwork and jewellery. There it could have been seen by the designers and manufacturers who were to make 'Holbeinesque' jewels ornamented with this four-lobed flowerlet motif, such a commonplace of mid-nineteenth century jewellery fashion. Both the portrait and the jewel were privately owned, by Lady Sophia des Voeux, whose first husband was Sir Roger Gresley, 8th Baronet, but like other historical sources, such as the portrait of Lady Jane Grey by Master John (see plate 50) it may well have been known to artists and designers interested in the Tudor period.

The parure was shown by Hancock's at the 1862 International Exhibition and was favourably mentioned by the jury.

THE DEVONSHIRE GEMS

SET BY

MR C F HANCOCK LONDON

Colour Plate 46 (Right). A stiff gold bangle by Skinner and Co., Silversmiths and Diamond Merchants, Orchard Street, London W1, decorated with translucent green and opaque white enamel, inlaid with gold paillons. The centre of the bracelet is set with a pink topaz and diamond cluster and the shoulders of the bangle are also set with diamonds. Engraved on the reverse is '10th June 1854. Beloved and worthy'. (Private Collection.)

    This jewel was presented to Sir Joseph Paxton's wife, Sarah, by the 6th Duke of Devonshire to celebrate the opening of the Crystal Palace at Sydenham on 10 June 1854. Unfortunately the Duke was seriously unwell having suffered a severe stroke some days earlier in which he lost the use of an arm and a leg. Queen Victoria's diary for that day carries the following entry: 'When Paxton came up the steps of the dais he was immensely cheered, but he himself was low and said, his dear and revered Master and benefactor, the Duke of Devonshire, having had a stroke, and though going on well, is still feeble and confined to bed'. A letter in the archives at Chatsworth from Lady Paxton, writing from Sydenham to the Duke on 11 June, reads 'My Lord Duke, It is with feelings of the deepest gratitude, that I write to acknowledge your Grace's unbounded generosity to myself in the gift of a magnificent bracelet, which for beauty and elegance surpasses anything of the kind I have ever seen, and I can only express my heartfelt thanks for it.'

105

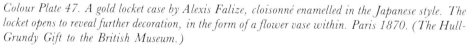

Colour Plate 47. A gold locket case by Alexis Falize, cloisonné enamelled in the Japanese style. The locket opens to reveal further decoration, in the form of a flower vase within. Paris 1870. (The Hull-Grundy Gift to the British Museum.)

As a result of the reopening of trade with Japan in the late 1850s the Parisian jewellers were fired with enthusiasm for the artefacts which found their way to Europe. They were especially fascinated by Oriental enamelling techniques and began to make pastiches, of which this is a particularly sophisticated example.

Colour Plate 48. A brooch and pendant in gold, set with enamelled miniatures in Japanese style each showing a figure in a garden, by Edwin Streeter, c.1880. The mounts are set with emeralds, rubies, sapphires, opals and pearls.

An enamelled silver brooch in the form of a fan decorated with a spray of flowers and a butterfly in the Japanese manner, by Edwin Umfreville, Birmingham, c.1879. (The Hull-Grundy Gift to the British Museum.) Compare these jewels with the similarly inspired locket by Alexis Falize in Colour Plate 47.

A brooch in coloured gold with a hammered finish in the form of a Japanese fan, made by Tiffany and Co., New York, c.1876. See the Catalogue of the Hull-Grundy Gift, *1984 no.1066. (The Hull-Grundy Gift to the British Museum.)*

Colour Plate 49. This portrait is by Lawrence Alma Tadema (1836-1912) and is of his second wife, Laura, in an 'aesthetic' dress, her hair bound with a golden 'Greek' fillet. Oil on canvas. (The Hague, Holland.)

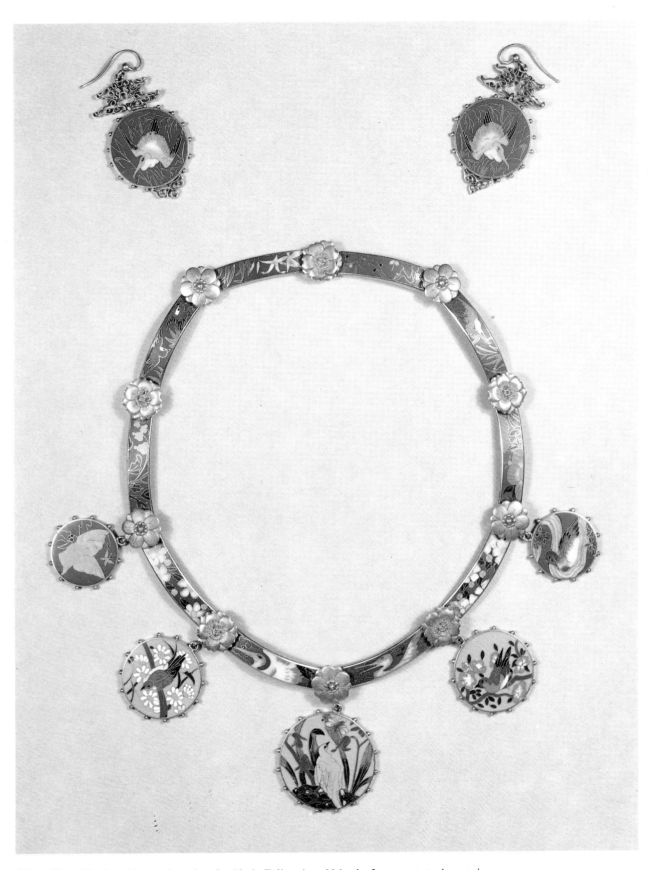

Colour Plate 50. A necklace and earrings by Alexis Falize, in gold in the Japanese taste decorated on both sides with cloisonné enamels. French, c.1869. (The Ashmolean Museum, Oxford.)

Colour Plate 51. 'Regina Cordium' by Dante Gabriel Rossetti. Signed with monogram and dated 1866. (The Glasgow Art Gallery and Museum.)

The model for this painting is Ada Vernon and she wears round her neck a heart shaped jewel pierced with arrows that is probably Spanish eighteenth century work. A similar heart but without the addition of arrows is in the collection of the Victoria and Albert Museum. The pendant in the background of the picture appears to be of rock-crystal, carved with a cupid (see From Slave to Siren *by Dora Jane Janson, the Duke University Museum of Art, Durham, North Carolina, 1973).*

CHAPTER IV
Dante Gabriel Rossetti and 'Pre-Raphaelite' Fashion

'I think there can be no doubt...of the influence in our time of what is commonly known as the Pre-Raphaelite school and its later representatives in this direction...But it is an influence which never owed anything to academic teaching. Under the new impulse, the new inspiration from the mid-century from the purer and simpler lines, forms and colours of medieval art, the dress of women in our own time may be seen to have been transformed for a while, and, though the pendulum of fashion swings to and fro, it does not much affect, except in small details, a distinct type of dress which has become associated with artistic people — those who seriously study and consider of the highest value and importance beautiful and harmonious surroundings in daily life...Beginning in the households of the artists themselves, the type of dress to which I allude, by imitation soon became spread about until in the 'seventies and early 'eighties we saw the fashionable world and stage aping, with more or less grotesque vulgarity, what it was fain to think were the fashions of the inner and most refined artistic cult.' In 1894 Walter Crane wrote the above on the 'Influence of the Pre-Raphaelites' for *Aglaia*, the magazine of the dress reform movement. He was not alone in recognising the source of artistic fashion as being the surroundings and dress of the artists and their families. The reason artistic fashion gained an unusually strong foothold in a very different social milieu to that inhabited by the artists themselves was a social revolution which permitted the leading hostesses of the day to receive artists, writers and musicians as guests.

Plate 58. *A pair of gold earrings decorated with black and white enamel and hung with pearls in the tradition of Italian peasant jewellery, by Giuliano. (The Victoria and Albert Museum.) These earrings were left in May Morris's will to a Mrs Trotter. However, the terms of the will were to be carried out by May's lifelong companion Miss M.F. Vivian Lobb, who fell ill very soon after her friend's death. In consequence the earrings came to the Victoria and Albert Museum with the majority of Janey Morris's jewellery (May's mother), as a gift from Miss Lobb. The original loops have been altered to screw fittings and it is possible that, because of this, the signatures usually found on Giuliano's jewellery were lost.*

Overleaf: Colour Plate 52. 'The Beloved' by Dante Gabriel Rossetti. The subject of this exotic and colourful oil painting is the bride from the 'Song of Solomon'. She is attended by fellow virgins and a slave boy. Textiles and jewels, mainly from Rossetti's own collection, clothe the models. Amongst the jewellery is a pair of early eighteenth century green paste earrings securing the veil of the girl on the extreme left. The bridesmaid who is third from the left at the back wears a seed pearl jewel to secure her veil, and Rossetti was especially fond of this pin. When he first acquired it he was so excited he summoned his friend Murray Marks to see it and to share his joy. The necklace which the slave boy wears as a frontlet was borrowed from Rossetti's friend, the painter George Price Boyce, who like Rossetti, had amassed a large collection of jewelled curiosities. A number were included in the 1872 Loan Exhibition at the South Kensington Museum. This one may well be the necklace and pendant of filigree and roses described as 'Danish, 18th century'.

About her wrist the bride wears a Burmese nineteenth century bracelet in the form of Makara, or water monsters, which was left to the Victoria and Albert Museum by May Morris in 1938. The head-dress of the bride is undoubtedly a Chinese jewel made of kingfisher feathers. Rossetti was not happy with their natural green blue colour and had decided to paint them as red. The whole picture is a rich harmony of textures and colours, of which jewellery is an important part. Rossetti took endless pains to gain the effects he wanted as the letter he wrote, when he was reworking the painting in March 1873 to his assistant, Treffry Dunn, shows: 'I am wanting a big showy looking jewel of the diamond kind (or yellowish would do, but I suppose glittering white would be best) to paint in the nigger boy's cup in the Beloved. *I dare say a theatrical jewel such as you could get for a few shillings in Bond Street would do quite well. It would be nice to have it heart-shaped, but that might be hard to find. Can you look me up one at once and send it.' (Letters, eds. Oswald Doughty and Wahl, Vol. III, 1965-7, p.1149).*

Colour Plate 52. 'The Beloved' by Dante Gabriel Rossetti, dated 1865-6. Oil on canvas. (The Tate Gallery, London.) See previous page for caption.

Colour Plate 53. ‘Monna Vanna’ by Dante Gabriel Rossetti, dated 1866. Oil on canvas. (The Tate Gallery, London.)

A sumptuous and decorative oil painting in celebration of female beauty, as with ‘The Beloved’ jewellery plays an important part in giving an exotic and textural quality to the subject. Rossetti’s favourite hair ornament appears again this time in conjunction with a rich display of corals. The model wears an Oriental gold bracelet with dog’s head terminals, and a green paste ring. At her neck hangs an Oriental rock-crystal heart-shaped pendant on a fine gold chain. The pendant was later owned by Sir Sidney Cockerell; it was stolen from a subsequent owner and so lost its association with the painter, the only thing of value attached to an otherwise commonplace example of a much repeated model.

Plate 59. Dante Gabriel Rossetti by William Holman Hunt, dated 1853. Oil on panel. (Birmingham City Museum and Art Gallery.)

In a letter Lady Carlisle wrote: 'Morris arrived early this morning — with such a diminutive carpet-bag — He was rather shy — and so was I — I felt he was taking an experimental plunge amongst the "barbarians", and was not sure what would be the resulting opinion in his mind. However, he has grown more urbane — and even 3 hours has worked off much of our mutual shyness.'

Plate 60. William Morris giving his fiancée Jane Burden an engagement ring, by Dante Gabriel Rossetti. (Birmingham City Museum and Art Gallery.)
It is interesting to compare this comic episode with the intensely refined and romantic drawing of Elizabeth Siddall contemplatively threading a scarf through a wedding ring (see plate 28). Rossetti's feelings for Jane Morris were to equal and even surpass those he cherished for his ill-fated wife, and it is the paintings of Janey which dominated the last period of his career and which provide the most potent model for the 'aesthetic' style.

Plate 61. 'May' Morris by Frederick Hollyer, dated 1886. (The National Portrait Gallery, London.) May wears a neoclassical fillet in her hair and a necklace of European peasant jewellery about her neck. An accomplished jeweller in the Arts and Crafts tradition, Miss Morris was also a collector of ethnic jewellery, some of which her father, William Morris, brought back from his travels as gifts.

The dresses of the women in the Pre-Raphaelite circle echo those of the painted figures in Rossetti's and Burne-Jones's paintings. It was as much the influence of the painted image as of the women themselves which determined the Pre-Raphaelite style. Sir Charles Dilke recognised this when writing a memoir of his wife after her death: 'The costume in which Mrs. Pattison was painted by Lady Trevelyan is that of the Venetian colour revival, inaugurated by Dante Rossetti and his friends.' His wife was first married to Mark Pattison, Rector of Lincoln College in Oxford and the model for George Eliot's Mr. Casaubon in *Middlemarch*. Mrs. Pattison was a distinguished scholar in her own right; her writings on art in eighteenth century France have stood the test of time and are still of considerable value today. She was also a perfect example of an aesthete in her dress; current fashion held no temptations for her and Sir Charles Dilke remembers her evening occupation, working at 'adapting historic costume to her own dress'. She liked antique jewellery, and two pieces which belonged to her were given by Sir Charles to the Victoria and Albert Museum in her memory. She also seems to have possessed that *sine qua non* of artistic taste in ornaments, a silver belt, much like Constance Wilde's no doubt. Mrs. Humphry Ward remembered her at Oxford: 'It was in '68 or '69 — I think I was seventeen — that I remember my first sight of a college garden

Plate 63. A silver and parcel gilt brooch in the form of an angel set with an opal and pearls, the head carved from ivory. English 1900-1901. Designed and made by A.C.C. Jahn who was principal of Wolverhampton School of Art. (The Victoria and Albert Museum.)

The inference that there is a relationship between this brooch and Rossetti's angel drawing in plate 62 seems inescapable. At the time when the drawings from Fairfax Murray's collection were being acquired by the Birmingham City Art Gallery through public subscription, Jahn was headmaster of the nearby Wolverhampton School of Art. It is even conceivable that his help may have been solicited in the task of raising the money to make this important purchase.

Plate 62. Design by Rossetti for a brooch in the form of a head of winged angel. (Birmingham City Museums and Art Gallery.)

This design is related to the frieze of heads of winged angels at the top of Rossetti's painting of 'Dante drawing the Angel on the Anniversary of Beatrice's Death' now in the Ashmolean Museum, Oxford. The inspiration for the motif is probably from Byzantine mosaic decoration. Burne-Jones alludes to this in his early jewellery designs (see plate 87) and in the designs for the mosaic decoration of G.E. Street's Protestant Episcopal church in Rome. Like the watch design, which seems to be Rossetti's only other jewellery project, this drawing belonged first to Fanny Cornforth and then to Fairfax Murray, before being acquired by the Birmingham City Art Gallery in 1903.

lying cool and shaded between grey college walls, and on the grass a figure that held me fascinated — a lady in a green brocade dress with a belt and chatelaine of Russian silver, who was playing croquet, then a novelty in Oxford, and seemed to me as I watched her, a perfect model of grace and vivacity.' (*A Writer's Recollections*, 1918, p.102.) This recollection comes from the period when Rossetti was establishing his later style of painting, the life-size half-length figures of beautiful women, heavily draped and bedecked with exotic stuffs and ornaments which were influenced by the portraits of the Venetian Renaissance. The dress adopted by Mrs. Pattison has parallels in Rossetti's

Plate 64. *An openwork gold necklace in the form of graduated bows and knots decorated with blue, white and black enamels and set with table cut diamonds. Beneath the unusually large central bow is a pearl and sapphire bead drop. Probably French, c.1660. (The Victoria and Albert Museum.)*

The necklace was bequeated to the Museum in 1909 by Lady Alma Tadema. In the later years of the nineteenth century the collecting of antique jewellery was a new enthusiasm, particularly in artistic circles. In the later years of his career Sir Lawrence Alma Tadema preferred to limit the artistic sources for his paintings to the ancient world but his early works include a number of subjects set in the seventeenth century. This jewel is an unusually good and complete example of that date.

Plate 65. *'Bianca' by William Holman Hunt (1827-1910). (Worthing Art Gallery, Sussex.) 'Bianca' recreates a portrait of the Renaissance, the sitter being dressed in the type of standing 'Medici' collar that Mrs Oscar Wilde adopted for her wedding dress, but Hunt seems to have borrowed Rossetti's Indian pearl ornaments for the model to wear as earrings which suggests that they may have been designed with clip fittings of some kind.*

works, and the taste for curious jewellery, shared by a number of women within the 'aesthetic' circle, comes from the same source. Fortunately we have a certain amount of information about Rossetti's jewellery, some of which survives, bequeathed to the Victoria and Albert Museum by William Morris's daughter May. (The bequest was discussed in detail by Shirley Bury in the *Burlington Magazine,* Vol. CXVIII, 1976, pp.96-102.) Of the pieces now in the Victoria and Albert Museum, nearly all have been convincingly matched to examples in the paintings, but there are many that are lost, notably the pearl ornament, possibly Indian, which features in so many of the pictures. It was

Plate 66. Charles Augustus Howell by Frederick Sandys. Coloured chalks on paper. Signed and dated 'F. Sandys 1882'. (Ashmolean Museum, Oxford.)

Charles Howell was an entrepreneur of considerable panache and charm but distinctly questionable moral values. In 1857 he had made the acquaintance of Rossetti and was later engaged as a secretary by John Ruskin. Georgina Burne-Jones wrote of him: 'He was one who came amongst us in friend's clothing but inwardly was a stranger to all our life meant.' By 1870 he was dismissed from Ruskin's service as a result of the influence of Edward Burne-Jones. Howell was also a picture dealer and collector of objets d'art. In this portrait we see him wearing a scarf ring set with a classical cameo, and on his right hand a ring set with a similar gem can just be made out. In 1875 Howell removed a seed pearl pin from Rossetti's home. The artist was inordinately fond of the jewel and used it in many of his pictures (see Colour Plate 52); Rossetti was furious and wrote to Howell asking for its return in the strongest terms. Howell said that his wife had worn the pin to a party and broken it and that the jeweller to whom he had entrusted it had taken especially long with the repair.

borrowed by the wife of Charles Augustus Howell, and while it was away Rossetti made many attempts to get it back as it was one of his most treasured and frequently used embellishments to the paintings of his later period. It was sold after his death with a number of other pieces which can be recognised as having featured in his paintings. Surprisingly for a man so interested in unusual jewellery Rossetti only made two designs, both for watch cases. One, at least, of these was made up, and was shown to the committee of the Ecclesiological Society in December 1868 by the owner E.R. Robson, architect

Plate 67. A photograph of William Morris's wife Jane (second from the left), in late middle age, with her daughters Mary known as May (first from the left) and Jane Alice, known as Jenny (third from left). Jenny was mentally disturbed and needed constant supervision hence the presence of the helper and companion to the right of the photograph.

The group is sitting in the garden at Kelmscott Manor and a small tame bird can just be seen at Mrs Morris's feet. Jenny is wearing a large brooch in the form of an elephant. It is tempting to link the form of this jewel with Dante Gabriel Rossetti's housekeeper, model and mistress Fanny Cornforth whose voluptuous figure had, in later years, become even more full. She was given the nickname of 'Dear Elephant' and it may be that Rossetti bought the jewel on impulse to give to Fanny but it remained undelivered. Several elephant jewels were at Kelmscott and only one seems certain to have belonged to Mrs Morris. It was bequeathed by her daughter May to Mrs Amy Tozer and three others were sold at auction at the Morris Memorial Hall at Kelmscott on 19 and 20 July 1939.

and patron of Rossetti's friend G.P. Boyce (see plate 70 and Colour Plate 55). The watch was a treasured possession of Robson and his descendants; it is celebrated in a poem of which a facsimile is illustrated in plate 69.

Holman Hunt, in *Pre-Raphaelites and the Pre-Raphaelite Brotherhood* (1905), wrote: 'My past experience in pattern designing, and my criticisms upon the base and vulgar forms and incoherent curves in contemporary furniture, to which I drew Rossetti's attention on his first visit to me, encouraged visions of reform in these particulars, and we speculated on improvement in all household objects, furniture, fabrics and other interior decorations. Nor did we pause till Rossetti enlarged upon the devising of ladies' dresses and the improvements of man's costume, determining to follow the example of early

Plate 68. Detail of plate 67 showing the elephant brooch more clearly.

WINGED TIME.

THOU wilt outlive me as thou didst outlive
        The architect belov'd to whom Rossetti
With lofty vision sure didst give—
But little recking all the debt he
Created by—this wond'rous gold invention,
With black inlays *en manière champlevé*,
Portraying all the Heav'nly constellation.
With Sol and Luna set in stars—*brevet
D'invention*. Precious are life's fleeting hours,
God's gift to use or waste ever striving
To follow that empyrean bird which dow'rs
The back. Elusive Time is on the wing !
May we of its creator's euphrasy
Draw tonic, then find added eucrasy.*

, * See frontispiece and note p. 74.

7

*Plate 69. 'Winged Time'
the poem by Philip Robson
dedicated to the watch
designed by Rossetti and
which is illustrated on plate
one of Robson's* Votarial
Verse and Arabesques,
1927.

*Colour Plate 54. 'Fair Rosamund' by Dante Gabriel Rossetti, 1861. Oil on canvas. (National
Museum of Wales, Cardiff.)*
*   Fanny Cornforth modelled for the painting and she is shown awaiting the arrival of her Royal
lover. The gold necklace, chosen to indicate the sumptuous destiny of the subject, may be filigree,
of European peasant origin or even Asiatic.*

artists not in one branch of taste only, but in all.' These revolutionary
achievements were not to be brought about by Rossetti, but by William Morris
whose wife Jane, with whom Rossetti was for many years obsessively
infatuated, was the perfect exemplar of artistic fashion.
    Janey Morris was described by Henry James in 1869. In a letter to his sister,
after a visit to Morris at Queen's Square in March, he wrote: 'Imagine a tall
lean woman in a long dress of some dead purple stuff, guiltless of hoops (or
of anything else, I should say), with a mass of crisp, black hair heaped into
great wavy projections on each side of her temples, a thin pale face, a pair of

Designed by Dante Gabriel Rossetti in 1862, and made by
Cozens, Matthews & Thorpe, London (No. 96674).   Never before illustrated.
Subject:—"Time on the Wing."   See Notes page 74.

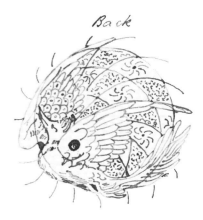

*Colour Plate 55. A slim gold pocket watch decorated with black champlevé enamel both on the case
and the dial, by Cozens, Matthews and Thorpe and numbered 96674. (Reproduced from the
frontispiece of* Votarial Verse and Arabesques *by Philip Appleby Robson, first published
1927.)*

*Edward Robert Robson, the architect, commissioned Dante Gabriel Rossetti to design this watch
and it was presumably made up shortly before Robson showed it to the Ecclesiological Society in
December 1863. When Robson died in 1917 the first line of his will directed that the watch should
pass to his son Philip Appleby Robson who illustrated the watch in his privately published anthology
of poetry. Despite exhaustive enquiries amongst the Robson family, the watch itself remains lost.
E.R. Robson was the architect of the New Gallery, which opened in Regent Street in 1888, where
Burne-Jones, Watts and Alma Tadema showed their work.*

*Plate 70. Rossetti's design
for the back and front of the
watch case made by Cozens
Mathews and Thorpe.
(Birmingham City Museum
and Art Galleries.)
In Pre-Raphaelite tradition,
Rossetti has drawn on two
completely disparate sources
for the design of this watch.
The face is strongly
medieval in flavour whilst
the back seems closely related
to Oriental themes and has
been said to derive from a
Japanese badge motif. The
drawing was one of those
given by Rossetti to Fanny
Cornforth, and later
acquired by Charles Fairfax
Murray, whose collection
was bought by the
Birmingham Art Gallery in
1903.*

strange, sad, deep, dark Swinburnian eyes, with great thick black oblique
brows, joined in the middle and tucking themselves away under her hair, a
mouth like "Oriana" in our illustrated Tennyson, a long neck, without any
collar, and in lieu thereof some dozen strings of outlandish beads.' The style
was instantly recognisable and easy to ridicule; Vernon Lee's *Miss Brown* has
surely been to the same modiste: 'the mediaeval sort of thing — no stays and
no petticoats, and slashing and tags and bootlaces in the sleeves, and a yard
of bedraggled train'. W. Graham Robertson, recognising the dangers of
eccentricity in dress, recommends the beauty of Marie Spartali with the
reassuring phrase: 'Mrs. Morris for beginners', and the mode that really
caught on was a modified form of artistic medievalising dress, with mere hints
of the more extreme adaptations; in the set of a sleeve or the discreet network
of criss-crossed ribbons; in the use of rich dark velvet or soft cashmere and silk;
worn with antique or traditional ornaments made, it was thought, by Italian

119

Plate 71. A portrait of George Eliot (Mrs Lewes) by Samuel Lawrence, dated 1857. (Girton College, Cambridge.)
In this portrait the novelist wears a shell cameo which was bought in Rome on 18 April 1860, at Neri's shop in the Piazza di Spagna. The Leweses took it immediately to the goldsmith C. Tombini in the Via del Babuino to be put into an Etruscan style mount which they chose for it. The cameo is of a bacchante scene. After George Eliot's death the brooch went to Lady Burne-Jones, from her it descended to Margaret Burne-Jones, and finally to her daughter Angela Thirkell.

peasants, but in reality probably by enterprising goldsmiths intent upon cashing in on the credulity of gullible visitors; a contrast indeed to the prevailing fashion. Estella Canziani, painter of 'The Piper of Dreams', once immensely popular but long since forgotten, was an avid collector of this kind of Italian gold jewellery (see Colour Plate 56). She records in her memoirs how her collection was given to the Birmingham Museum: 'The collection of peasant costumes, jewellery, metalwork, pottery and woodwork which I collected for my books led to the first beginning of an ethnological museum in England...S.C. Kaines Smith, Keeper of the Art Gallery and Museum, came to see me in London and asked for my collection to start a new department in the Museum. Altogether two vans of twenty tons, and one of ten tons of material and objects went to Birmingham.' (*Round About Three Palace Green*, 1939, pp.207-8.) Her interest in folk crafts and arts was first stimulated by visiting William Morris.

If Rossetti was to disappoint Holman Hunt's expectations as a designer, Burne-Jones surely would have exceeded his hopes at least as far as jewellery was concerned. Lady Burne-Jones in her life of her husband, *Memorials*, dates his interest in jewellery to the year when Ruskin persuaded him to provide a design for the Whitelands cross (plate 74).

Just over one hundred years ago, on 1st May 1881, the first May Queen was crowned at Whitelands College in Chelsea, and this ceremony, hardly altered in its essentials, has taken place every year since then. As well as being crowned with flowers the Queen receives a gold cross and a ring; in the first years she also had all the published works of John Ruskin to distribute among her friends. The occasion had been devised by Ruskin himself with the enthusiastic co-operation of John Faunthorpe, then principal of the College. The Whitelands archive contains many records of over a century of May Days, including wonderfully evocative photographs of the Queens and their attendants, and a group of the original crosses which have been returned to Whitelands by some of the former recipients or their families. Included are examples of all the different designs of the crosses which were used between 1881 and the 1920s, with one notable exception, the 1883 cross, made after a design by Burne-Jones, which was untraced for a century. This cross is described in the *Whitelands Annual* (1883, p.28), as follows: 'Presented by Mrs.

Colour Plate 57. Italian gold jewellery collected by Estella Canziani, the artist, and presented to the Birmingham City Museum and Art Gallery.
Estella Canziani's intention in collecting this jewellery was to preserve and demonstrate the fast disappearing forms of local and traditional ornaments. A respectable precedent exists in the vast collection made by the Castellani family which was exhibited at 'L'Exposition Universelle' in Paris in 1867 before being purchased by the South Kensington Museum (now the Victoria and Albert Museum). Clearly much of this work is somewhat debased contemporary 'archaeological' jewellery that was eagerly bought by tourists in Rome, but the taste for folk ornaments was a feature of the Pre-Raphaelite circle, and it may be that Mrs Heseltine believed, like Miss Canziani, that her jewels were of traditional workmanship. It seems unlikely that a man of Heseltine's means would have bought Italian tourist souvenirs.

Colour Plate 56. Portrait of Sarah Heseltine, wife of the collector and patron J.P. Heseltine, by Edward Poynter (1836-1919), signed and dated 1870. Watercolour. (Private Collection.)

Mrs Heseltine, appropriately for her setting among her husband's collection of blue and white porcelain and Morris and Co. furniture, is dressed in the height of 'aesthetic' taste. Her dress is of French silk in an eighteenth century rococo pattern with a belt embroidered in the style of Spitalfields silk ribbon and a collar and cuffs of antique lace. The gold jewellery is Italian of the type collected by Estella Canziani in the mistaken belief that it belonged to the folk tradition of local workmanship (see pp.120-1). Her hair is dressed in the neo-Greek fashion with a fillet, a style almost universally adopted in artistic circles at the time of the painting.

Colour Plate 58. A pair of enamelled gold earrings by Carlo Giuliano, in the form of Roman oil lamps, each set with a pearl. The fitted case for this jewel makes it possible to date the earrings between 1874 and 1895.

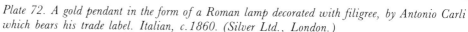

Colour Plate 59. 'A Lady with a Dove: Madame Loeser', by John Brett. Oil on canvas painted in 1864. (The Tate Gallery, London.) For this portrait Madame Loeser wears a dress of loosely Classical inspiration, a brooch set with mosaic in the Roman style and at her neck an archaeological style pendant in the form of an oil lamp much like the one shown in plate 72.

John Brett was in Florence in 1862 and in Naples for the winters of 1863 and 1864. Goldsmiths' work of classical inspiration like the Roman lamp pendant was to become a commonplace of Italian jewellery production in the second half of the nineteenth century, but at this date it must still have seemed highly innovative to English eyes. Castellani's Roman style jewellery was not well known outside Italy until after his participation in the International Exhibition in London in 1862.

This picture was sold in London in 1908 for 4 ¼ guineas. Latterly it was owned by Sir Charles Holroyd, Keeper of the Tate Gallery and, subsequently, Director of the National Gallery. He died in 1917 and Lady Holroyd presented it to the National Gallery for British Art (now the Tate Gallery) in 1919.

Plate 72. A gold pendant in the form of a Roman lamp decorated with filigree, by Antonio Carli which bears his trade label. Italian, c.1860. (Silver Ltd., London.)

Antonio Carli worked in Rome from c.1830 until some time after 1868. Like Castellani's, his shop at 76 Piazza S. Silvestro and later at 158 Via Babuino was a lure for the enormous number of tourists visiting Rome in the mid-nineteenth century. This is not a sophisticated archaeological style pastiche, rather its form is immediately evocative of the antique and it makes a readily appreciated souvenir.

Burne-Jones the cross is of the Greek pattern…its form almost hidden by entwining branches of May exquisitely wrought in gold; the leaves of a delicately greenish hue and the blossoms silvery pink'. On 1 May the delicately wrought and chased three-colour gold cross with hawthorn blossom ornament was given to the newly elected Queen. It remained with the family of the recipient, used only for special occasions such as weddings in succeeding generations, lost to sight to all intents and purposes for one hundred years, but it is now on loan to the British Museum.

The May Day ceremony at Whitelands realised ambitions which Ruskin had first cherished nearly twenty years earlier when he had thought of celebrating

Colour Plate 60. A cameo portrait of John Ruskin by Constantin Roesler Franz, in pink and white shell, which was cut in Rome between the end of December 1840 and January 1841.

In his famous autobiographical work entitled Praeterita, *Ruskin wrote: 'Among the living Roman arts of which polite travellers were expected to carry specimens home with them, one of the prettiest used to be the cutting of cameos out of pink shells. We bought, according to custom, some coquillage of Gods and Graces; but the Cameo cutters were also skilful in mortal portraiture, and papa and mamma, still expectant of my future greatness, resolved to have me carved in cameo… The cameo finished, I saw at a glance to be well cut; but the image it gave of me was not to my mind. I did not analyse its elements at the time, but should now describe it as a George the Third's penny, with a halfpenny worth of George the Fourth…'*

Colour Plate 61. The Whitelands Cross and chain of 1883, four colours of gold, in the form of a spray of hawthorn in bloom, contained within its original heart-shaped case, by London and Ryder. (Private Collection, at present on loan to the British Museum.) This jewel was the third in a series of crosses which were given annually by John Ruskin to the May Queen at Whitelands College. Strikingly original in conception, it presents a great contrast to the conventional gold cross used in the previous ceremonies. Burne-Jones seems to have been inspired by the form of the leafy carved stone bosses found at the junctions of the ribs in a medieval vaulted roof. It is the only Whitelands cross designed by Burne-Jones and was presented by his wife in Ruskin's name to Edith Martindale. It still belongs to her descendants and is worn by the bride at family weddings. However, its whereabouts were not known outside the family until one hundred years after its presentation when it was rediscovered. Ruskin was secretly dissatisfied with Burne-Jones's cross — perhaps stimulated by the expert appraisal of Edith Martindale's father, who was a botanist — and he was never asked to design another; the commission was given in subsequent years to Arthur Severn, the husband of Ruskin's beloved cousin Joan, who had designed the first cross in 1881.

the first of May at Winnington School, a venture which he described to Faunthorpe in the course of the correspondence over the Whitelands scheme.

Whitelands College was established in the 1840s by the high Anglican National Society to provide teachers for the Society's National schools, and the training was therefore strongly religious, the focal point of the May Day ceremony being a service in the Chapel. Indeed the emphasis in the choice of the Queen of the May was on the qualities which are looked on with favour by Christian teaching. Ruskin himself, on the other hand, expressed the wish that all the girls should show an interest in cooking and sewing and looking pretty!

Ruskin's correspondence with Faunthorpe over the plans for the May Day ceremony began on 25 January, 1881. He did not concern himself overmuch with the rigmarole of the procession and the Maypole dancing but he was

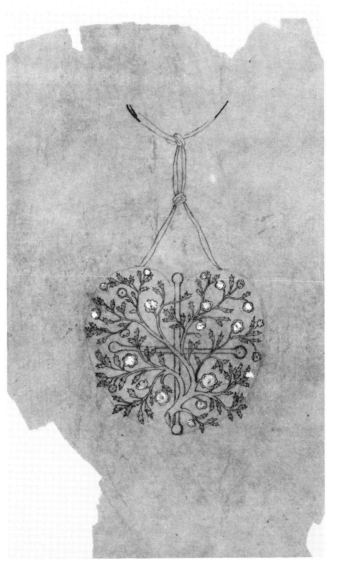

Plate 73. Three designs for the gold cross which John Ruskin commissioned Sir Edward Burne-Jones to design in 1883. The jewel was to be given at the May Queen's Festival instituted by Ruskin at Whitelands College in 1881. The design shown above was eventually chosen and the results can be seen in Colour Plate 61. (The Pierpont Morgan Library, New York.)

Burne-Jones maintained that this commission had cost him the most painful amount of work. These are three of fifty attempts, so he claimed, to arrive at a satisfactory design. The difficulty with which this modest little cross was achieved is surprising in a man with such a feeling for ornamental accessories and whose grandfather, Benjamin Coley, was a prominent Birmingham jeweller.

Plate 74. An openwork gold brooch by Carlo and Arthur Giuliano in the form of a web of clover leaves, enamelled translucent green and set with diamonds. Signed 'C. and A.G.' (Wartski, London.)

This jewel has strong stylistic affinities with those jewels designed by Sir Edward Burne-Jones, and most particularly with the Whitelands Cross of 1883 (see plate 73 and Colour Plate 61). In this brooch the relationship with medieval ecclesiastical ornament is more apparent than in the cross. A close parallel can be drawn with the leafy ornamented bosses at Ely Cathedral, but the precise source of inspiration is difficult to track down since Burne-Jones, in common with many of his fellow artists with medievalising tendencies, possessed an almost encyclopaedic knowledge of ecclesiastical architecture. Considering the relationship between the artist and Giuliano family it seems likely that his ideas permeated their commercial repertoire.

Plate 75. A watercolour of hawthorn by John Ruskin. (Private Collection. Photograph, Thomas Agnew and Sons.)

For Ruskin, hawthorn was a symbol of rebirth and he was especially fond of the flower. Following his unhappy relationship with Rose La Touche the plant became a poignant reminder of her death. In his diary the entry for the day she died is bordered with sketches of hawthorn and on 28 May 1875 he wrote to a friend, Susan Beevor: 'I've just heard that my poor little rose has gone to where the hawthorn blossoms go'. The Whitelands cross is in the form of hawthorn and its meaning is only faintly disguised.

Burne-Jones also felt strongly the romantic association of the hawthorn blossom, which plays a symbolic part in the story of Merlin and Nimuë from the Arthurian legends. Writing in 1893, to his friend Helen Mary Gaskell, about the model for Nimuë in his painting 'The Beguiling of Merlin' (shown at the first Grosvenor Gallery exhibition in 1877), he explained: 'The head of Nimuë in the picture called the Enchanting of Merlin was painted from the same portrait, and was very like — all the action is like — the name of her was Mary [Zambaco, his mistress]. Now isn't that very funny as she was born at the foot of Olympus and looked and was primeval and that's the head and the way of standing and turning... and I was being turned into a hawthorn bush in the forest of Broceliande — every year when the hawthorn bush buds it is the soul of Merlin trying to live again in the world and speak — for he left so much unsaid.' (Quoted in the catalogue Lord Leverhulme, A Great Edwardian Collector and Builder, *Royal Academy of Arts, 1980, no.5.) The meaning, in the language of flowers, of the may or hawthorn blossom is 'hope'. Burne-Jones seems to have been well aware of this as he painted a watercolour entitled 'Spes' showing a female allegorical figure bearing a large branch of flowering hawthorn. The painting was in the collection of Burne-Jones's patron Alexander Henderson of Buscot Park, for whom the decorative 'Briar Rose' series was painted.*

deeply interested in the symbolism of the crowning with flowers — for instance, the retiring Queen in later years was crowned with a wreath of forget-me-nots — and was also adamant on one matter, that at no point in the choosing of the Queen should the staff intervene. All the rest of the ceremony was devised by the members of the College, but the cross was a different matter and in this Ruskin accepted the whole responsibility for the design and all the arrangements with the goldsmith as well as the cost of providing a new one each year.

The first mention of the cross itself occurs in a latter to Faunthorpe written on 6 April, 1881: 'I've written today to a goldsmith to whom I have confidence about a little cross of gold and white May blossom in enamel for the Queen. I think it will be more proper for the kind of Collegiate Queen it is to be, than a crown or fillet for the hair.'

On 16 April, he wrote again: '...I console myself with conveyance of a piece of, to me, very pleasant news, that Mr. Severn has made a sketch of our hawthorn cross, which I think quite lovely, and I've sent it to be put in hand today'. This refers to Arthur Severn, the artist son of Keats's friend Joseph Severn, and husband of Joan Agnew, Ruskin's cousin and devoted companion. The jewel is a conventional gold cross with applied hawthorn blossoms. On 24 April Ruskin wrote again to Faunthorpe: '...The cross is sure to be ready in good time. I doubt not but the hawthorn blossom will only be in gold *this* time; I couldn't get enamel done safely.'

On 26 April he wrote in reply to Faunthorpe's query about the subsequent years: '...Of course there is to be a cross every year! Being the likeablest or nicest girl of one hundred and sixty is surely a thing which deserves memory — from all who care for her or will care — worth at least so much fastening of it as may be in a little gold trinket.'

Another two letters followed in quick succession, on 29 April and 1 May: '...The little cross is safe here, and will *do* for this year; but it may be much improved when I am able to see after it in time next year.'

'...I do hope no accident will hinder the arrival of the cross in due time, but in case mischance should befall, the girls can always make a crown of flowers which will do for the coronation. I am pleased with the chain now, and think it well worth the little risk of delay. Next year there shall be more than one *thorn* in the cross, however; it isn't moral to be all blossom and no prickle.'

After the ceremony had taken place Ruskin waited impatiently for the photographs of his Queen which he had been promised; they arrived towards the end of the month, and he wrote thanking Faunthorpe, but not concealing his disappointment at the appearance of the poor girl, in a letter dated 22 May: '...Photos both quite safe, but I'm rather frightened of my Queen. She looks to me between thirty-five and thirty-eight, and rather as if she would bring back trial by the rack. Photographs are horrid things!'

This May Queen was in fact about twenty, and she really does not look so severe as Ruskin's comments imply. She was in mourning, and the black dress would to a certain extent have conditioned Ruskin's reaction as he hated to see women in black clothes (see *The Professor,* p.131, Arthur Severn's memoir of Ruskin, edited by James Dearden and published in 1967). The dress for the Queen was to cause endless trouble. Since the identity of the girl and therefore her size and colouring were not known until the last minute, the devising of an all-purpose robe was the subject of much experimentation. Even Kate Greenaway's design, a somewhat shapeless garment with bands of embroidered violets, never really gave complete satisfaction to any of the participants.

Correspondence with Faunthorpe about the design of the next cross began in April, 1882. Ruskin wrote on the 26th as follows: '...Difficulties about the cross more than last year! English workmen getting every day, literally, more stupid and less docile, under the iron heel of — *No* Despotism. I may be reduced to sending you merely a pretty one out of Bond Street, but there's

Plate 76. *The May Queen of Whitelands College of 1887, with three former Queens in attendance. The retiring Queen (right) wears symbolic garlands of forget-me-nots. (Whitelands College, London.)*

Plate 77. A large gold pectoral cross by Hunt and Roskell (working 1843-1897) decorated with a stylised trailing plant and flowers, presumably that of the passion flower. The substantial gold chain from which the cross hangs is a later addition. The cross is apparently unmarked but is contained within its original fitted velvet case with the supplier's satin in the lid. Engraved on the reverse:
Ruskin's Cross
Whitelands College.
The Gift of
Ruskin's Godson
Henry Dyke Acland.
May Day 1932
Whitelands College
The applied ornament and filigree borders of this cross strongly recall the early work of Carlo Giuliano (c.1831-1895). Before he opened his premises at 115 Piccadilly in 1874, Giuliano was a supplier to Hunt and Roskell and one cannot discount the possibility that he is the maker of the jewel.
It was Henry Dyke Acland's wish that this cross should be worn by the principal at the Whitelands College May Queen's festival instituted there by John Ruskin. The festival has been celebrated annually without interruption and the cross has been worn since 1932.

some chance of hawthorn yet. Anyhow, you shall have it on Saturday morning.'

Three days later he confirmed his disappointment with the results: '. . . The cross is just as far from what we meant as last year; but I'll have the one for next year made (D.V.) before I leave London in the spring, and the first two Queens must be content to *be* the two first, though their crosses are, to me at least, more crosses than anything else.' The recalcitrant workmen referred to

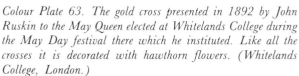

Colour Plate 62. The Whitelands May Queen's Cross in the form of a spray of hawthorn flowers and leaves, designed by Arthur Severn. Engraved on the reverse 'Ruskin Cross presented to E. Hand. May 1st 1893'. This is a similar model to the 1884 cross, the first with which John Ruskin, the originator of the Whitelands May Day festival, was completely satisfied. He continued to use the form of the jewel in subsequent May Day ceremonies for many years. (Private Collection.)

Colour Plate 63. The gold cross presented in 1892 by John Ruskin to the May Queen elected at Whitelands College during the May Day festival there which he instituted. Like all the crosses it is decorated with hawthorn flowers. (Whitelands College, London.)

The first cross, now lost, like so many subsequent examples was designed by the artist Arthur Severn (1842-1931), who was married to Ruskin's beloved cousin Joan (née Ruskin Agnew) and was himself the son of the artist Joseph Severn (1793-1879) a friend of John Keats. Despite Severn's obvious artistic capabilities Ruskin was displeased with it and was not satisfied by this second cross Severn designed, or even the third by Edward Burne-Jones in 1883 (see Colour Plate 61). However, in 1884 he asked again for Severn's help and between them they arrived at a design which pleased them both and which was used with little alteration for many years.

must have been employees of London and Ryder, the Bond Street jewellers to whom Ruskin entrusted the making of all the crosses in the early years.

The next year was, of course, to be the year of the Burne-Jones' cross. In choosing Burne-Jones in 1883, Ruskin must have hoped for great things, eagerly anticipating an ideal design for the May Queen's cross which would assuage the dissatisfactions of the first two years. He began discussing the cross with Burne-Jones as early as February, 1883, and by March Burne-Jones had decided that he ought to get on with it. 'What is the feast day you want it by?' he wrote, 'I'll do all I can for thee about the Cross. You shall talk it over with me when you come and tell me why hawthorns and how much work is to be in it.'

Possibly without realising it, Burne-Jones had asked a crucially significant question, and one which seems not to have occurred to Faunthorpe. In questioning the choice of hawthorn for the decoration of the cross he was in effect asking Ruskin about the significance of the whole ceremony. It is an unavoidable inference from the many but scattered clues which Ruskin let drop that the choosing of a May Queen and the reward of a gold cross entwined with hawthorn constituted a covert memorial to Rose La Touche, the young girl who was the great love of Ruskin's life and whose death in 1875 had driven him temporarily insane. On 28 May that year he wrote to a friend, Susan Beevor, 'I've just heard that my poor little Rose is gone where the hawthorn blossoms go', and his diary entry for the day of her death was bordered with hawthorn. Burne-Jones must have been enlightened as to the significance of the cross as a memorial to lost love, as he refers to this in a letter to Ruskin written in 1883 after he too had lost — this time only to marriage — his great love, Frances Horner. After deploring her choice of husband, he suggests that he should be awarded the cross which he was then designing as a consolation for his despair.

Ruskin remarked more than once on the absence of thorns on the hawthorn branches which decorated the successive crosses: 'as if a true queen's crown could ever be without a thorn'. The thorny cross would have appropriately expressed his unhappiness, and his perennial dissatisfaction with the designs show that he felt none of them could do justice to the complexity and intensity of his feelings. Evidently even Burne-Jones was not sufficiently impressed as to the necessity for thorns, but the hawthorn at least has been allowed to dominate the cross in all three versions of his design. Before this cross reappeared it was not known which, if any, of the three surviving designs had been used. It is not possible to see in the photographs of the May Queen what the cross looked like, except that it was smaller, lighter and more delicate than either the crosses of the preceding years or those that were to replace it later. The name of the Queen was recorded as Edith Martindale; her married name had also been noted, and from this tiny clue a descendant of Miss Martindale was identified and contacted. After some anxious negotiations, she produced, in an atmosphere of due ceremony, the heart-shaped velvet case in which the cross had remained for nearly a century. It was an exciting moment of anticipation to know that the fruit of this most significant collaboration was just about to be revealed. In fact the finished work of art is so close to the drawing that was finally settled upon that even the artist himself must have been astonished by how faithfully the goldsmith, Ryder of London and Ryder, managed to realise his conception of the May Queen's cross, with its subtle deployment of delicately coloured gold to suggest the different tints of the flowers and leaves.

This 'exquisite' jewel had caused much anguish to its designer. Burne-Jones, writing to Ruskin in April, says: 'You don't know how hard I find that little cross to do — I think I have made fifty designs — but yesterday I chose 3 for you — and I want you to say which you like best so I'll send them first to you at Brantwood.' Happily the three drawings have remained with the letter in spite of many changes of ownership over the years, and they are now safely in the Pierpont Morgan Library in New York. The designs show three very different crosses, two of them of Latin form with branching may blossoms wreathing round them, and one of Greek form almost entirely obscured by dense twigs of may in bloom. Ruskin chose the Greek cross, the most unconventional and the one incidentally which seems to accord least well with his own taste as exemplified by his heavy gold cross which he bequeathed to Whitelands College.

In none of the designs has Burne-Jones considered the technicalities of carrying out his ideas, and it may be that Ruskin's choice was to a certain extent dictated by expediency. Perhaps he hoped that this arrangement of two separate but complete elements, the cross and the overlying branch of hawthorn would be easier to achieve than the meandering branches which do not seem to attach anywhere on the other designs. Certain liberties have had to be taken with the way in which the cross is suspended, as the designer, defeated by the mechanics of his pretty notion of a knotted ribbon, has left the drawing deliberately vague. The solution arrived at by the goldsmith is not very happy, and the long oval of the suspension loop destroys the proportions of the cross, but in all other respects this cross is Burne-Jones's drawing exactly realised.

Ruskin professed himself delighted with the result, writing to Burne-Jones on May Day itself to congratulate him: 'The success of the Cross today is *perfect* — in all possible ways — and I cannot thank — nor enough congratulate you — them — and my little self on all the matter. Ryder will have credit out of it too, and lately *all's* well — AND ends well — or rather begins well — for there is no saying of how much this Whitelands cross, by your design is the beginning.' In spite of the exultant tone of the letter, Burne-Jones's cross was not used again. In January 1884 Ruskin began to worry about a replacement; writing to Arthur Severn's wife Joan, he says: 'I think the sooner the Whitelands cross is in hand now the better. . .if Arfie would make another drawing to change the present form of the useless cross it would beat Jones's

131

Plate 79. An undated photograph (c.1885) of the Cork Rose Queen and her attendants taken at the May Day festival which took place each year, under the patronage of John Ruskin, at Cork High School for Girls. (Whitelands College, London.)

which the Queen Regnant's father doesn't like — because it is not hawthorny enough'. This uncharacteristic deference to the preferences of Mr. Martindale, an amateur botanist, must indicate that Ruskin himself had grown dissatisfied with the jewel, which had seemed to please him so much hardly more than six months previously.

Ruskin's perceptions were acute but his taste was erratic. A streak of conventional sentimentality sometimes coloured his artistic opinions and never more so than when Rose La Touche's memory was being invoked. Ruskin rather mistrusted the jeweller's art, and he often voiced his preference for minerals and metals in their natural state, before they have been adulterated or fashioned by cutting. The experience of devising a jewel had not proved to be a happy one, and the design which Arthur Severn produced in 1884, which is a modified and tidied-up version of one of the Burne-Jones' drawings, was allowed to serve with few alterations until Ruskin's death in 1900.

At the time of Ruskin's death it was found that no provision had been made in his will to continue paying for the May Queen's cross, but after hurried

Colour Plate 64. A gold cross in the form of intertwined roses, contained within its emerald green velvet box. (Private Collection, presently on loan to the British Museum.)

This is one of the series of crosses awarded to the Queen of John Ruskin's May Day festival held at Cork College in Ireland. The Cork College May festival was instituted by Ruskin in 1885 and ran until his death. It was similar to the festival at the Whitelands College, but in Ireland, the celebrations were more overtly a memorial to his great love Rose la Touche, who was herself Irish. Those that would have been May Queens at Whitelands College were Rose Queens at Cork and the Whitelands hawthorn cross was paralleled by a rose cross. The vivid emerald green case is undoubtedly a reference to Ireland.

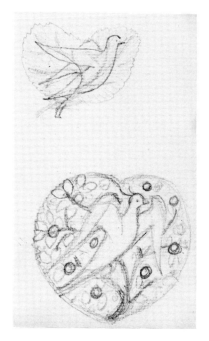

Plate 80. Wash studies of mosaics of olive trees and flowers for plate 4, Stones of Venice, *Vol. III, 1853. (The Brantwood Trust, Coniston, Cumbria.)*
These medieval mosaics may well have been the source of inspiration for the bird brooches which Sir Edward Burne-Jones asked Giuliano to make for him (plate 81). Whether or not the artist remembered them from his visit to Venice in 1862 will never be known but the fact that Burne-Jones owned a copy of The Stones of Venice *can hardly be doubted.*

consultations and the setting up of a fund to pay for the chain by a group of former Queens, the St. George's Guild, which had been founded and financed by Ruskin, took over the responsibility of providing the cross, which was made by Canon Rawnsley's Keswick School of Industrial Arts. After Canon Rawnsley's death the cross was made by Alwyn Carr to a very characteristic design in hammered gold, and it was not until the 'twenties that the College itself had to take over the cost of the undertaking.

Ultimately there were to be a number of May Queen ceremonies in National Society schools, instituted in some cases by Mrs Faunthorpe who herself presented a cross to the chosen Queen. These cannot have been as important and elaborate as the ceremony at Whitelands, but one which was started in 1885 by a Miss Martin, a former Whitelands Governess, at Cork County High School, also had the distinction of having a cross designed by Arthur Severn which was presented by Ruskin. Three examples at least survive, one in a private collection which is on loan to the British Museum, one at the Ruskin Galleries, Bembridge School, Isle of Wight, and the other at Cork Public Museum. All are contained within fitted green velvet cases, a colour wholly appropriate for an Irish recipient. The lid satin of the case at Bembridge bears the supplier's name and address: Edward Stow, 4-6 Camberwell Park. It may

Plate 81. Designs for jewels by Burne-Jones in the form of birds perched in trees and leaves, some with a heart shaped outline. These were presumably the preliminary designs for the bird brooches which were made up to his designs by Giuliano. (The Victoria and Albert Museum.)

Plate 83. A pencil portrait of Sir Edward Burne-Jones by George Howard, 9th Earl of Carlisle (1843-1915). (The Fine Art Society, London.)

Plate 82. A silver pendant by Child and Child in the form of a descending dove which holds a faceted garnet in its beak. This is one of the jewels from the commercial stock of Child and Child which seems to reflect the influence of Burne-Jones. (Private Collection.)

Plate 84. A photograph of Katharine Horner wearing the bird brooch designed by Sir Edward Burne-Jones which Laura Lyttleton left to Cicely Horner in 1885. Mrs Lyttleton died in 1885 after giving birth to her first child and made this special bequest to her god-daughter in her will which was quoted at length in The Autobiography of Margot Asquith *(1922): 'I want Alfred to give my god-child Cicely Horner the bird brooch Burne-Jones designed . . .' Cicely Horner, who later became the Honourable Mrs George Lambton, appears to have lent her sister the brooch for this sitting. (From* Time Remembered *by Frances Horner, 1933.)*

KATHARINE HORNER

Plate 85. Anatomy, lesson 1 and 2 — The Anatomy of a Good Man and a Good Woman, by Sir Edward Burne-Jones and dedicated to Philip Carr. (Reproduced from The Reminiscences of Mrs Comyns Carr, *1925.)*

In this pair of drawings Burne-Jones shows how the heart, sometimes winged, fascinated him. The upper torsos of both the good man and the good woman are almost entirely occupied by their hearts. The hand of the man seems literally to radiate sensitivity while that of the woman rests on a small tree where birds pair and nest. (For a comparison with the use of hearts in Burne-Jones's jewellery see plate 87, and for the use of the bird, Colour Plate 65.)

be that this jeweller received commissions for Cork and possibly Whitelands crosses owing to his close proximity to Ruskin's home in Herne Hill.

A letter from Miss Martin to Ruskin describing her May Day celebrations is printed in Ruskin's *Collected Works* in the Appendix to Volume XXX (which includes an account of the devising of the Whitelands ceremony and the designing of the cross) with the following rather cryptic note attached: 'The Queen in this case — for reasons which readers of *Praeterita* (iii, pp.51 ff) will guess — is a Rose Queen, instead of a Queen of the May.'

This rather veiled reference to Rose la Touche was as far as Cook and Wedderburn, Ruskin's meticulous editors, felt able to go at that date (the volumes in question appeared between 1903 and 1907) but much has been written since about this ultimately tragic relationship. Ruskin first met Rose in 1858 and she died in May 1875. The thorny cross was meant for Rose, and Ruskin's dissatisfaction with it mirrors his feelings about the other memorials: none could do justice to their intensity.

Burne-Jones, on the other hand, was undeterred by any of the set-backs which had occurred over the designing of the cross, even apparently coming to terms with the fifty discarded drawings that this commission had cost him. As Lady Burne-Jones remarks in *Memorials,* the Whitelands cross was indeed to be the beginning of an interest in jewellery design for Burne-Jones.

Lady Burne-Jones claimed that only one other jewel was actually executed, the coral and turquoise bird for which Burne-Jones made so many designs

Colour Plate 65 (Left). An openwork gold brooch pendant in the form of a bird on an olive branch by Carlo Giuliano, decorated with translucent green and red enamel and set with turquoise and coral cabochons, pearls and a single ruby. Designed by Sir Edward Burne-Jones. Stamped C.G. (Private Collection.)

A similar bird jewel is now on loan to the Victoria and Albert Museum. It belonged to Burne-Jones's granddaughter, Clare Mackail. The inspiration for these jewels seems likely to have come from late medieval mosaics in Venice which are also in the form of olive trees (see plate 80). Burne-Jones may have seen them when he was sent to Venice by Ruskin in 1862. Several designs, which reflect closely the form of this jewel, are preserved at the British Museum. The version which belonged to Margaret Burne-Jones was exhibited at the New Gallery in 1892-3.

(Right). An enamelled gold brooch by Carlo and Arthur Giuliano in the form of a blue bird pecking at berries of coral in an olive tree. The bird is set with a single cabochon garnet. (The Fitzwilliam Museum, Cambridge.)

Designed by Charles Ricketts, the jewel was probably inspired by the bird brooches of Sir Edward Burne-Jones, a version of which Ricketts must have seen at the New Gallery in 1892-3.

Colour Plate 66. A design for a brooch or pin in the form of two birds perched in a tree, by C.F.A. Voysey. It was to be made in pearls and enamel for the Revd. J. Tetley Rowe. (The Royal Institute of British Architects.)

The jewel is no longer in the Tetley Rowe family but this beautiful design suggests that it would be closely comparable with the bird brooches designed and made up by Giuliano for Sir Edward Burne-Jones and Charles Ricketts. The jewel bears such a close similarity to the Burne-Jones jewel in Colour Plate 65, that it is tempting to suggest that Voysey could have seen it at the New Gallery in 1892-3.

Colour Plate 67. An oval silver and gold brooch by John Paul Cooper, in the form of birds in a tree, the roots set with a single emerald. (Silver Ltd., London.)

Plate 87. Designs for pendants in the form of flaming and chained hearts by Sir Edward Burne-Jones. They are reproduced with base metal models of the crowns used in 'King Cophetua and the Beggar Maid' of 1884 (left, now in the Tate Gallery) and the 'Adoration of the Magi' (now in the Birmingham City Museum and Art Gallery). (From a photograph in 'The Decorative Art of Sir Edward Burne-Jones' in the Art Annual (Special Number) Christmas 1894.)

The designs for jewellery in the form of hearts are now kept in the Department of Prints and Drawings at the British Museum. The base metal crowns were inherited by Sir Philip Burne-Jones but are now lost; they are known to have been made for Burne-Jones by his friend the metalworker W.A.S. Benson, sometimes known as Brass Benson. Burne-Jones was particularly anxious to ensure that decorations used in his pictures should work and it was his habit to have appropriate models made up in this way. Even the fanciful armour in paintings such as 'The Arming of Perseus' (1877) was made up by Benson.

Plate 86. Front and back of a brooch in the form of an opal heart tied with chains, suspended from a pair of wings set with pearls and decorated with red enamel. The reverse of the setting for the opal heart is of pierced gold showing another heart within scrolling foliage. (Wartski, London.)

This jewel seems to echo the designs of jewellery made by Sir Edward Burne-Jones illustrated in plate 87 and there is some evidence to suggest that the pendant heart has been added to the enamelled gold wings at a later stage. Although the enamelled gold wings follow a convention in nineteenth century jewellery design, the symbolism of the bound heart has not been seen before and given the rarity of the device, an attribution to the artist seems convincing.

(Colour Plate 65). The brooch, which belonged to Margaret Burne-Jones and remained in her family after her death, is now on loan to the Victoria and Albert Museum, but it is not unique. At least two other versions have come to light. One bird brooch is recorded as having belonged to Laura Tennant, the sister of Margot Asquith who married Alfred Lyttelton, and whose beautiful features appear in paintings by Burne-Jones. In her will she left her bird brooch to Frances Horner's daughter Cicely, and her wishes seem to have been respected, as Cicely's sister Katharine is shown wearing it in a photograph which illustrates Frances Horner's book of reminiscences, *Time Remembered*. Margaret Burne-Jones's brooch was shown in the exhibition of her father's work which was held at the New Gallery in 1892, and it seems to have inspired the young artist Charles Ricketts to make his own version a few years later (Colour Plate 67).

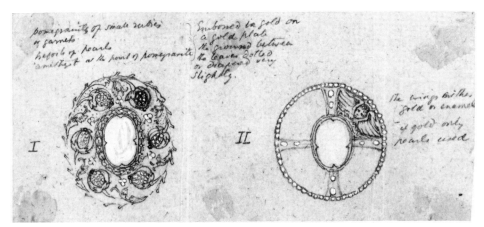

Plate 88. Four designs for jewels by Sir Edward Burne-Jones in Byzantine style. (The Pierpont Morgan Library, New York.)

The meticulous way in which these drawings are annotated for goldsmiths, leaves little doubt that they were eventually made up. They come from the same collection of papers in which Burne-Jones's design for Ruskin's Whitelands cross is found, and it may be that these drawings were also commissioned by Ruskin.

BROCHE
AVEC ÉMAUX BYZANTINS
par Coffignon.

Plate 89. An engraving of a brooch in the Byzantine taste by Coffignon, from La Bijouterie Française au XIXème Siècle by Henri Vever (Vol. II, p.192). The designer of this jewel seems to have drawn on the same Byzantine sources as Burne-Jones when he designed the brooches illustrated in plate 88.

Other pieces of jewellery designed by Burne-Jones are still owned by the family. Apart from the heart-shaped cuff-links made by Child and Child of Kensington which were shown in the Arts Council's Burne-Jones exhibition in 1975 (Colour Plate 74), there are rings and other trifles of deeply personal significance. Curiously none are connected with the many designs for jewellery which are scattered amongst his sketchbooks in the Victoria and Albert Museum, in the *Secret Book of Designs* now in the British Museum, and in one of the sketchbooks at Wightwick Manor in Wolverhampton. Most tantalising of all are the designs with detailed instructions for manufacture which are inexplicably with the letters to Ruskin at the Pierpont Morgan Library.

Both of the jewellers employed by Burne-Jones to make his designs were profoundly influenced by his ideas. The forms that he favoured, wings and hearts, reappear in a number of pieces that are modified versions of his commissions. One brooch, made by Child and Child, encompasses so neatly the form, material and symbolism typical of his work that it is tempting to ascribe the design to Burne-Jones himself. Made of green-stained ivory in the form of a flower-head with heart-shaped petals, the brooch is a marguerite, surely for Margaret Burne-Jones (later Mackail), the artist's beloved daughter

Colour Plate 68. Georgiana Burne-Jones by Sir Edward Poynter (1836-1919). Watercolour, inscribed 'Georgiana B-Jones 18 EP 70.' (Private Collection.)

This sensitive portrait of Edward Burne-Jones's wife is by her brother-in-law. Georgiana was one of the children of the Rev. George Macdonald and two of her sisters were also married to notable men: Agnes to Sir Edward Poynter and Alice to John Lockwood Kipling. In this portrait Georgiana wears a heart-shaped lapis-lazuli pendant surrounded by pearls. This was presumably the gift of her husband and is another example of his interest in the symbol of the heart which he used in his graphic and metalwork designs. At her waist is a watch which Georgiana wore constantly all her life. Her granddaughter, Angela Thirkell, described her thus in old age: 'She was a widow during the greater part of my recollection of her, and always wore much the same dress, very long full black gowns of velvet or satin with a little lace. A large watch all set with chrysolites which my grandfather had given her was always pinned at her waist. He had bought it for its beauty in their early married days with almost the last eight pounds in his possession. On her head she wore swathes of soft lace, pinned here and there with an old paste brooch, and on one hand an old diamond mourning ring... Otherwise my grandmother wore hardly any jewellery.' (Angela Thirkell, Three Houses, *1931, pp.50-51.)*

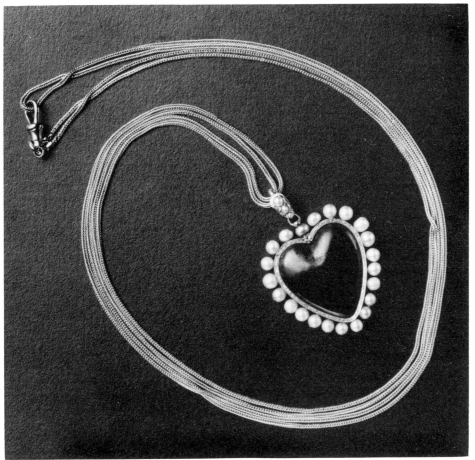

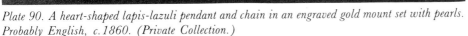

Plate 90. A heart-shaped lapis-lazuli pendant and chain in an engraved gold mount set with pearls. Probably English, c.1860. (Private Collection.)
    This jewel belonged to Georgiana Burne-Jones and she wears it in the portrait of her by Sir Edward Poynter (Colour Plate 68). It seems likely that the jewel was a gift from her husband Sir Edward Burne-Jones.

who was the recipient of many jewels from her father, some in stained ivory (see Colour Plate 75).

Child and Child also enjoyed the patronage of Edwin Lutyens, who employed them to make the silver and ebony crucifix illustrated in Colour Plate 79, which he designed for his future wife. It is tempting to see this as a further consequence of Burne-Jones's patronage.

Carlo Giuliano had already received the imprimatur of approval as an 'artistic' jeweller from Mrs. Haweis in 1878, but his employment by Burne-Jones was to lead to other commissions from artists. E.J. Poynter, a fellow artist and, incidentally, Lady Burne-Jones's brother-in-law, designed a jewel for the marriage of his son Hugh Poynter to Clara Bell in 1895 which was executed by Giuliano, who was to benefit from further interesting commissions

Plate 92. A late medieval gold love jewel in the form of a heart engraved with tears against a ground presumably prepared for enamel or niello, now completely lost. The reverse of the jewel is deeply engraved with an ivy leaf and the black letter inscription 'Tristes en plesire' (sadness in pleasure) which echoes the device of the tears on the front. (The British Museum)

The pendant brings together three significant motifs associated with late medieval jewellery: the heart, the ivy leaf and tears. The meaning of the heart and tears is obvious, but the ivy may represent womankind and that which medieval society saw as her clinging nature. The jewel, which is French and dates from the third quarter of the fifteenth century, was discovered in Rosklea Sands in Dorset in 1977.

Plate 93. Designs for a heart-shaped jewel by Federico Giuliano inscribed 'Haddon 1885-1894.' Pencil on card. (Private Collection.)

This heart-shaped locket was intended as a memorial for Lord Haddon who died tragically at the age of nine, after drinking laudanum from the medicine cupboard. He was the son of Violet Lindsay who had married Henry Manners, the heir to the Dukedom of Rutland in 1882. Violet, Duchess of Rutland, was an accomplished artist and was hailed as such by Auguste Rodin and Jacques-Emile Blanche. Lady Diana Cooper, her daughter, wrote: 'My Mother was in such an anguish of grief that she withdrew into her studio in London, when in her dreadful pain she was able to sculpt a recumbent figure of her dead son . . . All her artistic soul went into this tomb.' Another version was placed in the chapel at Haddon Hall. Tradition holds that the Giuliano jewel was placed inside the memorial by the grieving mother and this is substantiated by the fact that the jewel does not survive in the family. The heart-shaped locket covered with heart-shaped tears may be inspired by a medieval theme. (Compare with plate 92).

from Poynter's family. The choice of Giuliano was apt since this firm had the services of a gem-engraver who had made a speciality of working in relief in opal and must have been one of the very few competent to execute the opal angel.

In 1899 Charles Ricketts, consciously or unconsciously based his design for a bird brooch on Burne-Jones's bird, and followed his example in employing the Giuliano firm to make it (Colour Plate 67). By this time Carlo Giuliano had died and the business was in the hands of his two sons, Carlo and Arthur. In 1904 Ricketts was wrestling to obtain a worthy piece from Giuliano. In April he wrote: 'In the morning to see the Giuliano pendant and found it horribly chased up and spent the rest of the day scraping it with a knife, graver and nail and knocked some shape into it.' (For a detailed account of Ricketts' jewellery experiments see: Diana Scarisbrick, 'Charles Ricketts and his Designs for Jewellery', *Apollo,* September 1982, pp.163-9.)

Plate 94. A photographic reproduction of a pencil portrait of Lord Haddon by Violet, Duchess of Rutland. (Jeremy Luscombe.) The Duchess gave as presents these signed photographic prints of her work and they are almost indistinguishable from the original drawings.

Plate 95. An openwork gold pendant by Carlo and Arthur Giuliano in the form of a heart-shaped garland, set with emeralds and sapphires and hung with a single pearl. (Mrs Richard Dorment.)
This jewel is part of a series which is probably based on the designs of Sir Edward Burne-Jones. It is certainly related to the foliage which forms the background of the bird brooches which were designed by the artist (see plate 81).

Plate 96. Walter Child (1840-1930) and Harold Child (1848-1915), the proprietors of the firm of Child and Child which operated from 35 Alfred Place West from 1891 until Harold's death in 1915. The shop, now 35 Thurloe Street, which was a favourite of Sir Edward Burne-Jones, William Holman Hunt, and Sir Edwin Lutyens, was also patronised by the Edward Coterie known as 'The Souls'. Child and Child also boasted of the patronage of Queen Victoria, King Edward VII, and Queen Alexandra, King George V and Queen Mary, and Alexandra Empress of Russia, as well as 'The nobility, Gentry, the Army and Navy, and the most prominent men and women of the day in Society, Politics, Arts, Sciences and Literature.' (See 'Child and Child and Their Artistic Patronage' by Geoffrey Munn in the handbook of the Silver and Jewellery Fair, 1987.)

Plate 97. Two views of the watch by Child and Child illustrated in Colour Plate 20, here shown open and closed. (The Rt. Hon. The Viscount de Vesci.)

144

Colour Plate 69. A heart-shaped jewel box in green leather with gold tooling decoration of willow boughs and wreaths. The centre of the box is impressed with twinned hearts and around them can be read the inscription '1888 September Margaret Mackail'. Designed by Sir Edward Burne-Jones and possibly made by Sangorski and Sutcliffe the book binders. (Private Collection.) Burne-Jones was immensely fond of his beautiful daughter Margaret and she modelled for several of his major works. He wrote to Mrs Horner: 'I got her (Margaret) a moonstone that she might never know love and stay with me'. (Time Remembered by Frances Horner, 1933.) However, the charm failed and she married J.W. Mackail in 1887. Burne-Jones gave this jewel box to her on her first wedding anniversary.

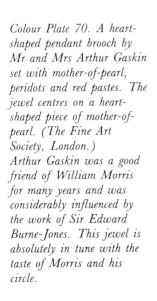

Colour Plate 70. A heart-shaped pendant brooch by Mr and Mrs Arthur Gaskin set with mother-of-pearl, peridots and red pastes. The jewel centres on a heart-shaped piece of mother-of-pearl. (The Fine Art Society, London.) Arthur Gaskin was a good friend of William Morris for many years and was considerably influenced by the work of Sir Edward Burne-Jones. This jewel is absolutely in tune with the taste of Morris and his circle.

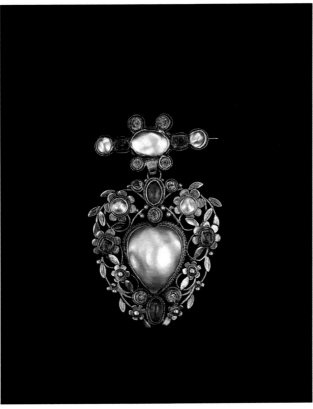

145

Plate 98. 'April Love' by Arthur Hughes, 1855 (detail). Oil on canvas. (The Tate Gallery, London.)

This is Hughes' idea of fragile young love. It was shown at the Royal Academy in 1856 with a quotation from one of the songs from Tennyson's 'The Miller's Daughter'. In this poem the young couple fear the passing of their love 'Love that has us in the net/ Can he pass, and we forget?' Hughes has placed his lovers in an ivy clad arbour and, as with many of his works, ivy is also used to embellish the frame. This may be a reference to the eternal qualities of the love which is the subject of the painting. The young girl wears a heart-shaped pendant at her neck.

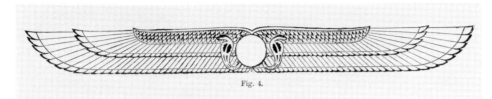

Fig. 4.

Plate 99. An engraving of the ancient Egyptian 'winged globe'. (Reproduced from Principles of Decorative Design *by Christopher Dresser, London, 1873.)*

Dresser was one of the most original and individual designers of the last decades of the nineteenth century and his influence was wide ranging. Although this device was well known to enthusiasts of ancient Egypt, by reproducing it in his anthology of design, Dresser undoubtedly made it popular with the goldsmiths and jewellers of London. All the examples of jewellery illustrated in this book which owe their form to the winged globe, are later than the publication date of Dresser's work.

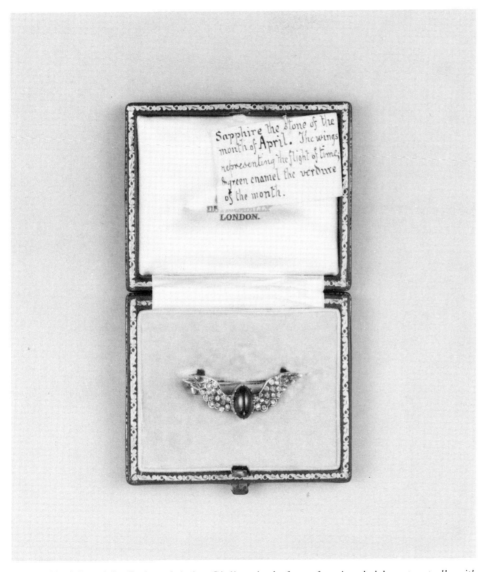

Plate 100. A brooch by Carlo and Arthur Giuliano in the form of a winged globe, set centrally with a cabochon sapphire and diamonds. The ends of the wings are picked out in green enamel. (Private Collection.)

This brooch was given by Constantine Ionides to his daughter, Lallie, for her birthday. According to the original label and invoice from Giuliano which accompany the jewel, its form is emblematic of the month of April.

147

148

The collaboration of these artists with Giuliano was to result in an elegant — even exquisite — hybrid: not Victorian revivalist, not Art Nouveau, not Arts and Crafts, but a style *hors catégorie* which has its roots in the Renaissance both formally and technically. It might be said to be the purest 'artistic' style, since the stylistic borrowings are submerged in the personal manner of the artists themselves the pastiche element so prevalent in nineteenth century jewellery is for once overcome.

Colour Plate 71. An unusually large engraved and enamelled silver and gold mounted brooch, set centrally with a sapphire, by Child and Child, c.1900. Signed with a monogram of two 'C's and a sunflower. (Editions Graphiques, London.)

This extraordinary jewel and the smaller version photographed with it are based on the Egyptian prophylactic symbol known as the 'winged globe' (see plate 99). This particular example is remarkable in that the wings are hinged and can be pitched at any angle to suit the owner's mood.

(Below). Another version of the 'winged globe' by Child and Child similarly engraved, enamelled and signed, c.1900. In this instance the globe itself has been replaced with a baroque pearl pendant. Although loosely based on an antique prototype these jewels are strongly Pre-Raphaelite in mood and seem to reflect the decorative work of Sir Edward Burne-Jones.

Colour Plate 72. A tiara by Carlo and Arthur Giuliano in the form of a pair of green enamelled gold wings centering on a star sapphire. This device, which may be unscrewed to form a brooch, is supported on two diamond set snakes with ruby set eyes. Signed 'C. and A.G.' (Wartski, London.)

Although it is not immediately obvious this jewel owes its origins to an ancient Egyptian prophylactic symbol known as the 'winged globe'. In antiquity it was believed to be such a strong charm against evil that if placed above a doorway nothing with evil intent could enter therein. In the nineteenth century its meaning was well understood and it was much used in the decoration of tombs and mausoleums. As a gift in the form of jewellery, it might be thought to protect and watch over the recipient. The globe itself is usually flanked by serpents' heads but in this instance the Giulianos have moved these down to form a support for the jewel. Nineteenth century jewellers were particularly fond of the 'winged globe' design and adapted it constantly, sometimes substituting a heart for the globe (see plates 99 and 100). The firm of Child and Child took the theme even further making a series of jewels in the form of wings which strongly recall the work of Sir Edward Burne-Jones (see Colour Plate 71.)

Colour Plate 74. A pair of green stained ivory cuff-links mounted in silver, by Child and Child. Signed with their trade mark; a monogram of two 'C's and a sunflower. (Private Collection.)

These links were designed by Sir Edward Burne-Jones for his own use and reflect his continued interest in the heart as a decorative device and as a symbol of love. His own finger ring in silver, centering on a heart-shaped baroque pearl was also made by Child and Child (see plate 91).

An openwork heart-shaped silver and gold pendant by Carlo and Arthur Giuliano decorated with green and white enamels and set with cabochon sapphires. Signed 'C. and A.G.' (Private Collection, Chicago.)

This is one of the jewels from the Giulianos' commercial repertoire which seems to show the influence of Sir Edward Burne-Jones. The parallels between this pendant and the cuff-links photographed with it are obvious, however the heart-shaped gem-set wreath seems to derive from the foliage employed by Burne-Jones in his famous bird brooch which was also made up by Giuliano (see Colour Plate 65.)

Colour Plate 75. A gold brooch in the form of a marguerite flower by Child and Child. The heart-shaped petals are of green stained ivory and the centre is set with a citrine. Signed with the monogram of two 'C's and a sunflower. (Geoffrey Munn.)

This brooch is without precise provenance but it has a strong resemblance to the heart-shaped green stained ivory cuff-links which Burne-Jones designed and had made for his own use by Child and Child (Colour Plate 74) that it must have also been made to his order. Burne-Jones was extremely fond of his daughter, Margaret, and the flower may be a rebus of her name. In Time Remembered (London 1933) Frances Horner remarked that Margaret Burne-Jones, like her father, preferred stained ivory to any precious stone.

Plate 101. A photograph of Margaret Burne-Jones aged twenty, by the Cameron Studios, 70 Mortimer Street, S.W. from the collection of Henry Holiday. (Jeremy Maas.)
Margaret Burne-Jones was her father's particular favourite and often modelled for him. He frequently gave her presents of jewellery. Here she is wearing a brooch in gold set with an amethyst which takes the form of a winged heart. The jewel remains in the Burne-Jones family and is reproduced in Colour Plate 73.

Colour Plate 73. (Centre). A faceted amethyst mounted in gold in the form of a winged and crowned heart. The design registry number, Rd 8032, reveals that it was made by Peter Westren of 27 Frederick Street, Edinburgh. He is recorded as a goldsmith and the design was registered on 9 June 1884.

Margaret Burne-Jones was unmarried when she first owned the jewel and it is reasonable to suppose that it was a gift from her father. If so, it again illustrates his fascination for the symbolism of the heart (see Colour Plates 74 and 75.)

(Outside). Nineteenth century Indian turquoise and gold necklace with pendant, the reverse decorated with bright polychrome enamels in Jaipur style. This necklace was in the collection of Margaret Burne-Jones and is kept within a fitted leather case from the firm of Child and Child. This is evidence that Child and Child were importing Oriental jewellery into London and selling it to the artistic community who had already begun to patronise Liberty's for these pieces.

151

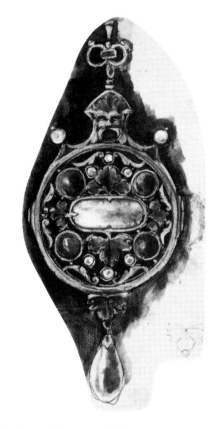

Plate 102. Design by Charles Ricketts for the jewel in the form of Pegasus drinking at the fountain of Hippocrene, which was made up by Giuliano in 1901. It was this jewel which was finally decided upon and contained the miniature of Edith Cooper.

Plate 103. Design for the front of a pendant jewel by Charles Ricketts decorated with enamelled vine leaves and set with mother-of-pearl and garnets. This was the first design for the jewel made to contain the miniature of Miss Edith Cooper which was commissioned in 1901. The link in the form of twinned rings from which the jewel hangs is the emblem of the poet who with her aunt Katherine Bradley, wrote under the name of Michael Field. (The British Museum.)

Plate 104. Design for a pendant in pen and ink by Charles Ricketts from the album in the British Museum. Ricketts has transformed the idea used for the relief profile portrait of Mrs Hacon, into a Medusa in the manner of Burne-Jones. The sketches of the head of Marie Zambaco, executed by Burne-Jones in a state of deep emotional involvement, were an important influence on his contemporaries. Other examples of the intense, romantic style of portrait with its nimbus of wind blown hair include the self-portrait by Violet, Duchess of Rutland.

Plate 105. *A photograph of Charles Ricketts. Photographer unknown. (Sotheby's.)*

Plate 106. *A jewel in the form of a pendant cockle shell, mounted in enamelled gold and hung with pearls and a pear-shaped cabochon. Designed by Charles Ricketts for Mrs. Furse. (The British Museum.)*

Colour Plate 76. Five jewels designed by Charles Ricketts and made by Carlo and Arthur Giuliano.

(Top left.) A gold locket in Renaissance style in the form of Pegasus drinking at the fountain of Hippocrene. The jewel is enamelled blue, green and white and is set with pearls, rubies, and garnets. The interior of the locket contains a miniature of Miss Edith Cooper in pencil and watercolour highlighted with gold (see plate 102). The reverse is decorated with a neo-Renaissance ornamental device in polychrome champleve enamels. (The Fitzwilliam Museum, Cambridge.) The Pegasus motif appears to derive from a gem in the Marlborough Collection. The jewel was made so that the poet, Katherine Bradley, could use it to hold a miniature of her niece Edith Cooper (by Ricketts). It was delivered in May 1901.

(Bottom left.) A gold pendant in the Art Nouveau style, enamelled green in black and set with a turquoise between two pearls, the drop being a gold mounted amethyst. (The Fitzwilliam Museum, Cambridge.) This jewel was designed by Ricketts to be worn by the model for Icarus in one of his paintings. On 5 December 1899 he gave it to Katherine Bradley.

(Centre.) An unusually large gold pendant enamelled blue, green and white and set with sapphires, emeralds, carbuncles, chrysolites, and a pink topaz. The jewel represents the descent of Psyche into Hell and the reverse is decorated with neo-Renaissance ornamental devices in polychrome champleve enamel. (The Fitzwilliam Museum, Cambridge.) This jewel was designed to celebrate

the betrothal of Maria Appia and Thomas Sturge Moore and was completed on 5 March 1904.
It was described by Ricketts as 'the pendant of pendants which will tear all lace and scratch babies'.

(Top right.) A gold brooch in the form of a dove decorated with blue and green enamel and set
with cabochon corals, a garnet and a pendant crystal. (The Fitzwilliam Museum, Cambridge.)
This is Rickett's version of the bird brooches designed by Sir Edward Burne-Jones which were also
made by Giuliano. Ricketts could have seen the version made for Margaret Burne-Jones when it was
shown at the New Gallery in 1892. One of Rickett's bird brooches was designed for Mrs Lawrence
Binyon but Ricketts was dissatisfied with the work and it was given to 'a model I rather dislike
and the four pale sapphires and one chrysolite like a star will glimmer unseen in the studios of sundry
bad landscape painters'.

(Bottom right.) A pendant jewel made in 1900, to contain a gold portrait medallion of Mrs
Llewelyn Hacon sculpted by her artist husband. Decorated with green and white enamel and set with
ruby, pearls and emeralds with three pearl drops attached. (Ashmolean Museum, Oxford.)

Colour Plate 77. The reverse of the jewels in Colour Plate 76 which are decorated front and back.
(The turquoise pendant and the bird brooch are hollow and therefore not included in this photograph.)

Plate 107. A gold ring designed by Charles Ricketts for William Morris's daughter May (Mary). The bezel of the ring is in the form of a domed turret and the dome itself set with a cabochon ruby. Possibly by Giuliano. (The Victoria and Albert Museum.)

Like the ring designed for Katherine Bradley (see plate 110), the form of the jewel is loosely based on a Jewish marriage ring. This ring was left to the Museum by May Morris when she died in 1938.

Plate 108. 'May' Morris by Frederick Hollyer, c.1830. (The National Portrait Gallery.)

Miss Morris is wearing a pectoral cross on a chain about her neck, the complicated construction of which suggests that it is part of her collection of European peasant jewellery.

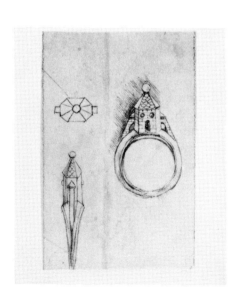
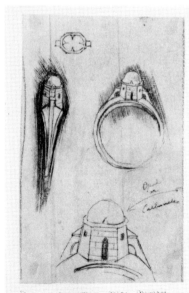
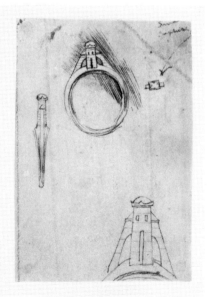

Plate 109. Designs for May Morris's ring by Charles Ricketts. (The British Museum.)

156

Plate 110. *A gold ring designed by Charles Ricketts in 1903 for his friend, the poet Katherine Bradley. (The Fitzwilliam Museum, Cambridge.)*

The jewel is inspired by the story of Sabbatai Sebi (1626-1676). He was a Jewish mystic who believed himself to be the Messiah but was later converted to Islam. The ring is inspired by that given by the Sultan of Constantinople which made Sabbatai change his mind. It symbolizes the Mosque of Omar supported by a shrine. The ring was complete by 8 January 1904 and on 5 February Ricketts presented it with the words 'Here is the distinguished stranger'. A star sapphire is set in the dome, and through the windows of the shrine a loose emerald can be heard and seen. The ring is designed to appeal to four senses and so the doors of the shrine are smeared with ambergris. The ring may have been made by Giuliano, but there is no proof of this.

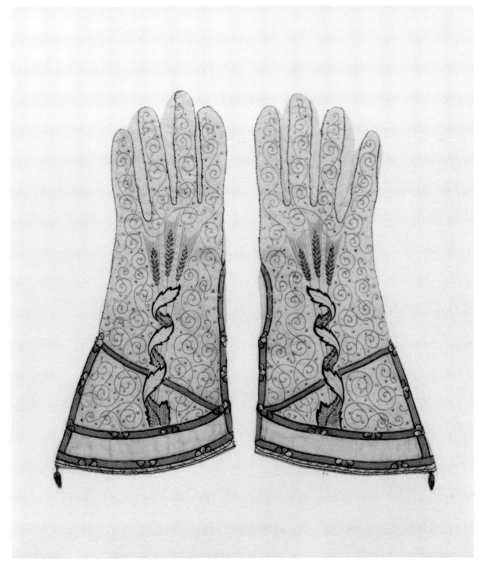

Plate 111. *A pair of episcopal gloves designed by Charles Ricketts and embroidered by May Morris, which were probably those exhibited at the 1899 Arts and Crafts Exhibition. Bequeathed to the Victoria and Albert Museum after May's death in 1938. (The Victoria and Albert Museum.)*

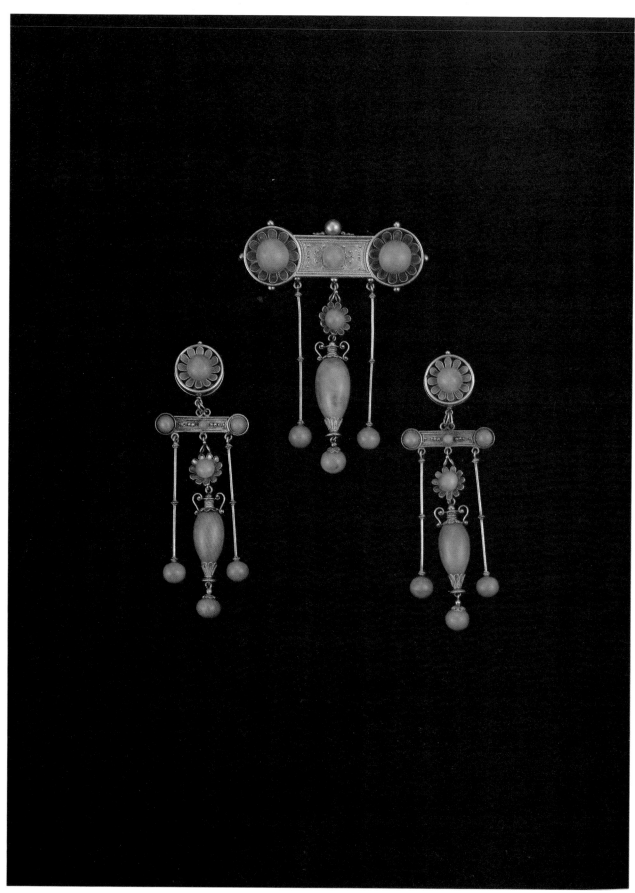

Colour Plate 79. A silver and ebony crucifix set with six pearls designed by Sir Edwin Lutyens and made by Child and Child. Signed with a monogram of a marigold and two 'C's. (Private Collection.)

    This cross was made as a gift for Lady Emily Lytton when Lutyens was courting her in 1896-7. It was contained within a casket filled with small treasures and love tokens which were contrived to win her hand. This jewel, indeed the whole casket (see plate 112), is very Pre-Raphaelite in spirit and appears to have strong parallels with the jewellery designs of Sir Edward Burne-Jones, who also employed Child and Child. The firm of Child and Child is believed to be a successor of Sir Francis Child's jewellery firm which flourished under the patronage of King William III in the last quarter of the seventeenth century. Sir Francis converted the plateworkers and jewellers Blanchard and Child into one of the most successful banks in the City by the time of his death in 1712. However, despite the marigold sign common to both the bankers and the nineteenth century jewellers Child and Child, the connection remains tenuous and unproven to date. (See 'At the Sign of the Marigold' in The Three Banks Review, *September 1969, and 'Sir Francis Child's Jewellery Business' by Edgar R. Samuel, in the same magazine, March 1977).*

Colour Plate 78. A gold-mounted coral demi-parure in the archaeological taste. English, c.1870. (Wartski, London.)

    Engraved on the reverse 'Ned to Georgie'; almost certainly a gift from Sir Edward Burne-Jones to his wife Georgiana, who was one of the celebrated MacDonald sisters. The artist was particularly interested in precious materials gathered from the depths of the sea, and was known to value coral above most other precious stones. (See Time Remembered, *by Frances Horner, London 1933.)*

Plate 112. A painted wood and leather casket with brass mounts designed by Sir Edwin Lutyens c.1896 as a gift for Lady Emily Lytton before they became engaged. It is decorated with gold tooling in a diaper pattern and the alternating initials of the couple are to be found in the resulting diamond shape. The casket was made to contain small treasures symbolic of the couple's future wedded state and amongst them is the ebony and silver crucifix designed by Lutyens and made up by Child and Child which bears the maker's monogram of two 'C's and a sunflower (see Colour Plate 79). It was Lutyens' intention to woo Lady Emily with the casket and it worked. They married on 4 August, 1897. (The Rt. Hon. Nicholas Ridley and Miss Mary Lutyens.)

Plate 113. A wooden trinket box covered in brown shagreen and bound in silver decorated with filigree, by John Paul Cooper (1869-1933). (By Gracious Permission of Her Majesty Queen Elizabeth the Queen Mother.)

This box is a particularly sophisticated example of Cooper's work in shagreen of which he was very fond. It was a gift from Mr and Mrs McEwen Marchmont to Her Majesty and the late King.

Plate 114. A wooden jewel casket bound with iron strips in medieval style. The panels were painted by Dante Gabriel Rossetti and Elizabeth Siddall as a wedding gift to William Morris's wife, Janey, who he married in 1859. (The Society of Antiquaries, Kelmscott Manor.)

The painted scenes which decorate the casket are taken from various late medieval sources including an illuminated manuscript called the Poems of Christine de Pisan *which is French and datable to about 1403. It is now in the British Library. For a detailed examination of the aesthetic ancestry of the casket see 'Janey Morris's Jewel Casket' by Jennifer Harris in the* Antique Collector, *December 1984.*

Colour Plate 80. A gold and enamelled pendant in Renaissance style by Henry Wilson, made for Douglas Strahan, the Aberdeen stained glass artist. (The Fine Art Society). The design for the pendant is shown in Colour Plate 81, opposite.

Douglas Strahan was the most famous and prolific Scottish stained glass artist of the early twentieth century. He was the first east coast designer to incorporate Arts and Crafts motifs and innovatory techniques into his work. Like Cromar Watt, a fellow teacher at the Edinburgh College of Art, he had made contact with Henry Wilson in London, possibly through the Central School of Art. Strahan's work was strongly influenced by Wilson, and his admiration for Wilson resulted in this commission, the subject matter of which reflects Strahan's own craft.

CHAPTER V
The Craft Revival

Pevsner has said (in the Introduction to *The Anti-Rationalists,* a collection of articles on Modern Movement architecture and decorative art), that the first Art Nouveau work was the design for the title page of *Wren's City Churches,* made in 1883 by Arthur Heygate Mackmurdo, founder of the Century Guild and editor of *The Hobby Horse.* However, his later development as a designer shows that he was more in sympathy with the Arts and Crafts Movement than with the Continental Art Nouveau. His small structure designed as the Century Guild stand for the Liverpool International Exhibition in 1886 incorporates many of the characteristic elements of Glasgow School architecture, with the strong verticals reminiscent of Japanese buildings and the recessed decorative panels. Even if it is difficult to accept Mackmurdo on his own as the very first in the field, it is true that from this date the activity in the Craft Revival field became increasingly frenzied as Guilds and craft workshops were set up in quick succession.

The Century Guild was formed by Mackmurdo with Selwyn Image, Herbert Horne, Frederick Shields and Clement Heaton, in about 1882. It was one of the few craft guilds not to produce jewellery and silverwork, although Clement Heaton was responsible for the enamel work on Alfred Gilbert's mayoral chain for the Preston Corporation (1897) and also carried out a number of Mackmurdo's designs in cloisonné enamels, a technique which was rarely used in England at that date except by Elkington's. The Guild was disbanded in 1888, and Heaton set up his own firm, Cloisonné Metals Ltd. He went to Switzerland in the 'nineties, and carried out a series of elaborate

Colour Plate 81. The design for the pendant in Colour Plate 80, from Henry Wilson's album, now in the Victoria and Albert Museum. (The Victoria and Albert Museum.)

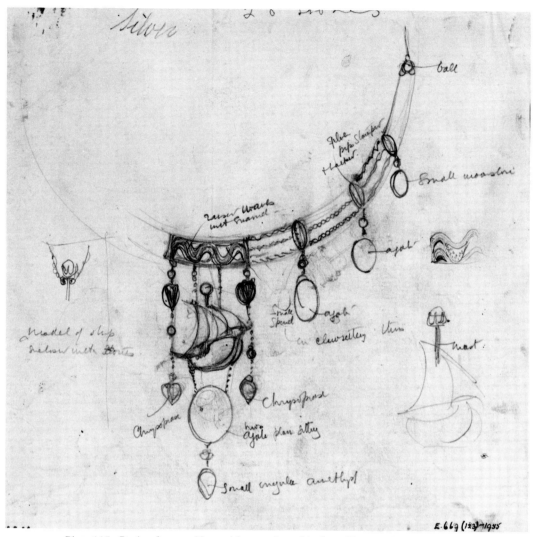

Plate 115. Design for a necklace with a pendant ship from Henry Wilson's album in the Victoria and Albert Museum.

large scale decorations for the Municipal Museum at Neuchâtel in cloisonné and stained glass. He emigrated to America in 1912.

In the year following the appearance of Mackmurdo's book on the Wren churches the Art Workers' Guild was founded. The Art Workers' Guild is remarkable not only in having been among the first of the craft guilds to be established but also in being still in existence today. The Guild was founded by five architects, Horsley, Lethaby, Newton, Macartney and Prior, all members or former members of the staff of Norman Shaw's office in Bloomsbury Square. The original members were joined soon afterwards by the 'Fifteen', an informal group of artists which included L.F. Day and Walter Crane. Among the founder members was the architect J.D. Sedding, master of both Henry Wilson and J. Paul Cooper who were to become outstanding Craft Revival jewellers and silversmiths. At the risk of making a generalisation, it seems reasonable to claim that all the artists of any importance who were involved in the Arts and Crafts Movement belonged for some period of their working lives to the Art Workers' Guild. A record of all the members and an account of the Guild's activities from 1884-1934 exist in

Plate 116. A silver pendant by Henry Wilson, in the form of a ship encircled by formalised waves. (Hessisches Landesmuseum, Darmstadt.)

The Art Workers' Guild, by H.J.L. Massé, and it is instructive to note the dates at which the various members joined the Guild. The Guild's centenary was celebrated by an exhibition at the Brighton Museum and Art Gallery which demonstrated its relevance to the continuance of the Craft Guild ethos.

The Arts and Crafts Exhibition Society was founded three years later in 1887 by W.A.S. Benson, the metalworker, to provide a showcase for the craftsmen connected with the Art Workers' Guild. Walter Crane was the first president, and the first exhibition was held at the New Gallery in 1888. The rules of the Society were strict and exhibiting craftsmen had to demonstrate their right to show work in the exhibitions by assuring the committee that exhibits were entirely hand-made. The prestige attached to exhibiting with the Society was considerable, and when Arthur Lasenby Liberty wanted to exhibit metalwork at an Arts and Crafts show at the turn of the century he had to come to a special arrangement with Archibald Knox, his chief designer, to show specially made pieces in Knox's name, a remarkable reversal of his usual policy of anonymity for his designers (see *Archibald Knox* by A. Tilbroke, 1975).

In the 'eighties a number of Guilds and craft classes were set up in an attempt to realise one of the chief aims of the Craft Revival, i.e. to bring the pleasure of original creative activity into the lives of the men and women of the working classes, and to relieve the monotony to which repetitive mechanical labour condemned them for the greater part of their waking hours. Silverwork and jewellery were produced by a number of these schools and Guilds, among them the Keswick School of Industrial Art, which was started by Canon and Mrs. Rawnsley as an evening institute in 1884; the Duchess of Sutherland's Cripples Guild, whose mark (D S C G) appears mainly on silver-plated copper wares of very simple design, and the Birmingham Guild of Handicraft, which Arthur Dixon, a jeweller and silversmith who had trained as an architect, founded in 1890 in imitation of C.R. Ashbee's Guild of Handicraft, which later expanded into a Limited Company and was successfully commercialised.

Plate 117. A pencil design for a pendant by Henry Wilson from the album in the Victoria and Albert Museum. This design unites the two most important influences in English Art Nouveau jewellery, Alfred Gilbert and Edward Burne-Jones. The figure recalls the mermaid in Burne-Jones's 1887 painting entitled 'The Depths of the Sea', which forms part of the European Symbolist Movement. Symbolist designs for jewellery are rare, especially in England, and this group of figural jewellery designed by sculptors, which includes the 'Psyche' pendant by Ricketts illustrated in Colour Plate 76 and the Watercolour Society and Architectural Society badges by Alfred Gilbert and Walter Gilbert (plates 4 and 14), is very important for this reason. The closest parallels in Symbolist terms are the designs of the Glasgow School artists, but none of these British designs can match in suggestive mystery the jewellery made by Vever to the designs of Eugène Grasset.

Plate 118. A silver pendant by Henry Wilson in the form of an angel in a boat navigating with the aid of a moonstone. The jewel hangs from a circular plaque set with another moonstone. (The Rt. Hon. the Viscount de Vesci.)

The Guild of Handicraft was started by Ashbee a year after he had set up his School of Handicraft at Toynbee Hall in 1887 (the School was closed in 1895). Charles Robert Ashbee (1863-1942) trained as an architect like so many of the Craft Revival silversmiths. He was articled to G.F. Bodley, a close associate of Morris and the founder of Watts and Co., the church furnishing firm for whom he designed a number of pieces of ecclesiastical metalwork in the revived Gothic style. Ashbee's work, though flowing and sinuous in form, is not without its Gothic side, an aspect of his inspiration which is perhaps best demonstrated by the designs for sporting trophies and cups, table silver and, predictably enough, the church metalwork.

The Guild of Handicraft moved in 1890 to Essex House, a 'spacious Georgian mansion' in the Mile End Road: here the presses and type used by the Kelmscott Press, which were acquired after Morris's death in 1896, were installed. Both Ashbee's translation of the *Notebooks* of Cellini and his book on *Modern English Silverwork* were published by the Essex House Press. During this period at Essex House, and before the Guild moved to Chipping Camden in 1902, the showrooms in Bond Street were acquired, the two marks used by Ashbee and the Guild were registered with the Goldsmiths' Company, and the

Plate 119. The design for the pendant in plate 118. (The Victoria and Albert Museum.)

166

Guild became a Limited Company. Although the competition from the trade in general and firms like Liberty's in particular was always a serious threat to the prosperity of the Guild, it was from the time of the move to Gloucestershire that the financial position became really serious. In 1908 the Guild went into voluntary liquidation and was formally disbanded, though some work continued to be produced, and marked, by the Guildsmen. In 1907 a catalogue of jewellery was produced offering the stock at very reduced prices, and much of it must have been cleared in this way, though it seems that certain pieces remained in Ashbee's possession until much later, and some of them with dated inscriptions were presented to friends long after the dissolution of the Guild. Four pieces designed in the 'nineties which belonged to Ashbee's wife are illustrated in *Victorian Jewellery* by Margaret Flower, 1951.

The Guildsmen employed by the Guild of Handicraft were not professional silversmiths and were mainly without training of any kind. The early work was produced by a system of trial and error, many of the techniques being based on those described by Cellini, and bearing this fact in mind the complexity of some of the work is quite remarkable. The names of a number of the Guildsmen are known; the jewellers included W.A. White, F.C. Varley (a descendant of the watercolour painter, who made a speciality of landscape enamels), W. Mark (an enamellist), A. Gebhardt (who is usually credited with the design of one of the famous peacocks), A. Cameron, J. Baily, S. Viner, A. Toy, and Fred Partridge, a chemist's son from Devon who went with Ashbee to Chipping Camden and married May Hart, the enamellist. Ashbee is usually understood to have provided the designs for the work produced by the Guild, though some of the pieces illustrated in *The Studio* are attributed to the other craftsmen on information presumably provided by Ashbee himself, and the three pieces belonging to the Countess of Cranbrook illustrated in *Victorian Jewellery* (op. cit. pp.227 and 233) are said to be by Ashbee's friend Hugh Seebohm. The drawings now in the Public Library in Chelsea are by Ashbee himself and are fully annotated for the craftsman. There can have been no need of any further intervention by another designer.

The importance of the Guild to the Craft Revival in England was considerable. Many similar ventures, as well as the Birmingham Guild, were based on Ashbee's practical demonstration of Ruskin's theories, and on the Continent the famous Viennese craft workshops, the Wiener Werkstätte, were set up in imitation of the Guild of Handicraft after Josef Hoffmann had met and talked to Ashbee, and invited him to exhibit with the Vienna Secession.

Not all the Guilds set up at this time adhered to the rigid formula (similar to that which theoretically rules the modern 'commune') set out by Ruskin and used by Ashbee. The Bromsgrove Guild of Applied Art, which was formed by Walter Gilbert (a pupil and associate of Alfred Gilbert, the sculptor), employed craftsmen and designers as the occasion demanded and thus provided work for the large number of craft metalworkers who remained independent of the Guilds.

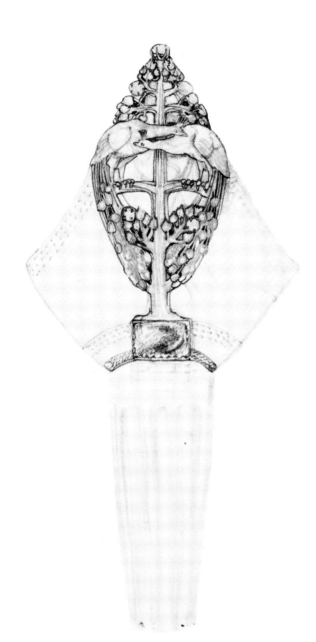

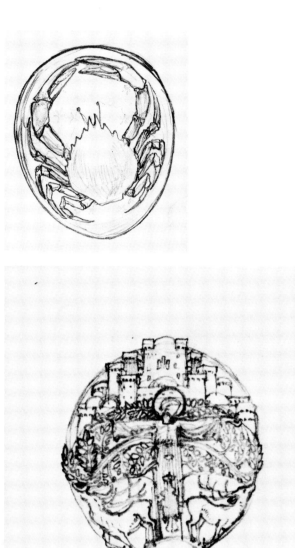

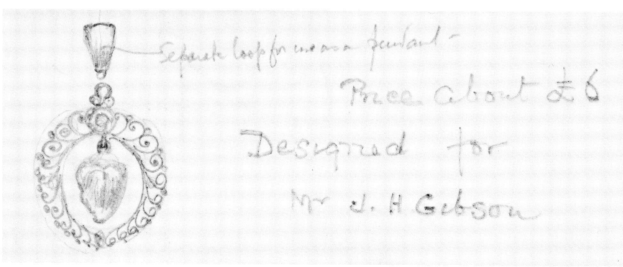

Separate loop for use as a pendant —

Price about £6

Designed for

Mr J. H Gibson

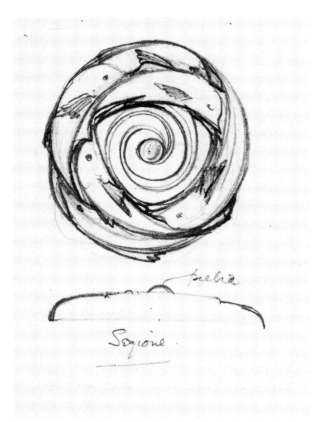

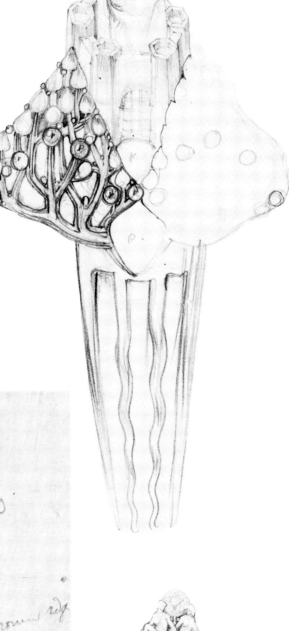

Plate 120. A selection of drawings from Henry Wilson's album, now in the Victoria and Albert Museum.

The morse shown opposite (centre), which was made from this design in enamelled gold, formerly in the Handley-Read Collection, is now in the Victoria and Albert Museum.

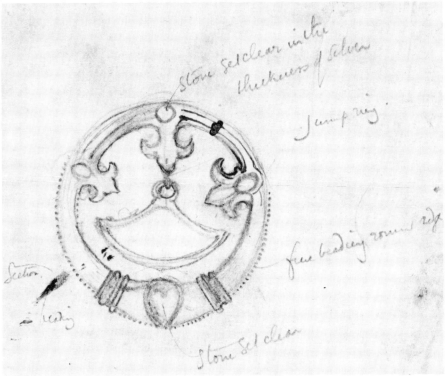

Colour Plate 82. Design for a belt, emblematic of the four seasons, by Henry Wilson, in repoussé silver or gold on a silk band. (The Victoria and Albert Museum.)

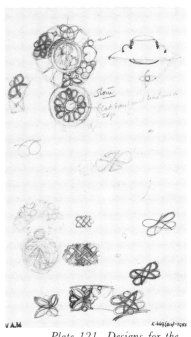

Plate 121. Designs for the necklace shown in Colour Plate 83. (The Victoria and Albert Museum.)

Colour Plate 83. An enamelled gold necklace in Renaissance style, by Henry Wilson, set with cabochon emeralds. (Hancock's, London.)

Colour Plate 84. A cloisonné enamelled gold pendant by Henry Wilson, set with cabochon sapphires, emeralds, moonstones and a garnet. The bezel which contains the centre stone is hinged and opens to reveal a compartment for a souvenir. (Christie's, London.)

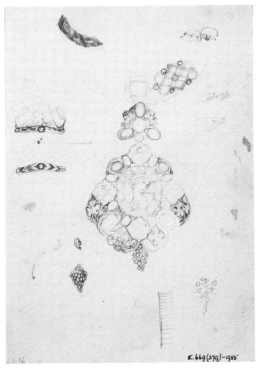

E.669(379)-1955

E.669(380)-1955

Plate 122. Designs for the pendant shown in Colour Plate 84. (The Victoria and Albert Museum.)

171

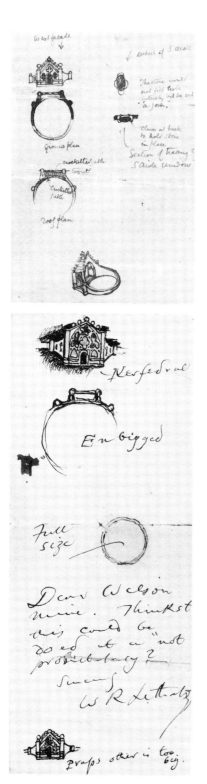

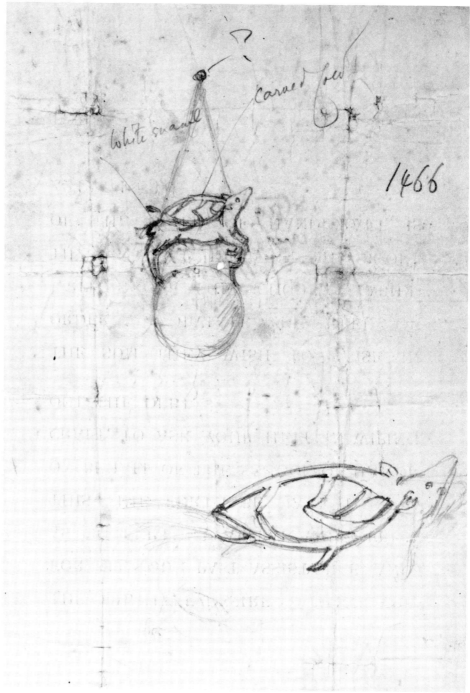

Plate 123. Designs for an architectonic ring by Henry Wilson for W.R. Lethaby, comparable with Rickett's design for a ring for May Morris in plate 109. (The Victoria and Albert Museum.)

172

Plate 124. Designs for jewels incorporating a stag, by Henry Wilson (see plate 125), from the album in the Victoria and Albert Museum.

Plate 125. A pendant by Henry Wilson, incorporating the stag motif, which hangs from a seed pearl necklace set with star rubies, emeralds and moonstones. (The Victoria and Albert Museum.)

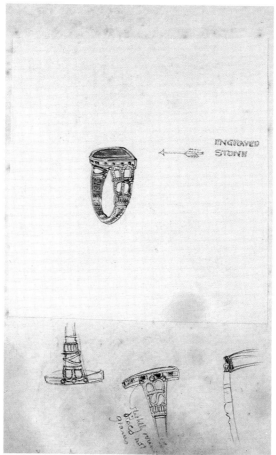

Colour Plate 85. A jade and rock crystal plaque de collier by Henry Wilson, the gold mounts enamelled in translucent green and set with a moonstone. From the centre of the jewel hangs a gold crescent which encircles a model of a leaping stag in repoussé gold. (Wartski, London.) This jewel exemplifies the medievalism so often found in Henry Wilson's work.

The form of this jewel closely reflects that of a hat badge designed by Albrecht Dürer (1471-1528), illustrated above left in black and white, which is now kept in the Musée du Louvre, Paris.

Colour Plate 86. Designs for a ring set with a shield-shaped engraved opal in the medieval taste, by Henry Wilson. The shoulders are pierced with the initials SB VB; the inside of the shank engraved Sep. 23, 1913. (Private Collection.)

Colour Plate 87. An unusually large breast ornament in gold, set with moonstones, rubies, chrysoprase and abalone shell, by John Paul Cooper, 1908. (John Jesse.)

Plate 126. The design for a pendant in the form of a triple turreted castle by John Paul Cooper. From an entry in the artist's stock book dated 1913. (The Cooper Family.)

From the early years of the Arts and Crafts Exhibition Society until well into the present century it was apparent that silverwork and jewellery were to play an important part in the Craft Revival, more important in that the pieces are generally more recognisably the products of small workshops than the furniture or fabrics, and immensely superior numerically. The sheer weight of production in jewellery and silver meant, both at the time and in terms of survival to the present day, that much work of indifferent artistic and technical quality sheltered under the umbrella of serious intent erected by the craft workers.

Henry Wilson was trained as an architect and after completing his articles he worked first with John Oldrid Scott and then with J.D. Sedding, whose chief assistant he became, taking over the practice at the time of Sedding's early death from influenza in 1891. Wilson became interested in metalworking shortly before Sedding's death, and set up a workshop in a house at Vicarage Gate in Kensington where he entered briefly into a partnership with Alexander Fisher. The two men were temperamentally incompatible and the relationship did not last long, but Wilson continued to run the metalworking workshop in the basement of the Vicarage Gate House (the architectural practice was installed on the ground floor and Wilson's own studio was in a north-lit room at the top of the house), with at least two of Fisher's assistants, Luigi Movio, an Italian aged about sixty who became the first foreman, and Lorenzo Colarossi, a general worker, then still a young boy. J. Paul Cooper was taught jewellery-making in Wilson's workshop by two of his assistants, Movio and John Innocent, a jeweller who had been trained in the trade, and who added some useful professional knowledge to the usual trial and error methods of the craft workshop. Wilson joined the Art Workers' Guild in 1892 and became Master in 1917; he taught metalworking at the L.C.C. Central School of Arts and Crafts from 1896 (the year of its foundation). He went on to teach at the Royal College of Art in about 1901 and while there (in 1903) published his masterly textbook, *Silverwork and Jewellery*. He exhibited more than twenty-five items of jewellery and other metalwork at the exhibition of *Arts et Métiers de la Grande Bretagne* in Paris in 1914, and was the chairman of the committee selecting the British metalwork exhibits at the *Arts Décoratifs* exhibition in Paris in 1925, an appointment reflected in the choice of objects shown.

The design of Wilson's jewellery and silverwork reflects with some fidelity the influences of his artistic contacts throughout his career, with traces of the pure Gothic which characterised Sedding's metalwork designs, the range of intense jewel-like colours to his enamels which presumably results from his partnership with Alexander Fisher, and his interest in the use of unusual and subtly coloured stones which probably arises from his close contact with J.P. Cooper.

Wilson's career follows a pattern which was to become familiar in the Arts and Crafts Movement in the wielding of influence through the twin outlets of the workshop and the classroom, and it is this pattern so often repeated which explains the wide influence of the craft metalworkers in their own sphere and the comparative longevity of the movement as an identifiable commercial force. The influence of the craft ethic continued long after Continental Art Nouveau was a spent force, and can be seen in the work of many present-day designers, who are not simply making a pastiche of an obsolete style, but drawing on it as a continuing source of inspiration.

J. Paul Cooper, like Ashbee, Wilson and Nelson Dawson, also trained as an architect, he was articled to Sedding in 1889 and completed his articles under Henry Wilson after Sedding's death. Cooper's interest in craft work dates from the early 'nineties and he exhibited silverwork at the Arts and Crafts Society show in 1894. In 1897 he moved to a house in Aubrey Walk (no. 16), near to Wilson's office and workshop at Vicarage Gate, where he was able to establish his own studio and workshop. In 1899 he began to work with shagreen, which he used mainly for boxes mounted in silver, and which he made his speciality. These silver-mounted shagreen pieces were very popular and sold well throughout the whole of his career. In 1900 he began to take lessons in jewellery-making from John Innocent at Wilson's studio, and in 1901 he was appointed head of the metalwork department at the Birmingham School of Art. He seems to have started working on a regular basis at Birmingham in 1902, and he took the young Lorenzo Colarossi from Wilson's workshop to help with the practical work at the Art School. In 1907 he was getting sufficient work from private commissions to feel justified in giving up his teaching, and he moved back to the south of England, first to Hunton, near Maidstone, and then to a house with a studio and workshop which he designed for himself at Westerham, also in Kent. While having certain recognisable characteristics, particularly in the use of foliage and flowers as ornament, Cooper's work is always influenced by his early training in Wilson's studio; he in his turn was to have enormous influence on the work of Edward Spencer, presumably through the pieces he made for the Artificers' Guild for whom he worked from 1899 until 1910, supplying them direct during that period with about 225 items.

While in Birmingham Cooper would have become acquainted with Arthur Gaskin, who was from 1902 head of the recently opened Vittoria Street School for Silversmiths and Jewellers from 1902. Gaskin, who was first a student and then a teacher at the Birmingham School of Art and a member of the Birmingham Group of Painters and Craftsmen, had first started making jewellery and silverwork in partnership with his wife, Georgie Cave France, who was also a former student of the art school, in 1899. Some simple pieces of jewellery were exhibited with the Arts and Crafts Society by the Gaskins in that same year, and a further twenty-six pieces in 1901. Gaskin exhibited widely during the next fifteen or sixteen years, while also executing a number of private commissions, including two for the Birmingham City Corporation (a casket and an elaborate enamelled and jewelled necklace for Queen Alexandra), and also working for the Bromsgrove Guild of Applied Art with

Pendant in gold, enamelled and set with minute gemstones from the design (left) by John Paul Cooper. (John Jesse.)

whom he exhibited at the Centennial Exposition in Paris in 1900. He remained the head of the Vittoria Street School until 1924, influencing several generations of students during that time, and his characteristic use of flowers and leaves in gold or silver, set with small coloured stones and sometimes decorated with opaque enamels in pale colours, occurs in the work of many Birmingham-trained jewellers at the turn of the century.

It is understandable that much of the activity in the field of craft jewellery should have been centred on Birmingham, traditionally the home of the jewellery trade since the eighteenth century, and is proof that the craft ethic could survive the close proximity of commercial reality; this makes it all the more curious that the other metalworking centre, Sheffield, should not have been equally productive of craftsmen. The only students of the Sheffield School of Art to achieve a wide reputation in the Arts and Crafts movement were Omar Ramsden and Alwyn Carr, who came to London and set up a partnership in 1898. From the early years of the partnership a large number of assistants were employed in the studio, and it seems probable that little or no actual metalworking was done after his student days by Ramsden, though Carr may have kept up his skill as he continued to work as a silversmith after the dissolution of the partnership in 1919. Much of the work by Ramsden and Carr is in the style now identified as 'Craft Revival', but the application of the ornament is often somewhat mechanical, and the design of some of the larger pieces verges on the showy, both these characteristics perhaps being responsible for the undoubted commercial success of their products.

Another partnership similar to the Gaskins', was that of Nelson Dawson and his wife Edith. They met while Dawson, who had studied painting at the South Kensington Schools in London, was working in an art shop in Scarborough. Dawson came back to London in 1891 and took up metalworking, meanwhile attending a series of lectures on enamelling given by Alexander Fisher. The Dawsons were married in 1893, and Nelson taught his wife enamelling which was to become her speciality. Edith Dawson's enamels are amongst the most accomplished produced at this time. Much less ambitious in conception than Fisher's or those of Fisher's pupils who worked in his style (e.g. Ernestine Mills and Mrs. Percy Wyndham) they are correspondingly more successful. Most of the designs are inspired by nature in the best Ruskinian tradition, and the flowers and insects have a delicate jewel-like quality which is easily recognisable. Mrs. Dawson was a great perfectionist and many apparently perfectly satisfactory pieces of enamelling were rejected by her as being below the standard required.

In 1900 the Dawsons had an exhibition at the Fine Art Society in Bond Street at which no less than 125 pieces of jewellery were shown. The explorer Sir Arthur Stanley's widow (who before her marriage had been the painter Miss Dorothy Tennant, and the daughter of a notable member of the aesthetic circle which included Burne-Jones and Leighton), married for the second time a certain Dr. Curtis who ordered each year from Nelson Dawson an elaborate necklace for his wife. The style of the enamelling is the only indication that these very grand, sometimes diamond-set, pieces are the product of the Craft Revival ethic. During the busiest years Dawson's workshop in Chiswick employed up to twenty craftsmen, and the strain of maintaining the operation with its heavy wage bill was considerable. It was with relief that he was able to give up the business in about 1914 and return to the painting which he had abandoned so many years before. Idealism had led Dawson many years before to try and turn his workshop into a Guild, where there would be no distinctions between employer and employees, but it was doomed to failure through the usual Guild disease of financial problems.

In 1901 Nelson Dawson founded the Artificers' Guild, binding himself to work only for the Guild for five years, and one of his workshop employees, Edward Spencer, became a Guildsman as well. By 1903 the Guild was in serious financial trouble, and Montague Fordham was able to acquire control of it and remove the whole operation to his gallery in Maddox Street. Edward Spencer elected to remain with the Guild, and he became Fordham's chief designer. Henry Wilson and J. Paul Cooper both sold work through the Fordham Gallery, which was now called the Artificers' Guild, and Spencer produced numbers of designs which were made up by the Guild metalworkers. Among the silversmiths employed by the Guild were E.R. Minns and the prizewinning Liverpool student J.C. Bonner, who subsequently set up on his own as a silversmith and jeweller. Spencer also employed a number of orphan boys for idealistic reasons, and they were trained as metalworkers. The bulk of the production was always in domestic metalwork and silverware, but Spencer himself designed several ambitious and elaborate pieces of jewellery which were illustrated in *The Studio,* including the 'Tree of Life' necklace incorporating a phoenix in gold rising from flames of opal, the tree of life itself being carried out in gold, silver, diamond and opals. This necklace appeared on the market in London a few years ago, as did the 'Ariadne' necklace made at about the same date; others, it is to be hoped, may turn up as well. If wide exposure in the illustrated magazines of the period is any indication of success, it must be assumed that the metalwork produced by the Artificers' Guild was very popular indeed. Up until the First World War the Guild's work appears with almost monotonous regularity in *The Studio* and the *Yearbook of Decorative Design.* After the war the Guild moved from Maddox Street to 4 Conduit Street, and remained there until 1942. During the period between the wars interest in the Guild diminished considerably, largely due, no doubt, to an inability to adapt to changing taste.

Bernard Cuzner was born in Redditch the son of a watchmaker and served his apprenticeship with his father as well as studying watchmaking and silversmithing at Redditch School of Art before moving to Birmingham to work and study at the Vittoria Street School under R. Catterson-Smith and Arthur Gaskin. He taught for some years at the Vittoria Street School, and later became head of the metalwork department at the Birmingham School of Art

Plate 127. A circular pendant by John Paul Cooper, in silver and gold with a central section suspended in a circle of stars showing the Virgin and Child in a niche. Set with cabochon sapphires, chrysoprases, opals, aquamarines and garnets, datable to 1906. Provenance: Handley Read Collection. (The Victoria and Albert Museum.) Cooper's medievalising style is clearly apparent in this jewel.

179

in Margaret Street, where he remained until 1942, thus providing an unbroken link with the craft revival at the turn of the century until the craft revival of the present day. He designed for Liberty's, and ran his own silversmithing workshop. He had a short-lived partnership with A.H. Jones, a fellow pupil at the Vittoria Street School who also made designs for Liberty's 'Cymric' range of silver and jewellery. At his best Cuzner rivals the foremost of the English Art Nouveau designers who worked for Liberty, and he was one of the few of the silversmiths who received their training in the early years of the century to make a successful transition to the changed post-war styles in silverwork (the other designer to make this stylistic shift with complete conviction was H.G. Murphy), but the cheap silver jewellery he produced in his workshop which is advertised in the pre-First War issues of *The Studio* is trivial and banal to a depressing degree. Dresser's conviction that the only way to produce well-designed goods at a really cheap price was by mass-production is proved correct again and again by the experiences of the Craft Revival designers.

The so-called 'gold rush' in 1922, when the rise in the price of gold saw the destruction of enormous quantities of unfashionable antique jewellery, seems to have affected both Craft Revival and Art Nouveau pieces surprisingly little, largely because of the lower content in these of precious metal, and the high incidence of enamelled decoration. Collectors in this rewarding field have had opportunities to acquire work by all the major designers and makers to an extent which does not occur with the much more intrinsically valuable products of the great nineteenth century commercial firms.

The Arts and Crafts movement in America can be seen as a development roughly parallel both in time and in basic intentions to the English Craft Revival, but with the important difference that silverwork and jewellery play a far less important part in the American scheme than in England or on the Continent. In the 'nineties a number of craft organisations and co-operatives were set up in America, notably in Boston, Chicago and Minneapolis, on the example of the Arts and Crafts Exhibition Society in London and through the influence of the teachings of William Morris who was greatly admired in the United States. It is significant that many of the leading figures in the American craft movement had met Morris and discussed with him the role of the crafts-man in the modern world of applied art, notably the architect H.H. Richardson and Elbert Hubbard of the Roycroft Shops, East Aurora, N.Y. Gustav Stickley, editor of the highly influential *Craftsman* magazine, was deeply imbued with the teaching of Morris, and when he visited Europe in 1898 he also met C.F.A. Voysey and C.R. Ashbee and discussed the role of the craft-worker with them.

The Centennial Exposition which took place in Philadelphia in 1876 is generally regarded as a turning point in the development of American decorative art, the date at which the American search for an artistic identity, freed from the enervating dependence on European inspiration, took an added

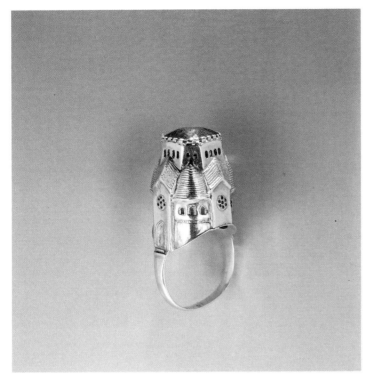

Colour Plate 88. An openwork gold ring by John Paul Cooper in the form of a castle, the top set with a green paste, made for Ellen Terry. (The National Trust.)

Ellen Terry was not only a patron of John Paul Cooper in life: when she died in 1928, her son Edward Gordon Craig turned to Cooper to provide a casket for her ashes which was needed in a hurry. Fortunately, a suitable octagonal casket, decorated with repoussé panels of birds and foliage, was available and it is now in St. Anne's Church, Soho.

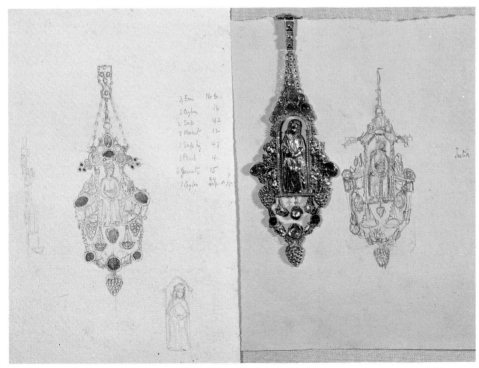

Colour Plate 89. A gold pendant set with emeralds, sapphires, moonstones and garnets designed and made by John Paul Cooper, c.1910. The finished jewel is shown against preparatory designs by him. (Birmingham City Museum and Art Gallery.)

impetus from national pride in the American exhibits which were shown alongside those of their greatest rivals in Europe. In 1879 L.C. Tiffany founded his interior decorating firm, Associated Artists, in New York, with the avowed intention of showing Americans that the luxurious decorative objects which they were accustomed to order from European firms could be produced just as successfully in the United States. In 1902 the name of the firm was officially changed to Tiffany Studios, and a certain amount of jewellery was produced at this period. Tiffany's remarkable jewellery is not easily classifiable; it is not really comparable with any of the English Craft Revival work with the possible exception of the more elaborate pieces by Henry Wilson. Nor is it really the same as the Continental work of the period, being quite different in colour range (the colour range in Continental Art Nouveau jewellery is surprisingly consistent being mainly bright and pale rather than bright and strong like English Gothic-inspired work) and in inspiration, which in Tiffany's work is a type of sombre Byzantinism rather than the rich neo-Renaissance or Romantic sources of mainstream Art Nouveau, as in the work of Lalique or Wolfers. Tiffany's contact with Bing, who stocked Tiffany glass at his Maison de L'Art Nouveau in Paris, would seem to make him more an Art Nouveau designer, but it would be very wrong to classify him as such in an American context as the development of Art Nouveau in America was almost entirely on a strictly commercial basis, using models which were copied from French work almost without alteration, much of the material being mass-produced by the cheapest possible methods (cf. Unger Brothers and Wm. Kerr & Co.). Alphonse Mucha claimed that his designs had been pirated more or less wholesale, and was surprised to find pieces on sale in America when he went there in 1904. It is difficult to understand Mucha's surprise, since his large pattern book of Art Nouveau designs, *Documents Décoratifs,* had appeared in 1902, and had almost certainly begun to circulate in the jewellery firms almost immediately. Mucha is said to have collaborated with Tiffany over a number of pieces of jewellery of which one example, which is illustrated in Jiri Mucha's life of his father, still survives.

One American silversmithing firm which made a genuine attempt to realise some of the ideals of the English Craft Revivalists was the Gorham Manufacturing Company. The Company had been in existence since the beginning of the nineteenth century, and had also been one of the first silver manufacturing companies in the United States to employ mass-production methods in the workshops. It was thus in a spirit of considerable trepidation that they set up a special design group, under William Codman, an English silversmith who had been employed by Cox and Co. before emigrating to America in the 'eighties. His brief was to produce a special range of jewellery and silverwork in the craft tradition. The most technically promising of the Gorham apprentices were put into the group, and a range of largely hand-finished silver and jewellery was produced and sold under the trademark 'Martelé', a suitable label in view of the hammered finish of many of the

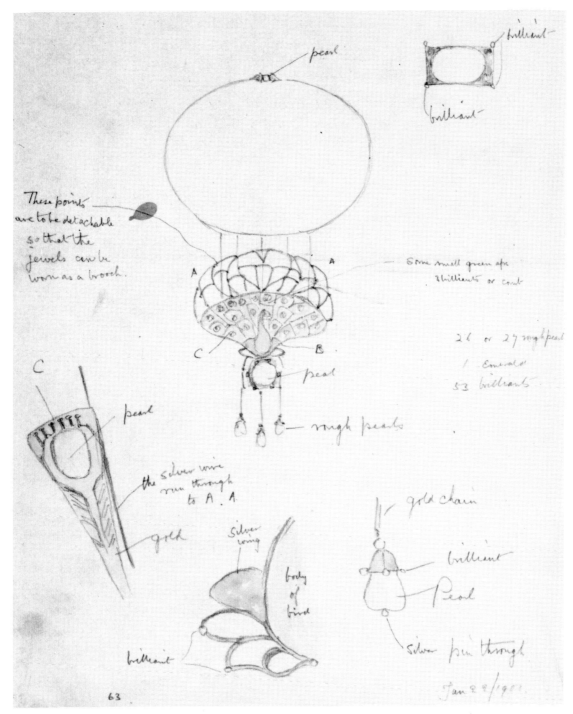

Plate 128. Drawings by C.R. Ashbee from the album in the Chelsea Library, for the peacock necklace in the Victoria and Albert Museum. (Royal Borough of Kensington and Chelsea.)

pieces. William Codman's own designs were in the English naturalistic tradition; they compare closely with those of an English Craft Revival silversmith, Gilbert Marks, in using a somewhat timorous Art Nouveau vocabulary, but the caskets and buckles in mixed metals are pure Arts and Crafts in inspiration. The designers, apart from Codman, are not named, and may not have been of the stature, in the American craft revival, of the artists

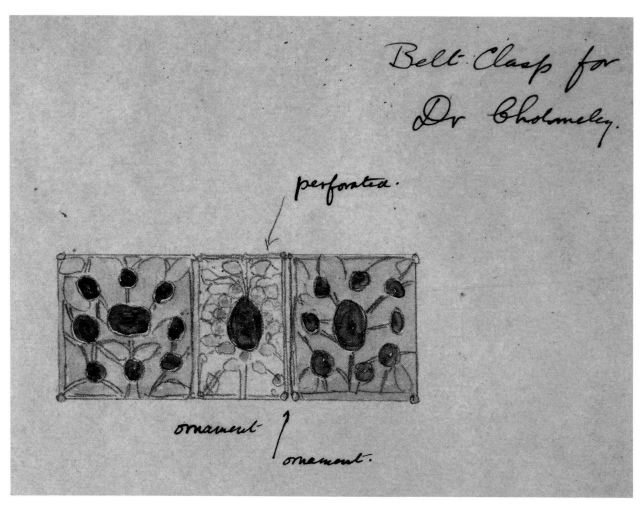

Belt Clasp for Dr Cholmeley.

perforated.

ornament.
ornament.

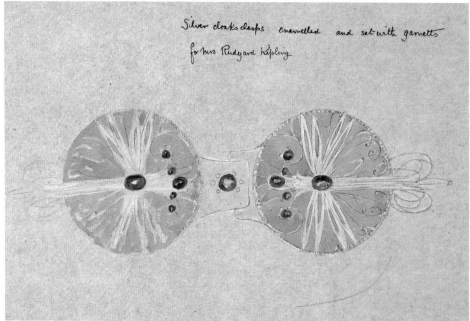

Silver cloak clasps enamelled and set with garnets for Mrs Rudyard Kipling

Colour Plate 90. Designs by C.R. Ashbee for jewellery from an album of drawings found amongst material from his studio at his house in Cheyne Walk. (Royal Borough of Kensington and Chelsea.) The designs include commissions for Mrs Rudyard Kipling, the Guild of Handicraft, Miss Tree, C.R. Strauss and Dr. Cholmeley, which are, as yet, untraced (see also plate 129, p.186).

184

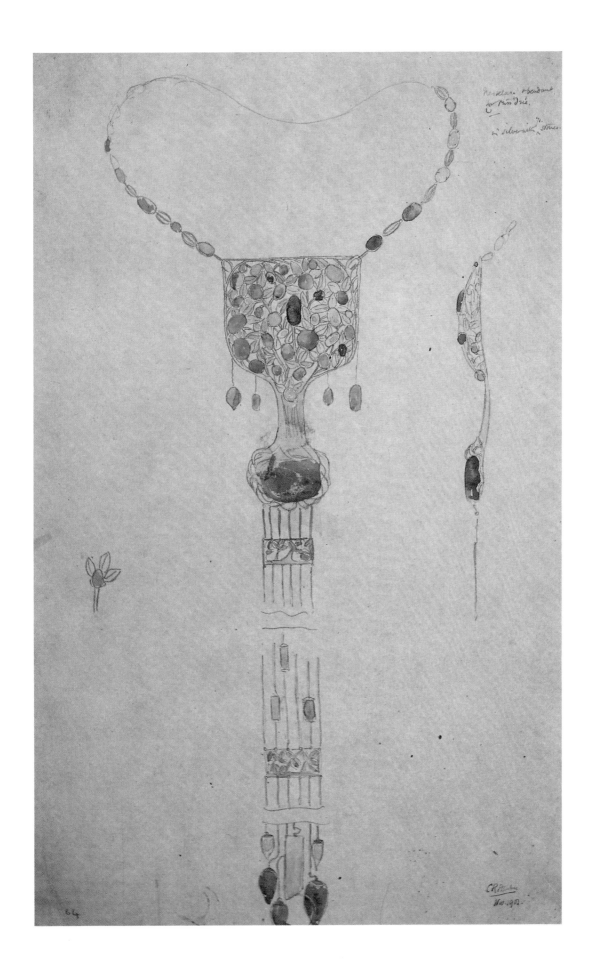

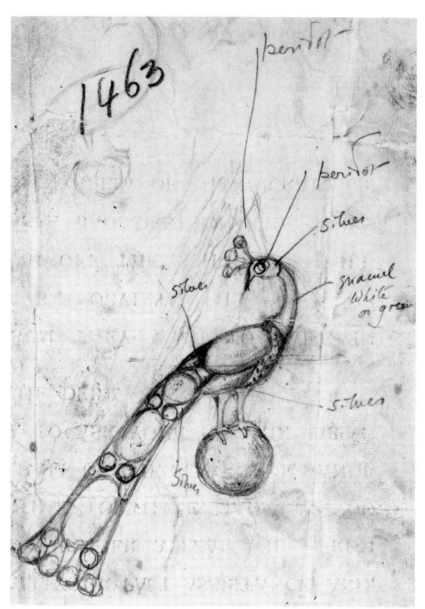

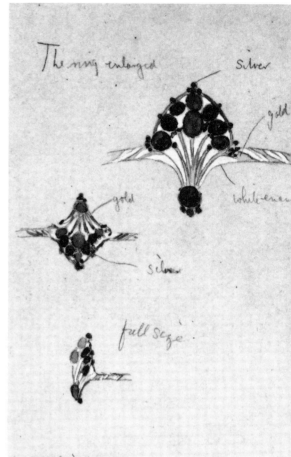

Plate 129. Further designs from C.R. Ashbee's album of drawings. (Royal Borough of Kensington and Chelsea.)

employed by Liberty's, though the 'Martelé' venture must have been much like Liberty's own 'Cymric' undertaking.

The names are known of fewer independent silversmiths and jewellers in the American craft movement than in the English equivalent. Work survives by Robert R. Jarvie, Mrs. Florence Koehler, Clara Barck Welles and Mrs. Frances Glessner of Chicago, Elizabeth Copeland and Edward Everett Oakes of Boston; drawings by Charles Boleshka and George Germer are preserved in the Cooper-Hewitt Museum in New York, and illustrations of pieces appear in *The Craftsman* (1901-16), among them the work of Brainerd Bresher who was strongly influenced by Edward Colonna, one of the most important designers to be involved in the American Craft Movement.

Colonna was born in Germany in 1862 and began to train as an architect in Belgium, but he emigrated to America at the very early age (in 1882) and spent most of the rest of his life there, living first in New York where he joined Tiffany's Associated Artists, and then at Dayton, Ohio, where he wrote his revolutionary *Essay on Broom Corn,* an Art Nouveau pattern book in pamphlet

186

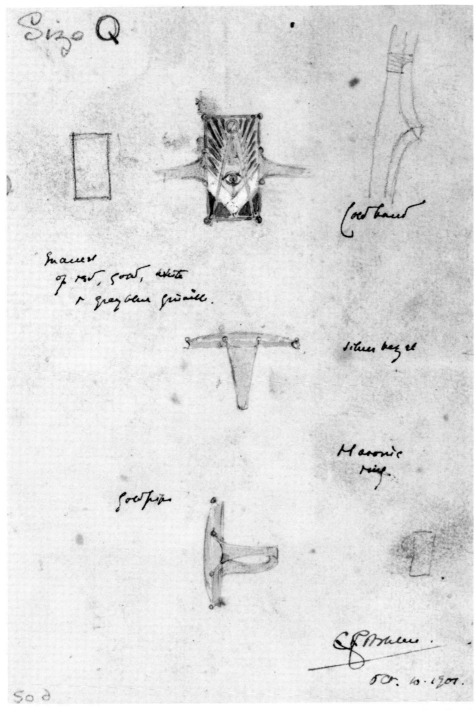

form which predates the work of almost all the Continental designers involved with the movement. Colonna's contact with Tiffany's Associated Artists may well have been his introduction to Siegfried Bing, whose Maison de l'Art Nouveau stocked both the work of the Tiffany firm and furniture and jewellery designed by Colonna. Colonna is said to have returned to Europe during the period when his work was stocked by Bing (i.e. 1898-1905), and his address is given as 22 Rue de Provence, in other words the premises of Bing's L'Art Nouveau, so there is no indication of where he lived. The designs for his jewellery and furniture (which are now preserved in the archive of the Public Library in Newark, New Jersey, where Colonna lived until his death) are

Plate 130. *Christobel Pankhurst, a watercolour attributed to Sylvia Pankhurst. (The Museum of London.)*

In this delicate and sensitive portrait Miss Pankhurst is wearing an enamelled pendant and a spiralling gem-set brooch, both of which can be attributed to C.R. Ashbee (1863-1942). The brooch is very similar to that illustrated in Colour Plate 91. So closely does it echo the brooch in the drawing that it may be safe to say that it is one and the same jewel.

Colour Plate 91. *The brooch illustrated in plate 130, worn by Christobel Pankhurst.*

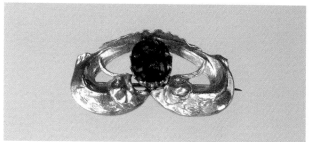

Colour Plate 92. *A repoussé gold brooch in the form of two fishes contesting a faceted garnet, by Edgar Simpson. (Wartski, London.)*

Colour Plate 93. *A tortoiseshell comb by James Cromar Watt (1862-1940). The gold mount is decorated with enamel, Mexican fine opals, and mother-of-pearl. Signed with monogram. (Wartski, London.)*

Cromar Watt was a trained architect with wide ranging artistic interests, amongst them metalwork and enamelling. Amongst the larger pieces of his work which are recorded, are an alms dish at King's College Chapel, the mace used by the Students' Representative Council, and a tablet in enamel and bronze over the fireplace in the Court Room. Dr. Watt made a special study of Chinese art and amassed a large collection of porcelain, jade and silk paintings, most of which he gave to the Aberdeen Art Gallery.

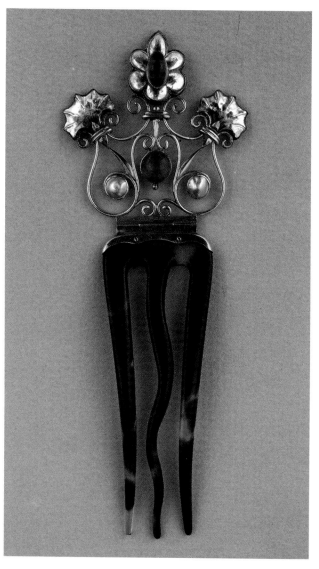

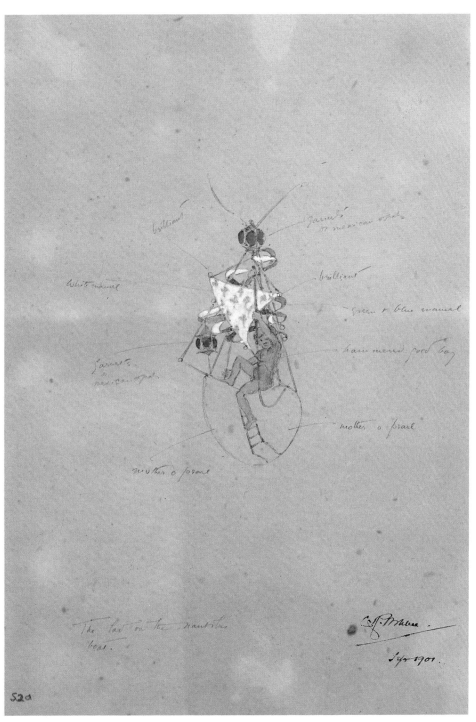

Colour Plate 94. An annotated design by C.R. Ashbee, dated 1901, for a jewel in the form of a putto climbing rigging, to be decorated with enamel and set with mother-of-pearl, opals, brilliant diamonds, garnets or Mexican fire opals. (Royal Borough of Kensington and Chelsea.)

Plate 131. Design by C.R. Ashbee for a pendant. (Royal Borough of Kensington and Chelsa.)

189

followed line for line in the finished objects and are certainly clear enough to have been used by the maker without close personal supervision. The jewellery at least is very like other pieces made for Bing from designs by other artists (e.g. Marcel Dufrêne) and has somewhat the appearance of having been made in Germany, where jewellery in the Art Nouveau style was made in large quantities and was almost certainly partly destined for the Parisian market. It is possible that Colonna also designed jewellery for the Tiffany Studios. Marcus and Co. are said to have made jewellery from Tiffany Studio designs, and these are close in form to the Colonna pieces for the Maison de l'Art Nouveau. Colonna's jewellery was widely commended for being more wearable than the work of most of his French contemporaries; possibly for this reason his influence is also apparent in the work of such French firms as Arnould Frères and Piel Frères, the enamellists, and there is also something of Colonna's flowing line in the better Art Nouveau designs of Wm. Kerr and Co. and Unger Bros. Colonna later ventured, somewhat tentatively, into designing in a modified geometric style, but this later work lacks the conviction of the *Broom Corn* designs and remains an uneasy compromise with fashion.

It is surprising that, with so much activity in the Craft Revival movement in America, the two most influential figures in the field of precious metalwork should be firmly identified with the Art Nouveau movement in Europe. Some idea of what might have been the style and technique of American Arts and Crafts silver can be gained from the surviving pieces in bronze, brass and copper produced by Stickley's Craftsman workshops, the Roycrofters, George Elmslie for Louis Sullivan, Frank Lloyd Wright, and Dick van Erp. These pieces are closely identifiable with the Arts and Crafts Movement in England, or in the case of Frank Lloyd Wright with the work of the Glasgow School artists (i.e. C.R. Mackintosh, J.H. McNair and the Macdonald sisters) in Scotland. A detailed account of the work of these and other designers connected with the American Arts and Crafts movement can be found in the catalogue of an exhibition held in 1972/3.

As in England the Craft Revival in America long outlived the taste for European Art Nouveau. The annual exhibitions of decorative art first held at the Art Institute in Chicago in 1902 continued until the 1920s. Clara Barck Welles' Kalo Shops in Chicago, which were established in 1900, survived even her retirement in 1940 and did not close down until 1970, and her designs were employed throughout the years, the succeeding generations of craftsmen using and reusing her original line drawings. One piece by Edward Everett Oakes was bought from the Society of Arts and Crafts exhibition in Boston as late as 1923, and Elbert Hubbard's Roycroft Shop only succumbed to the financial pressures of the Depression in 1938, having survived Hubbard's death on the *Lusitania* in 1915. It is significant that neither in America nor in England was there ever a truly distinguished body of designers creating the exciting new geometric designs that emerged after the war in Paris from jewellers like Raymond Templier, Jean Fouquet, Jean Puiforcat and Paul Brandt. This so-

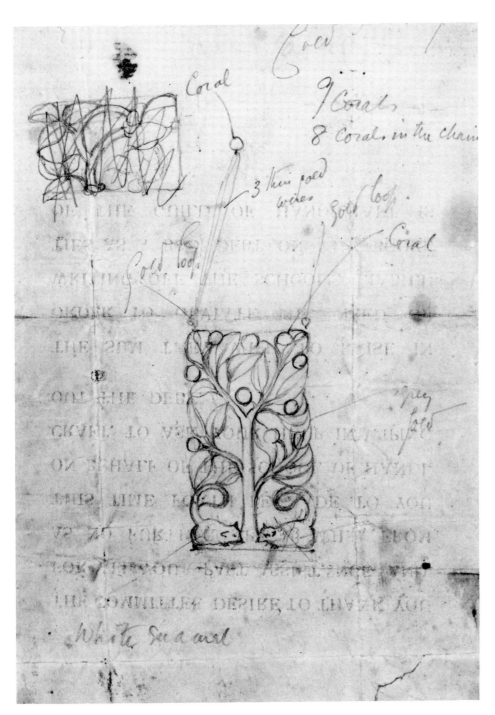

Plate 132. Design by C.R. Ashbee for a pendant with careful and detailed instructions for its manufacture, from the album found in his Chelsea house. (Royal Borough of Kensington and Chelsea.)

called 'Art Deco' style was to remain in both countries the prerogative of the large jewellery firms like Van Cleef and Arpels, Cartier, Mauboussin and Boucheron, who, despite their many branches throughout the world, remained temperamentally entirely Parisian.

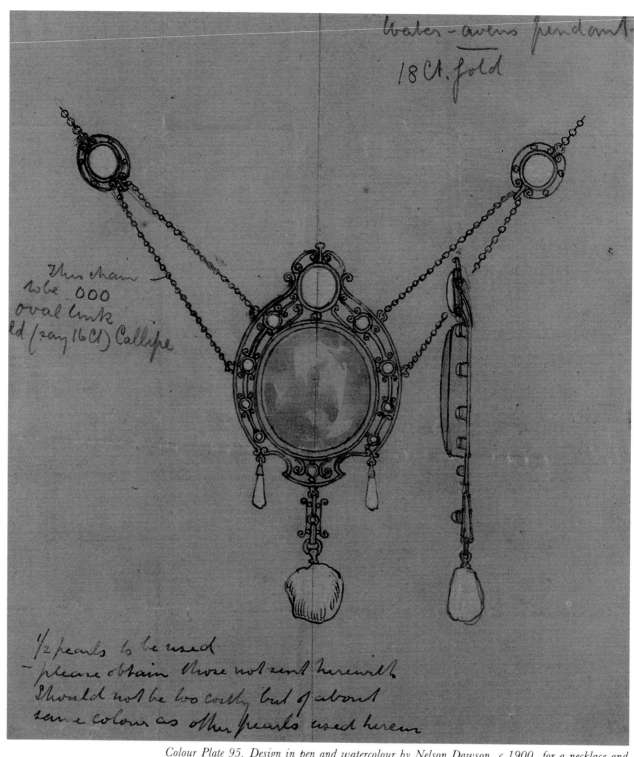

water-avens pendant

18 Ct. gold

This chain to be .000 oval link ld (say 16 Ct) Callipe

½ pearls to be used — please obtain those not sent herewith Should not be too costly but of about same colour as other pearls used herein

Colour Plate 95. Design in pen and watercolour by Nelson Dawson, c.1900, for a necklace and pendant, with detailed instructions to the goldsmith. (Photograph courtesy of the Fine Art Society. Private Collection.)

Colour Plate 96. Necklace and pendant in gold, set with aquamarines and pearls, the pendant set with a plaque of iridescent enamel. Made by the Guild of Handicraft and designed by C.R. Ashbee, c.1900. (Wartski, London.)

Plate 133. An unusually large gold cloak clasp or morse in the form of St. George and the Dragon, designed by Sir Ninian Comper (1864-1960) and made by Barkentin and Krall for the consecration of the Bishop of Norwich. The perimeter of the jewel is set with Russian coloured stone cabochons and is hung with a very large faceted cairngorm. (Norwich Cathedral Treasury.)

Sir Ninian Comper has been described as the last Gothic church architect and designer and his work is invariably based on medieval sources. Barkentin and Krall are noted gold and silversmiths who supplied church furnishings in the second half of the nineteenth century. Their most prominent patron was the architect and designer William Burges; they ceased trading between 1932 and 1935.

The commission for the design for the morse shown above was accepted by Comper in 1901. (The Royal Institute of British Architects, Drawings Collection.)

CHAPTER VI
Art Nouveau and Jugendstil

The publication, in 1964, of Robert Schmutzler's *Art Nouveau* confirmed the growth of interest in this phenomenon, which had begun some eight years earlier. This lavishly illustrated work had been preceded by *Sources of Art Nouveau,* by S. Tschudi Madsen (1956), and *The Sources of Modern Art,* by J. Cassou, E. Langui and N. Pevsner (published in 1962 but based on the catalogue of an exhibition of the same name held in Paris in 1960-1); it was to be succeeded by *L'Art 1900* by Maurice Rheims (1965) and S. Tschudi Madsen's *Art Nouveau* (1967), to name only two titles out of what was to become a veritable flood of books on the subject, culminating in 1985 with a publication devoted solely to jewellery, *Art Nouveau Jewellery* by Vivienne Becker. Most of these books deal deliberately with the subject as a whole, illustrating the work of Ashbee beside that of Lalique, and the designs of Mucha beside those of Toorop and the Glasgow School. While this serves the admirable purpose of showing the work of all these diverse artists in the context of the period, and incidentally pointing up the similarities in the sources of inspiration, it does tend to diminish the significance of the great ideological gulf which separated the Craft Revival artists on the one hand and the Art Nouveau artists on the other. The great difference in approach between work done in England and on the Continent was demonstrated early on by *The Studio* special number, *Modern Design in Jewellery and Fans* which appeared in the winter of 1901, a publication which certainly brought work in this new genre to the attention of a wide public.

The deep suspicion with which the 'New Art' was regarded is expressed in the strongest possible terms by W.R. Lethaby in his introduction to Henry Wilson's *Silverwork and Jewellery* (1903):

'Work in the precious metals, the subject which is dealt with in the present volume, seems especially to have suffered from the slavish methods introduced, perhaps, to compete with machinery, and from the general benumbing of the aptitude for design which affected so many of the artistic crafts during the course of the last century. On the other hand, there have been signs of a danger that these crafts may be victimised by glaring affectations in design and by unashamed crudeness of manipulation. Of the two vulgarities — that of commercial dullness, and that of blandishments which assume the name of ''new art'' — the latter is likely to be far the worse. On this question of design it is essential to guard oneself from a merely capricious originality, a striving for exaggerated elegance, and an endeavour to suggest ideas of luxury, which last is probably the most enervating and repulsive characteristic of certain forms of modern taste.'

A symposium on the subject of 'Art Nouveau, what it is and what is thought of it', in which the views of no less than thirty-seven distinguished painters, designers, architects and sculptors of the period were aired and published in the *Magazine of Art* in 1904, proposed such definitions of the 'new art' as Alfred Gilbert's famous and much quoted 'L'Art Nouveau forsooth! Absolute nonsense!' Gilbert's reaction might be considered inappropriate. He is one of

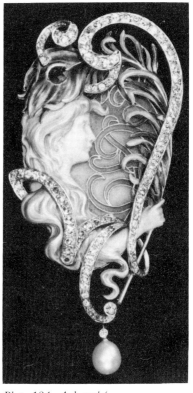

Plate 134. A brooch/ pendant, gold set with diamonds and a sapphire, a pearl pendant hanging from the diamond scroll, the enamelled profile head against a plique-à-jour enamel background. Designed and made for the Parisian jeweller Louis Aucoc, c.1900. (Hancocks, London.)

Colour Plate 97. A gold brooch in the form of an orchid, decorated with enamel and set with diamonds, attributed to Henri Vever, Paris, c.1900. (Wartski, London.)

the few English artists to be identified with Art Nouveau, and his was the only contemporary name to be mentioned in the same context as the French designers, albeit as a practitioner with superior taste and artistic ability to his counterparts in France. Since the revival of interest in Art Nouveau, Gilbert's work has frequently been bracketed with that of the familiar heroes of the movement, generally with the qualification that his style is not in the mainstream of Art Nouveau development, but his magnificently sculptural table-centre, the epergne executed for Queen Victoria in 1890, was included in Les Sources du XXᶜ Siècle, the exhibition which first put the movement into its art historical context.

Alfred Gilbert made many designs for jewels, but few seem to have been executed. It is possible to visualise their intended weight and quality of high relief from the extant examples, the magnificent Mayoral chain for the Corporation of Preston in Lancashire (1892) and the more modest Presidential badge and chain for the Royal Society of Painters in Watercolour illustrated in plate 4. At intervals throughout his career Gilbert made rapidly executed wirework jewels, whose apparently random form belies the subtlety of their design. These were not first designed on paper, but evolved in the artist's hand, it seems without premeditation (see plate 3). The surviving designs that are not connected with the mayoral chain or the badge are tantalising. Many suggest a form and technique using delicate openwork and enamel close in style to the work of Giuliano's maturity, and it is perhaps not too fanciful to suggest that examples of Gilbert's work exist but are still unrecognised.

Almost without exception the quoted views of the artists consulted for the *Magazine of Art* symposium are violently derogatory, ranging from T.G. Jackson's contention that '...the main motive of the designs was a conscious striving after novelty and eccentricity, which is the basest of all motives in Art', through Walter Crane's remark, 'my impression is that what is generally understood by *l'Art Nouveau* is already *old*', to George Frampton's caustic comment, 'I have nothing to say about *l'Art Nouveau* as I do not know exactly what it means. I believe it is made on the Continent, and used by parents and others to frighten naughty children...' It might be assumed that if the whole of the artistic establishment was so opposed to the art of the Continental designers then the reviews of such work as was exhibited in London would be highly critical, but this was not always the case. When confronted with the actual object, in the case of Lalique's jewellery at least, the critic is disarmed by the beautiful quality and the sheer inventiveness of the objects displayed and the notices of both the Grafton Gallery and the Agnew exhibitions of his work in the English press were highly adulatory. The anonymous, but presumably English, critic in *The Studio* (vol. 37, pp.127-134, 1905), speaks of: 'The variety which M. Lalique introduces in his materials, as much as anything else, shows the daring originality of the man as a designer... His cunning as a jewel-designer is almost eclipsed by his power as a sculptor and the resource with which he plays the one form of his art into the service of the other is wonderful and reveals to us the minuteness and skill of his jewellery work in the same object as he proves himself a brilliant sculptor. Lalique's work has become a model for other designers, and much of the inspiration for modern jewellery finds its source direct in his work.' Lalique's earlier exhibition at the Grafton Galleries had prompted the sort of comparison with contemporary English work which is rather unexpected in view of the wholesale condemnation, by the English artistic establishment, of all he stood for. A critic writing of the 1903 National Competition of Schools of Art says: 'Miss Linnell's designs for brooches etc., which appropriately come from Birmingham, the centre of the jewellery trade, are beautiful drawings, but if the young lady could see the recently exhibited jewels of M. Lalique she would quickly learn that the art contains possibilities far beyond anything that she has been taught to produce.'

The hostility to the Continental work shown by the English artists who attended the Symposium is all the more inexplicable when viewed through the eyes of modern students of the Art Nouveau movement, since it has become a commonplace of the present-day literature on the subject to find the early

Plate 135. Silver and ivory haircomb by L. Zenthal, made in U.S.A., c.1915. (John Jesse.)

sources of the movement in the work of the English nineteenth century Romantics, beginning with Blake and then traced through the work of the Pre-Raphaelite painters to William Morris and the Arts and Crafts Movement. The French *fin de siècle* obsession with flowing hair is usually traced to the later portraits by D.G. Rossetti, which date from the 1860s until his death in 1882, which do indeed contain the elements of exoticism and the faint air of decadence which characterise the jewellery designs of Lalique and his contemporaries. This idea is carried even further into abstraction by the Dutch artist, Jan Toorop, whose picture 'The Three Brides' was reproduced in an early number of *The Studio* (September 1893) in the year that it was painted, can be seen to have had an almost immediate influence on the work of the Glasgow School artists as well as on his Continental contemporaries. Even without the publicity of the illustration in *The Studio,* Toorop's work would have become widely known through his famous graphic designs, the best-known probably being the Delftsche Slaolie advertisement, now regarded as a seminal Art Nouveau object, which was designed in 1895.

The poster was obviously one of the most effective vehicles for the dissemination of an artistic idea, and it was his position as one of the outstanding poster artists of the period that made Alphonse Mucha such a widely influential figure. The story of the painter de Brunhof's discovery of Mucha's unrivalled talent for poster design, when at Christmas in 1894 he was desperate for a new poster for Sardou's play *Gismonda* in which Sarah Bernhardt was starring, is too well known to need repetition here; suffice it to say that Mucha's work for Bernhardt, in the designing of posters and of costumes and jewellery for her theatrical appearances made his name and established a style, rightly named 'le style Mucha', which embodies the very essence of Continental Art Nouveau. As well as the jewellery designed for Sarah Bernhardt (the famous snake bracelet which concealed an arthritic wrist can be seen on the *Medée* poster of 1898), Mucha designed pieces for Georges Fouquet (who had already executed the snake bracelet for Bernhardt) which reflect his contact with her in their use of an idealised female face which closely resembles her features and expression, though Mucha denied that these were intended as portraits.

In 1900 Mucha designed the interior, the furniture and decorations, and the façade for Fouquet's shop in the Rue Royale; many of the fittings survive and are preserved in the Musée Carnavalet in Paris. In 1902 his *Documents Décoratifs* was published, a collection of designs by him to supply the apparently insatiable public demand for them, and to be applied to every conceivable item of decorative and domestic use, so that no manufacturer need be at a loss for an Art Nouveau model for his jewellery, furniture, cutlery, carpet, screen or fan. The enormous success of this album can be judged from the wide use which was made of it throughout Europe and in the United States. In spite of his part in forming the Art Nouveau style and subsequently in popularising it, Mucha denied any involvement with the movement as such, saying, 'Art is eternal, it cannot be new', an unconscious paraphrase of George Clausen, who attended the Symposium mentioned above and is quoted as saying, 'Is it so new?' He also said, surprisingly, 'I have seen some very beautiful things in jewellery in this style'. Mucha remarked with indisputable logic, 'I do things in my own way' (see *Alphonse Mucha,* by Jiri Mucha, Marina Henderson and Aaron Scharf, Academy Editions 1971). The fact that so many other people wanted to do things in the same way as both Mucha and Lalique ensured for them an unassailable position in the forefront of the movement.

René Jules Lalique, who occupies a position of importance in the Art Nouveau movement comparable to or even greater than that of Mucha, was born in 1860, the son of a dealer in the charming but inexpensive trifles known as *articles de Paris.* His father died when he was sixteen and he was immediately apprenticed to the Parisian jeweller, Louis Aucoc; his work of around this period, which is illustrated in Vever's book (see plate 19), gives little or no indication of the talent that was to flower at the turn of the century, consisting as it does mainly of 'novelties' in diamonds of the most banal kind. He spent two years in England (1878-80) at the private art school in Sydenham. He also studied at the École des Arts Décoratifs in Paris and worked for various jewellers, among them his old master Aucoc, as well as Cartier, Boucheron, Gariod and Hamelin, providing designs for them and for the magazine of the jewellery trade, *Le Bijou.* In 1884 he was introduced to Jules Déstape, the proprietor of a small but successful jewellery atelier, and he did designs and work for him. Déstape was anxious to retire, and in 1886 offered Lalique the opportunity to buy the business at a reasonable price, an offer which Lalique wisely accepted. Lalique continued to supply the trade for some years after he had acquired his own atelier, with success, as can be inferred from the fact that he moved twice to larger premises before 1891, the year in which he started the series of commissions for Sarah Bernhardt's stage jewellery which were to lead to his exhibiting in his own name in 1894. From this date his success was assured; in 1895 he won third prize at the Paris Salon and in 1897 he became a Chevalier de la Legion d'Honneur even before his name became a household word, which it inevitably did after his startling and spectacular display at the Centennial Exposition in Paris in 1900. Like many successful men, Lalique was not without enemies. Dora Jane Janson includes in the notes at the end of her catalogue, *From Slave to Siren* (1971), an unpublished attack on the master by J. Marest, secretary of the Chambre Syndicale des Bijoutiers at the time (1900) which accuses Lalique of exhibiting pieces in the Paris Exposition which were not new and were already owned by eminent personages who had simply lent them for the duration of the exhibition. This accusation was perfectly just. Lalique appears to have started assembling the pieces for the exhibition in 1896, and many of the exhibited pieces were commissions from his patron Calouste Gulbenkian.

Lalique's greatest works were undoubtedly those done for Gulbenkian; being commissioned pieces they enabled him to concentrate on the design without the endless mundane preoccupations which accompany the creation of unconventional jewellery for general sale. He was occupied, on and off, between 1895 and 1912 with the work for Gulbenkian, who was eventually to be the owner of no less than 145 pieces (now in the Paombel Palace in Lisbon). Lalique's success allowed him to build his magnificent house and studio at 2 Cour la Reine, which is almost like a piece of sculpture in itself. At his best Lalique is sublime, as anyone who has visited the Gulbenkian collection in Lisbon will confirm (at his worst he is probably being faked, the dubious compliment which tends to be paid to the greatest names in any art movement); it is unlikely that anyone would seriously dispute his position as the greatest jeweller of the *fin de siècle,* but there were other Continental jewellers who bid fair to be close rivals.

Several names command almost the same respect as that of Lalique (and similarly large prices in the sale rooms), among them Georges Fouquet, for whom Mucha made some of his most spectacular designs; Vever, who shrewdly employed Eugène Grasset to provide the designs for jewellery which most nearly approach the subtlety and significance of symbolist art; Eugène Feuillâtre, the outstanding enamellist who while employed by Lalique investigated techniques for enamelling on silver, before setting up on his own, and Lucien Gaillard, a silversmith who was persuaded to take up jewellery making by Lalique.

Gaillard was a year younger than Lalique, but he made his name earlier, with a highly praised exhibit of silver in the Paris exhibition of 1889. Lalique also exhibited in this year, but still anonymously. Gaillard's chief interest throughout his career was in the subtle effects which could be achieved with the patination and colouring of metals in the Oriental manner, and Dora Jane Janson has also suggested that his work in horn (in the form of carved hair-combs when it is sometimes combined with gold and set with gems) may well predate his serious interest in jewellery, which dates from the time of his move from the Rue du Temple to spacious and well equipped premises at 107 Rue de Boetie in 1900. Gaillard seemed destined to assume the mantle which Lalique gradually let drop as his interest in jewellery design diminished and his energies were more and more concentrated on his experiments with glass. As early as 1904, the year in which Gaillard won a medal for his jewellery at the Paris Salon, one critic was prepared to suggest that his work surpassed that of Lalique, and there is certainly a quality of consistency in Gaillard's work (and absent from Lalique's) which makes this claim seem almost justified. All the same it is impossible to ignore the prior claim of the greatest innovator in jewellery design of the period, and there is something very slightly unoriginal about Gaillard's ideas which must invalidate his claim to first place.

If the period when Art Nouveau was at the peak of its influence was brief (it is generally acceped as having lasted from the opening of Bing's shop in 1895 until the complete falling off of critical interest about 1908-10), it was correspondingly fierce in its excitement, provoking intense feelings of either partisanship or disgust and attracting a predictably large number of commercial imitators. The earliest date of much commercial exploitation of the more obvious attributes of the Art Nouveau style, the female head surrounded by a mane of flowing hair, the peacock-tail decoration, and the orchid and iris designs, can be pin-pointed fairly accurately to the first moment at which professional visitors to the 1900 exhibition in Paris could get the original designs copied and on to the production line. For instance Luis Masriera, who had inherited with his brother the family jewellery firm in Barcelona, is reputed to have returned from the Paris exhibition so deeply impressed by the new art that he closed the shop, melted down the firm's entire stock which consisted of the traditional Spanish ornaments which had been their speciality for many years, and after six months reopened with an entirely new range of Art Nouveau pieces which were all sold within the week! Masriera's designs were used by the firm until 1922, with a visible diminution of quality in the later years, and after an interval of just over half a century they are being used again today. The quality of workmanship in these modern versions of Masriera's Art Nouveau jewels is extremely high. In order to protect the collector of antique jewellery a special system of marketing these modern pieces has been devised. The modern mark of the firm is used, i.e. Masriera y Carreras. Until their amalgamation with the Carreras firm in 1915 the mark used was Masriera Hermanos. Whether it will continue to be possible to distinguish between the early pieces and the modern ones is questionable. This thought is hardly encouraging in a field where there is already a large number of fakes and any unmarked piece which turns up immediately acquires a suitable distinguished 'signature'.

If Siegfried Bing was responsible both for giving a name to the applied art movement in France and for establishing, through the articles exhibited in his shop, a visual vocabulary for the style, the credit for inspiring Bing must go to Henri van de Velde (1863-1957), one of the greatest decorative artists of the period, who studied architecture and painting in Paris and Antwerp, and seemed destined to be one of the most talented of the Belgian painters of a period already rich in young and promising artists. He was forced through ill-health to abandon painting and he turned his formidable artistic abilities to the field of decorative art. His jewellery designs with their flowing linear composition are quintessentially Art Nouveau in inspiration, but the discreet use of materials has more in common with the Craft Revival jewellery being made in England. The Belgian decorative art movement in the late nineteenth century was more involved with English Pre-Raphaelite and Ruskinian inspiration than with the more spectacular work being carried out in France, and van de Velde's work can be seen to have been more influential in certain areas than that of many of his French contemporaries. He designed rooms for both La Maison de l'Art Nouveau (in 1894/5) and later for Meier-Graefe's Maison Moderne, which was opened in 1899. Van de Velde's contact with Meier-Graefe introduced him to rich and influential patrons in Germany, and

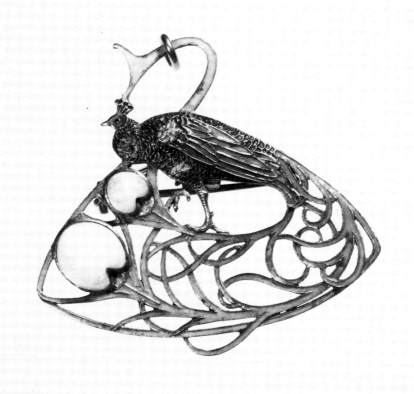

Plate 136. A peacock brooch of blue and green enamel, gold and opals, in the Art Nouveau style, c.1900, by René Lalique (1860-1945). (Musée des Arts Décoratifs, Paris.)

he was later to spend many years in Berlin; his linear forms were widely copied by designers in both Germany and Austria after the turn of the century. The other outstanding Belgian Art Nouveau jewellery designer, Philippe Wolfers, shows a far greater affinity with the work of French artists like Lalique and Vever, principally in the use of the rich materials which were almost universally eschewed in England and Germany.

Wolfers was a sculptor by inclination and training and he studied at the Académie Royal des Beaux Arts in Brussels and with the sculptor, Isidor de Rudder, before entering his father's jewellery firm, the famous Belgian Court jewellers, Wolfers Frères. There he designed some silverware as well as his spectacular series of unique pieces of jewellery, of which only 109 are recorded and which are all marked 'P.W., *exemplaire unique*', to denote their special place in the work of the firm. From 1893 much of Wolfers' work incorporated the beautiful ivory from the Congo which the Belgian Government offered to the artists of the period, in an attempt to popularise this material which was potentially a source of revenue to Belgium. At about this time Wolfers set up his own studio and workshop in the Square Marie Louise in Brussels, where he worked on jewellery and silver designs until about 1908, when he began to devote most of his time to sculpture. Wolfers' pieces do not really compare in exoticism with those of Lalique, but the workmanship is very refined, and in some ways the complete piece is more satisfactory as a piece of jewellery.

Of the few artists in Germany working in the Art Nouveau style closest to Lalique and the French School are Robert Koch, who made elaborate *plaques de cou* (the central ornament of the 'dog-collar') in enamelled gold set with diamonds and coloured precious stones, and Wilhelm Lucas von Cranach, the painter, interior decorator and jeweller who claimed descent from Lucas

Cranach, the painter. His designs for jewellery have a truly sinister quality which is rarely found in comparable French work: the 'Gorgon' or 'Medusa Head' brooch has an implacable quality which is not to be found in the more ingratiating expressions usually worn by the women in the French jewels. Cranach's jewels were designed as *objets d'art;* he at least had resolved the dilemma which was to plague many of his contemporaries, who remained undecided on this crucial issue, at times producing totally unwearable but magnificent objects, as well as opting on other occasions for rather more costume type pieces.

As well as this parade of names from the mainstream of Art Nouveau design, all now well-known and correspondingly highly valued in the saleroom, there existed a considerable body of what might be termed the unknowns, many of them equally well regarded during their own careers, but now in obscurity. Of the designers in the Lalique style there were Dabault, whose snake-entwined female figures are particularly close to certain of Lalique's more exotic designs; Paul Liénard, who uses the bee motif which occurs in some of the more modest Lalique pieces; Paul Follot, who was basically a *pasticheur* as his ability to design in any fashionable style shows; George Henry, a painter of English extraction whose designs are very much in Lalique's style, and L. Zorra, whose characteristic half-smiling female faces are the most recognisable among these otherwise rather confusingly similar designs. Many of the old-established firms, whose main business continued to be in the production of traditional diamond jewellery of immense intrinsic value and correspondingly high price, had the wits to foresee at an early stage the popularity of artistic jewellery, and they employed artists specifically to provide the exotic designs demanded by the new fashion. Georges Fouquet, for instance, took over the management of the family firm in 1895, and immediately set about modernising production, employing, as well as Mucha, Charles Desrosiers and the enamellist, Tourette, who also worked for Lalique. André Falize, son and grandson of famous French jewellers, worked in an Art Nouveau style based on botanical and other natural forms. Vever's employment of Eugène Grasset, which produced some of the most inward-looking and intellectual designs ever used for jewellery, has already been mentioned, and Vever also made up designs by Gautrait, who was the chief engraver of the Parisian firm, Léon Gariod, and a not undistinguished Art Nouveau designer. The name of Boucheron is not often associated with Art Nouveau though the firm made some of the most elegant of the jewellery in this style, and in a very sophisticated technique using either pavé-set diamonds or sharply sculpted gold. Many of these pieces were designed by Lucien Hirtz who was briefly associated with Lucien Falize in the 1890s and had once been employed by Boucheron, but by this period had set up his own independent atelier. Louis Rault, another former employee of Boucheron now in his own atelier, also produced a number of Art Nouveau jewellery designs for which the wax models still exist in the museum at the Hôtel Lambinet in Versailles.

In a field such as jewellery where so little is signed, confusion about the contribution of each individual designer sets in after a very short space of time. Much of the surviving unmarked work may in time be correctly attributed since so much work of the period was illustrated, but in the meantime it is advisable to view unsupported attributions to the more famous designers with some degree of scepticism.

As well as those designers whose names have been lost through their similarity to more famous contemporary figures, there exists a group of jewellers whose work seems to have been neglected because it does not fall into any accepted modern idea of what Art Nouveau should look like. Of these probably the best known during his lifetime, to judge from the frequency with which his work appears in contemporary periodicals, was Charles Boutet de Monvel. His work is much less smooth both technically and artistically, than that of Lalique, and is in many ways much closer to the English and American Craft Revival jewellers in inspiration and in the use of non-precious materials. Boutet de Monvel often uses the combination so much favoured by the English craftsmen of silver with either mother-of-pearl or large irregularly-shaped freshwater pearls. The forms in this work, as with the rest of the group of French designers whose work is very similar to that of Boutet de Monvel (e.g. Charles Rivaud, E. Mangeant, T. Lambert and the Belgian Paul Dubois), are almost always taken from botanical or other naturalistic sources, and the execution has a rough handmade look quite uncharacteristic of the other French jewellery of the period.

Many reasons have been put forward to explain the very brief flowering of Art Nouveau in France. The intensity of the reactions with which it was first received explain the rapidity with which it spread commercially, and part of the disenchantment with the style which could be sensed even as early as 1908 certainly came from boredom following this over-exposure. It seems indisputable that the ill-conceived and technically inferior copies of the more spectacular pieces were responsible for turning away public interest. In its more superficial aspects the Art Nouveau style was fatally viable commercially; it was said of Bing's Maison de l'Art Nouveau that it was too successful, and indiscriminate copying of the exhibits led to the closure of the firm in 1905, leaving the field to the purveyors of mass-produced novelties in the Art Nouveau manner.

While the French were stunning the public with the visual excitements of Art Nouveau, a much quieter artistic revolution was taking place in Austria — quieter possibly, and certainly attracting much less attendant publicity, but none the less radical in its effects. Like the Arts and Crafts movement in England this art movement in Vienna was to prove to have greater staying power than the French style and to be more far-reaching in terms of altering the appearance of everyday objects. It is no longer fashionable to see the roots of the Modern Movement in the great design theorists of the nineteenth century; Ruskin and Morris are now considered by many to represent the most

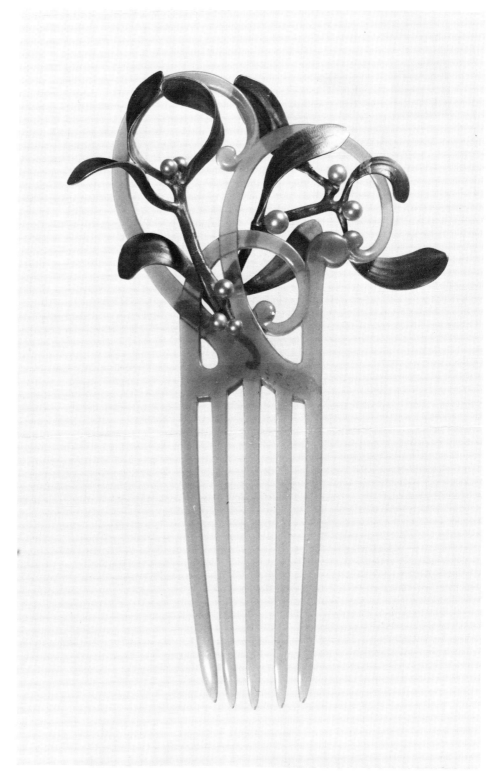

Plate 137. A tortoiseshell comb by Henri Vever (1854-1942) decorated with enamel and set with pearls. (Private Collection.)

serious threat to progress towards an identifiable Modern Movement that the nineteenth century produced, and it is true that much of the work done under the influence of their teaching or their example has more than a touch of the neo-Renaissance about it, hardly a revolutionary new style at this date. It is also true that some of the staunchest supporters of the Craft Revival later recanted many of their passionately held beliefs about the uninspiring nature of mechanical methods of production, and came to support the movement for the improvement of design in industry. J.D. Sedding, who was a founder member of the Arts Workers' Guild, wrote as early as the 1880s: 'Let us not suppose that machinery will be discontinued. Manufacture cannot be organised on any other basis. We had better recognise this, better make life square with the facts, rather than rebel against the actual and inevitable, in striving for the ideal.' Sedding, like Christopher Dresser, was prepared to recognise the 'actual and inevitable' long before the majority of his fellow artists in England, and it is to the credit of the founders of the Wiener Werkstätte that, although the inspiration for the workshops came from similar establishments in England, they were prepared to dispense with the English idealism which insisted on trying to recreate, in hopelessly inimical economic conditions, the pattern of work supposedly followed in the medieval craftsman's workshop. The fact that the Wiener Werkstätte survived into the 1930s is surely an indication that the more realistic approach to production methods, which was to be widely adopted in England after the First World War was already overdue at the turn of the century.

In the short essay on 'Modern Austrian Jewellery' which appeared in *Modern Design in Jewellery and Fans* in 1902, the writer (W. Fred) claims that: 'The art of jewellery in Austria remained under French influence almost to the present day — in fact, throughout the whole of the nineteenth century — and it has only been in the last year that Austrian art-industries have been set free from the foreign yoke which so long oppressed them, so that the true Viennese style of jewellery has but rarely come to the fore.' In fact the currently fashionable style in Vienna, even in so-called 'artistic' jewellery, was not so liberated from French influence as the above passage claims. The use of *plique à jour* (or openbacked) enamel was widespread, as in French Art Nouveau, and the jewellery of Rozet and Fischmeister, a firm producing quite avant-garde designs some of which were supplied by Koloman Moser and Otto Prutscher, both members of the breakaway Vienna Secession movement, bears a strong resemblance to that of Boucheron, using a rather watered down Art Nouveau idiom carried out in diamonds set in platinum and gold, or carved gold work in the manner of Lucien Hirtz. The designers whose work is commended by Mr. W. Fred for its elegance and originality, Elsa Unger, Anna Wagner, Franz Mesmer and E. Holzinger, were all trained at the famous Imperial Arts and Crafts School in Vienna, where a number of the artists connected with the Secession Movement were to teach in the early years of the century.

The principal artists who formed the Wiener Sezession in April 1897 were Gustav Klimt, Koloman Moser, Otto Wagner, Joseph Maria Olbrich, Josef Hoffmann and Egon Schiele. A year later, in the spring of 1898, their first major exhibition was held in the building specially designed for the group by Olbrich. By 1900 they were already mounting their eighth exhibition, in which

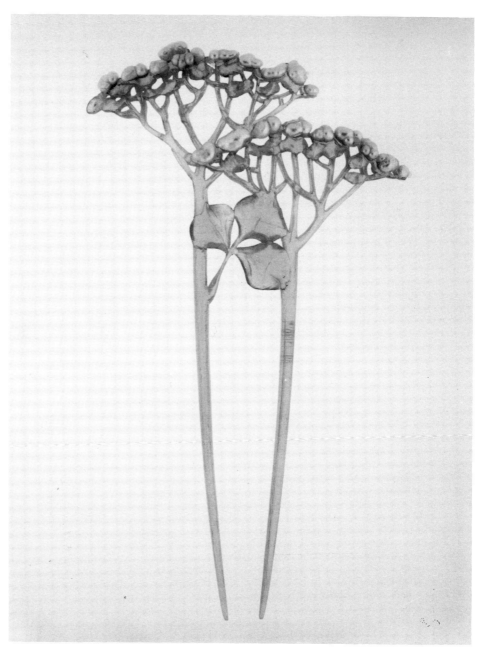

Plate 138. A tortoiseshell comb by Fred Partridge in the form of umbelliferous flower heads set with pearls. (Private Collection.)

a series of rooms, furnished and decorated by the Sezession artists, were shown with the work of foreign artists whò had been invited to exhibit, among them Charles Rennie Mackintosh and his wife Margaret Macdonald, Charles Robert Ashbee, founder of the Guild of Handicraft, and Henri van de Velde, whose participation in the Applied Art Exhibition in Dresden in 1897 had already resulted in a number of commissions from German patrons and from Meier-Graefe's Maison Moderne. Mackintosh's white tearoom was an immediate success with the Viennese public and commissions for decorative schemes followed. The cross-fertilisation of ideas between Mackintosh and van de Velde, the two giants of the modern decorative revival, was to have far-reaching results on the work of Hoffman, whose elongated, linear style must surely owe a great deal to Mackintosh's example. If Mackintosh can be seen as the most important stylistic influence, Ashbee must be accepted as the most important practical influence, as it was his own Guild of Handicraft which inspired the formation of the Wiener Werkstätte in 1903. Josef Hoffmann and Koloman Moser were the artistic directors, and the banker and *amateur* of art Fritz Wärndorfer was the financial director. Although based in theory on Ashbee's Guild of Handicraft the Wiener Werkstätte differed in one very important respect from this and all the other craft guilds in England: the designs provided by the artists were not carried out by them but by fully trained workmen who had served their long and arduous apprenticeships and gained their Masters' certificates. Among the trained craftsmen employed in the goldsmiths' department was the youthful Naum Slutzky later to became a distinguished designer on his own account. Carl Otto Czeschka joined the Wiener Werkstätte soon after it was founded and Eduard Wimmer became a member in 1907. The style of jewellery produced in the workshops is very recognisable, using the linear elements which characterise Hoffmann's work in other spheres of decorative design, allied to formalised natural ornament of leaves, flowers and animals. The early work is more abstract, with the emphasis in the post-war period on a more romantic style with the natural ornament predominating, the style associated with Dagobert Pêche who joined the workshops in 1917.

In Germany the modern decorative movement was not based on one city, nor did it have a truly national identity at the turn of the century. Little pockets of activity in various parts of the country were only united in 1907 with the founding of the Deutsche Werkbund. At the turn of the century Munich, Darmstadt, Weimar and Berlin all had small but flourishing centres where the craft revival or some other aspect of the Modern Movement was investigated and where experimental work in decorative design was carried out. The Münchener Sezession movement slightly predates the similar Wiener Sezession, and similarly the 1897 Munich Vereinigte Werkstätten für Kunst im Handwerk, of which Richard Riemerschmid was a founding member with Peter Behrens, Pankok, Hermann Obrist and Bruno Paul, predate by five years the establishment in Vienna of the Wiener Werkstätte. Ferdinand Hauser, the Viennese goldsmith, worked in Munich in the early years of the century, and many of the members of the Darmstadt artists' colony (see below) studied or worked in Munich, among them Patriz Huber and Ernst Reigel. Munich-based designers were quick to understand the importance of the Art Nouveau work being produced in Paris and Belgium. Examples of silver in a botanical Art Nouveau style were made from the designs of the Munich artist, A. Strobl, by E. Wollenwerber, the Munich silversmith and jeweller.

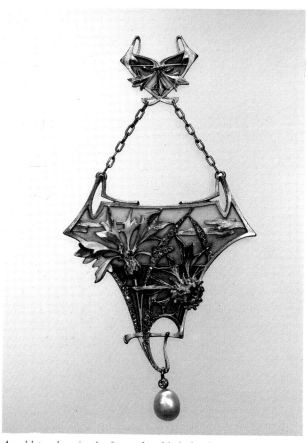

Colour Plate 98. A gold pendant in the form of a thistle head seen against a landscape, decorated with plique-à-jour enamel and set with diamonds and a pearl, by Gautrait, Paris, c.1900. (Private Collection.)

In Weimar the Grand Duke of Saxe-Weimar-Eisenach retained Henri van de Velde as his architectural adviser, and in 1901 asked him to consider the reform of the schools of applied art. Van de Velde began teaching his own seminar in Weimar, which expanded to became the Weimar School of Arts and Crafts in 1902, and was only closed in 1915 when Van de Velde left Germany for Switzerland; his school, combined with the old Weimar Academy, was later used by Walter Gropius as the basis on which he was to establish the Weimar Bauhaus in 1919.

In Darmstadt the Grand Duke of Hesse-Darmstadt was busy creating his artists' colony at Matildenhohe, building specially designed studio/houses for the artists and craftsmen who were invited to establish themselves as members of the colony. A number of the most famous decorative artists of the turn of the century spent some time at the colony in Darmstadt, among them Peter Behrens, Josef Olbrich, and Prof. Ernst Reigel. Olbrich's designs for jewellery are very spare in form, with all the restraint that has come to be associated with the Jugendstil work, while Ernst Reigel's jewellery and silverwork is almost neo-Renaissance in its elaboration, much closer in spirit to the work of the Scandinavian designers like Torilf Prytz or Gustav Gaudernack than to the work of his fellow Germans like Patriz Huber, whose designs are simplified to an unusual degree even for a Jugendstil artist, or Peter Behrens, whose silver designs rely almost entirely on form with minimal surface ornament.

In Berlin after the turn of the century a number of the artists involved with the expressionist movement made brief forays into the world of decorative design. Erich Heckel, Ernst Ludwig Kirchner, Emil Nolde and Karl Schmidt-Rottluff, members of the Brücke group, all designed a number of pieces of jewellery, mainly in silver or non-precious metal and semi-precious stones. The Deutsche Werkbund, which was founded to bring order, unity and commercial support to all these disparate groups, grew out of a lecture given by Hermann Muthesius at the newly founded Trade School in Berlin in June 1907, in which he recommended a more realistic and use-orientated approach to decorative design. The director of Peter Bruckmann und Sohn, one of Germany's largest silver manufacturing firms, gave Muthesius his support, and became the first president of the Werkbund, which was formed only four months later. Founding members included such major figures in the Kunsthandwerk world as Peter Behrens (who had already transferred his allegiance to the concept of Art in Industry and was working for the electrical firm of A.E.G.), Bruno Paul, Richard Riemerschmid, Josef Hoffman and Josef Olbrich. Later catalogues of Werkbund gold and silverwork show examples by Emil Lettré, the Berlin artist-craftsman and jeweller; Emmy Roth and Paula Straus; Johann Wilm and Ernst Schmidt, both of Berlin; Dagobert Pêche of the Wiener Werkstätte; Theodor Wende and Alfons Ungerer, both professors at the Kunstgewerbeschule in Pforzheim; Philipp Oberle of Pforzheim, who like Johann Wilm was researching into techniques of granulation in the 'twenties, and Kurt Bauer of Frankfurt. In 1908 the membership of the Werkbund stood at 492, by 1912 it had nearly doubled (971) and by 1930 there were no less than 3,000 members. If this were not proof enough that the venture was well timed, there are other pointers to indicate this incontestable fact, one being the declining interest in the Arts and Crafts Society exhibitions, culminating in the financial disaster of the 1912 show, which contrasted with the great success of the Werkbund exhibition in Cologne in the following year. In 1914 the Arts and Crafts designers recovered some lost ground with the *succès d'estime* of the British Decorative Art exhibition which was held at the Louvre, though many of the exhibits remained unsold, and by the following year *The Studio* was campaigning vigorously for the setting up of some body concerned with the decorative arts which could match the challenge thrown out by the Deutsche Werkbund. This campaign, coupled with the realisation on the part of many of the English artist-craftsmen that the improvement of art in industry was the only possible salvation for the deteriorating decorative arts in this country, was to result in the foundation of the Design and Industries Association in 1915. As with the Deutsche Werkbund, many of the founding members were originally prominent figures in the Craft Revival Movement. Owing to the total economic collapse of Germany as a result of the war, this late start on the part of the English group was to be less of a handicap that might have been expected, though the results of the war were to be disastrous for the decorative arts throughout Europe. It is not surprising that this world-wide cataclysm should have produced a stylistic watershed which makes it quite logical to talk of a 'post-war' style.

CHAPTER VII

Post~War Postscript

The most immediately striking feature of post-War fashion design — and thus also of post-War jewellery design — is the designers' concern for the whole effect, which gave a coherence to the ensemble so conspicuously lacking in the fashionable bits and pieces worn by the turn-of-the-century society lady. Thorstein Veblen, writing on economics in 1881, speaks of the woman of fashion as a 'monument of conspicuous consumption', an apt description of the dresses and cloaks lavishly decorated with elaborate panels of hand embroidery and flounces and fichus of hand-made lace, all hung about with jewels of every description. The most successful exponents of this elaborate style were the French designers, among them and notably Callot Soeurs. The three daughters of a Parisian antique dealer, whose speciality was old fabrics, embroideries and lace. The eldest sister and chief designer, Mme. Gerber, successfully incorporated these into the famous simple yet sumptuous *robes d'interieurs* by Callot Soeurs, the carefully thought-out designs were free of the more exuberant *nouveau riche* elaboration which still tended to characterise the work of the House of Worth, a legacy of the expansive personality of the founder, Charles Frederick, one of the most successful couturiers of the Second Empire. In less than skilful hands this over-decorated and jewel-laden style fully merited the dismissive criticisms of Paul Poiret, who described the woman of the *belle époque* as a 'decorated bundle'. It was Poiret himself who was to be responsible to a large extent for rationalising the 'bundle', with his introduction of the one-piece dress, constructed with a continuous flowing line from collar to hem, the fabric in a design which was exploited by the shape of the whole dress. This concern with the dress as a carefully planned work of art, whose fastenings, pleatings and trimmings were all of equal importance to the whole design, was also a characteristic of the work of Mariano Fortuny y de Madrazo, the Spanish artist and designer, who worked in Venice devising the secret, subtle dyeing processes and the complex pleating techniques which made his designs famous. An almost exact contemporary of Poiret, he established his Venetian workshops in the Palazzo Orfei in 1907, just three years after the opening of Poiret's Paris salon.

Although Poiret had opened his salon as early as 1904, his revolutionary ideas about dress design hardly penetrated beyond the small avant-garde circle in Paris by whom he was admired from the earliest years until well after the First World War. By the time the Poiret/Fortuny style had gained acceptance, if only in the very modified form of which the commerical dress manufacturer was capable, it was painfully apparent that the fantasies of the Edwardian jewellery designer were no longer a practical proposition as ornaments or accessories. It was customary for a female guest at a Court function in the early years of the century to wear as much precious jewellery, preferably of diamonds, as she could possibly cram on to the bodice of her dress and on to her elaborate coiffure. Anyone familiar with the Court photographs of Queen Alexandra will immediately be able to visualise the general effect towards which each guest was striving, with a success which varied according to the state of the family bank balance, thus proving the validity of Veblen's theory about conspicuous consumption. The idea of the dress itself as a work of art, as envisaged by Poiret and Fortuny, made this style of ornamentation unsuitable, not to say impossible, as the unboned bodice of the dress could not support the weight of a large amount of miscellaneous jewellery. It is possible to deduce from the Georges Barbier illustrations of Poiret dresses in the *Gazette de Bon Ton* that the two pieces of jewellery which were now essential to the aspiring woman of fashion were an immensely long string of beads in some subtle and understated colour possibly of amber or jade, and a large decorative brooch, to be worn not in the conventional fashion in the bodice or at the neck, but on the hat or headband to secure an exotic aigrette of feathers or flowers.

To compensate for the absence of the ten brooches at least and two or three necklaces (including the elaborate dog-collar with a pierced and decorated gem-set central *plaque-de-cou*) which had previously been *de rigeur* for all full dress social occasions, the evening handbag now began to assume increasing importance as a jewelled ornament, with a gem-set frame of precious metal. This type of evening bag was supplanted in the 'twenties by the *minaudière,* a special type of flat, compartmented vanity case made of gold or gilt-metal and usually decorated with enamels, which was invented by the firm of Van Cleef and Arpels. The contents of the bag or *minaudière* — cigarette case, powder compact, lipstick case etc. — would also be made of precious metal and decorated with enamel, lacquer, *coquille d'oeuf* and pavé-set stones. The French jewellery designers of the 'twenties made a speciality of the decoration of these cases and compacts, using mainly a flat, geometric idiom which is, perhaps, the most characteristic expression of the Art Deco style. The best known and most widely imitated exponent of this form of decoration was Raymond Templier, some of whose elegant, geometric-design pieces of jewellery were bought by the French Government from the French decorative art exhibition in 1937. Templier's work was extensively illustrated in Jean Fouquet's large format album of *Bijoux et Orfèvrerie,* published in 1928, which provided an accessible source of design ideas to a host of imitators.

Tony Bouilhet, Director and President of L'Orfèvrerie Christofle, wrote in 1940 of the period immediately after the First World War as follows, 'L'ornement semblait prendre un revanche sur les temps inhumains que l'on venait de traverser', a profound reflection on the times which could equally be applied to fashion in dress — what could be more frivolous and impractical than the harem trousers and hobble skirts devised by Poiret before the war but still in fashion in the early 'twenties? But in many other respects it is not true at all. The war had profoundly altered women's views of their potential and their position in the social structure of their time. How to keep women of the moneyed and leisured classes in idleness in the drawing-room after they had proved themselves able to do a complex or physically taxing job? Such was the dilemma of the early inter-war period, and the questioning of the classic and accepted role of the economically secure woman is reflected in the fashions of the period. However much the belted, waterproofed trench-coat might seem to be a reminder of the horrors of war, 'les temps inhumains' so recently passed through, the eminent practicality of the garment ensured its survival in fashion. The long trailing draperies of 1910 disappeared, and with them the heavy and uncomfortable tiaras and head-ornaments of the Edwardian period. These were abandoned for all except the most formal social occasions, in exact imitation of the situation in the early nineteenth century, when very cumbersome and long outmoded dress of far greater elaboration than the current neo-classic mode was still worn at Court. With few exceptions (e.g. Queen Alexandra and the late Duchess of Kent) it seems not to have been the destiny of the women of the English Royal family to influence fashion. Very stylish appearance is often connected in the popular imagination with a more raffish and unstable mode of life, with the result that the most influential fashion leaders of the 'twenties and 'thirties were probably the great stars of the cinema. The extreme smartness and refined artificially of her appearance probably predisposed public opinion against Wallis Simpson, whereas the unchanging and unfashionable clothes worn by Queen Mary seemed utterly reassuring.

In England where 'Courts' were held with the full panoply of head ornaments and feathers right up until 1939 many jewellery firms still had a fairly regular flow of commissions for tiaras. Hennell, Fraser and Haws (a firm which, having been in business in London since 1736, was well placed to record the vagaries of fashion and public demand) executed a small but steady stream of such commissions throughout the between-war period. In 1935 and 1937 the demand was slightly increased, firstly by the Royal Silver Jubilee and secondly by the coronation of George VI. In 1936, according to the reminiscences of a recent member of the firm, no less than three tiaras were in the course of production. Since the war only one tiara has been made by this particular firm. Even the tiaras commissioned in the late nineteenth century had an element of practical thinking in the design, being made to adapt to other more useful functions, and by the 'thirties this was an almost universal feature of tiara design. These composite pieces were a great speciality of Hennell's chief designer in the 'thirties, Charles Bruno, who excelled in the ingenious construction which their multiple function demanded. Instructions for dismounting the piece had to be sent out with the most elaborate of these jewels since it was otherwise almost impossible to find the concealed clasps which allowed them to be separated into as many as six different parts, including a necklace, a pair of bracelets, a pair of clips and a brooch/pendant. The entire design had to be reversible so that it could be worn either way up, in the form of a 'collar' necklace or a tiara, and the construction of all the settings had to allow for their being visible when the piece was dismounted into its many component parts. Few of these remarkable objects survive since the stones were of fine quality and the characteristic link and ribbon-interlace forms of 'thirties jewellery design have only very recently begun to be appreciated with the revival of interest in the whole period.

The effect on jewellery design of the new attitude to the domestic and social role of women was curious. The most glittering and showy effect had previously been the goal of the designer, but as a result of the newly-developed manufacture of blatantly unreal but dazzling costume jewellery the exact opposite became the object with the fashionable customer. The most exquisite workmanship and the most valuable materials were combined to make jewels of understated refinement and great simplicity; only in this way could they advertise their genuineness. A leading French couturier of the period is said to have remarked, 'It doesn't matter if it's real so long as it looks like junk,' thus voicing the ultimate concept for Veblen's theory of conspicuous consumption, and it became quite natural to assume that jewellery made of very large stones was false.

It has recently become common practice in the antique trade to speak of the decorative style of the inter-war period as being Art Deco and to describe, for instance, pieces of jewellery or silver as being Art Deco to indicate date rather than style. At this point, therefore, it becomes essential to ask the question, 'What is Art Deco?' The easiest way to answer this would be to assume that some exact definition of the term 'art nouveau' is actually possible, and then to say that where Art Nouveau ends, there Art Deco begins. The effect of this over-simplification of the problem would be to end up with an Art Deco period stretching from 1910 to c.1935, which in turn would lead to, indeed has led to, a tendency to misdate and misattribute objects which do not conform to the accepted idea of the Art Deco style. The amazing staying-power of the Craft Revival style both in Britain and in America is conveniently ignored and little of the unmarked jewellery or metalwork in the Arts and Crafts style is dated after 1912 in auction catalogues.

The concept of Art Deco as an identifiable decorative movement has twice been defined by Bevis Hillier, first in a pioneering study published in 1968 (*Art Deco*, Studio Vista), and later, with rethinking of the original thesis, in a more detailed and discriminating exhibition catalogue (*The World of Art Deco*, Minneapolis Institute of Arts, 1971), subsequently published in hardcover to provide one of the few sources of reference for this enigmatic period. In the introductory essay to this catalogue he discusses the date-range of the movement in some detail, and makes out a case for including both the 'twenties and the 'thirties, but to add further confusion to this question he includes works by Christopher Dresser dating from the late 1870s as 'Art Nouveau designs' and thus presumably as influential precursors of the style, as well as jewels by Jensen which were first in production before the First World War and furniture by Carlo Bugatti dating from 1913. In all fairness it should be pointed out that the most successful of the Jensen designs have been made continuously since the early years of the firm's existence, and are still made today. There is no way of telling the date of manufacture of these pieces since they do not bear a year-mark, so strictly speaking only designs

215

which were actually evolved during the period in question should be called 'Art Deco'. It is interesting to note how well these particular pieces have stood the test of time, a test which few of the contemporaneous designs of the English commercial manufacturers would pass, from the point of view either of design or workmanship, if they were to be produced today.

The term 'Art Deco' was first evolved simply as a convenient shortening of the rather ponderous title given to the large decorative art exhibition held in Paris in 1925, the *Exposition Internationale des Arts Decoratifs et Industriels Modernes.* If the term 'Art Deco' were to be confined to objects either shown in that exhibition or directly related to them stylistically, this would leave a large body of work in an aesthetic limbo whence it would have been rescured by the invention of a new term. For one thing the economically shattered German nation did not exhibit, and two years were to pass before the general public in Europe were to be able to judge the quality of the work of the Deutsche Werkbund which at this period is quintessentially in the style now known as 'Art Deco'. Equally a considerably body of work which is never described as Art Deco was shown in Paris; this was the work of the English designers selected by a committee which included as chairman of the metalwork section the archetypal craft revivalist Henry Wilson. The work shown by the English Arts and Crafts designers was in a style still used, with the rarest exceptions, by most of the leading figures in the field of decorative art. The exceptions include, of course, Harold Stabler, whose enamels show an early appreciation of more experimental trends in European design, and Harry Murphy, originally employed in Henry Wilson's workshop as an errand boy, and whose silver designs show the greatest affinity with the geometric French work of the period. Murphy was the living proof that Pugin's ironical joke about the office boy who designed in his spare time was not so absurd as he believed.

The best of the geometric Art Deco work in metalwork and jewellery is unquestionably French. The jewellery and personal ornaments produced by the French designers of the 'twenties set the style for the whole of the fashionable world and were inevitably widely imitated, with a greater or lesser degree of success, by manufacturers in England and America, by Swiss watch-makers, and by German and Czech costume jewellers. With few exceptions the commercial section of the trade interpreted these designs in such a modified form that much of the rigorous geometry of the originals was lost or obscured; the silver jewellery produced for Liberty's at this period is a particularly good example of the style in its most diluted form. In 1930 Raymond Templier published a treatise on design entitled *La Forme sans Ornement,* a concept that was incomprehensible to the jewellery manufacturers in Birmingham and Pforzheim.

In England the Craft Revival style continued to have an apparently undiminished influence on the appearance of 'artistic' handmade jewellery well into the thirties. It is interesting and instructive to contrast the work done by J.P. Cooper or Edward Spencer for the Artificers' Guild with designs of the same date produced by Jean Després or Raymond Templier. Even René Lalique widely acknowledged as the greatest Art Nouveau jewellery designer, made a successful transition to a different, and noticeably more modern, style for his designs in the 'twenties. It is perhaps because the creative impetus behind the Art Nouveau style diminished so rapidly after 1910 that the French were able to approach the new design problems with their minds uncluttered by the left overs of a previous style, whereas the English Craft Revival movement was still stumbling on supported by a faithful if diminishing body of admirers and fed by new recruits who were to ensure its survival until the outbreak of war and even beyond. The work of the inter-war designers like George Hunt and Sybil Dunlop, while making considerable concessions to the new ideas in materials and stone-setting techniques, remains basically Craft Revival inspired. Both these artists remain almost exclusively faithful to nature as a source of ideas, and the most noticeable difference between their jewellery and that of their Arts and Crafts predecessors is in the polychromy, achieved by an apparently haphazard selection of coloured stones, quite unlike the subtly calculated effects in the polychrome work of Henry Wilson or J.P. Cooper, both of whose work is distinguished by the most beautiful use of colour.

It is significant that at this period, as in the whole of the preceding century, the great jewellery designers in France (and thus by implication the great designers in the whole of Europe) should almost all bear names associated with famous and old-established firms. Cartier for instance, a name that is synonymous with the most refined jewellery work of the 'twenties, was established by Louis-François Cartier in 1859. Maison Chaumet, whose work is recognisable by the refinement of technique in the stone setting, already existed under the directorship of Etiènne Nitot during the reign of Napoleon I. Raymond Templier, who is unquestionably one of the most significant figures of the period, worked within the framework of the firm established in 1849 by his grandfather, carrying on the tradition of *avant garde* design established before the turn of the century by his father Paul Templier, who produced pieces designed by Theodore Lambert in a very advanced Art Nouveau idiom. Similarly Jean Fouquet, a figure of almost equal significance in the development of the vocabulary of geometric motifs, worked with his father in the family firm which had been established by his grandfather in the 1860s. The parallels go further than this, as Georges Fouquet had also laid the foundations of the firm's reputation for producing experimental modernistic work before the turn of the century, a reputation which both he and Jean sustained throughout the 'twenties with their designs in unusual combinations of materials, such as onyx with lacquer and two colours of gold, and black onyx and coral with diamonds, one bizarre piece consisting of a jade and diamond mask inlaid with black onyx eyes. Boucheron also maintained throughout this period the reputation established in the previous century, producing pieces of great value somewhat in the manner of Cartier, but lacking the panache of the

Cartier designs. Their clientele consisted largely, as in the past, of millionaires of conservative taste, a taste which is reflected in the rather modified use of the currently fashionable geometric style. Van Cleef and Arpels and Maison Mauboussin, both of much more recent foundation (in both cases the late 'nineties, though Mauboussin claimed to be the successors of a firm established in 1827, and gave this earlier date for their foundation on their publicity material), quickly established enviable reputations as fashionable jewellers.

As well as ensuring a thorough understanding of jewellery design, in terms of the possibilities and the limitations of materials and techniques, learned through years of experience, this design movement originating from within the highest class of the trade produced metalwork distinguished by the most impeccable workmanship. Technically the best jewellery of this period, like that of the previous thirty years, is of a quallity which, it is now freely acknowledged in the trade, will never be seen again, particularly from the point of view of the stone setting. Old men who have been in the trade since the 'twenties or 'thirties still maintain that, given the time and the money, the same quality of work could still be produced, but this is generally accepted as a nostalgic fantasy. The quality of work produced by a firm like Cartier, who disdained the limitations imposed by working to a price and made only pieces in keeping with their reputation, is perfectly flawless, in the matching of the stones and the precision of the metalworking. Each piece made in the London workshops is said to have been overseen and inspected on completion by Jacques Cartier himself, and the results of this careful surveillance are apparent in the surviving pieces, each one of which is a reminder of the reason why the name Cartier should enhance the value of every piece to which it is attached.

The establishment in Germany of the Deutsche Werkbund was intended to exploit this kind of technical experience by amalgamating the varied talents of old established firms with the design talents of the leading decorative artists of the period, and thus to ensure that avant garde work by designers like Kurt Baer, Philipp Oberle and Johann Wilm should be made to a high technical standard. Since their foundation the Wiener Werkstätte had employed fully trained craftsmen to make up the designs of Hoffmann and his fellow designers, with the result that the pieces produced by the Werkstätte have a professional finish not normally associated with craft workshop work.

The situation in England was entirely different. The distribution of patronage between the two diametric opposites in the jewellery trade, the craft jewellers on the one hand and the expensive retail trade on the other, had the effect of ensuring that no recognisably English style of Art Deco could emerge. The craft jewellers remained faithful to the Morris/Ashbee tradition of inspiration from nature, while the colonisation policy of the great French firms, a number of whom opened branches in London and New York at the turn of the century, ensured that the designs used for expensive jewellery destined for a rich and fashionable clientele were entirely under the influence

Colour Plate 99. Five brooches convertible to a tiara, set with aquamarines, pearls and diamonds, by Georges Fouquet. Signed G. Fouquet. Paris 1908. A very similar, possibly the same tiara was shown by Fouquet at the International Exhibition in Brussels in 1910. (Wartski, London.)

of French taste. Only towards the end of the inter-war period did a characteristically American style begin to emerge, with the work on unusual geometric cuts and combinations of coloured stones, randomly arranged in heavy, visible claw settings, which characterises the work of, for example, Harry Winston. The intrinsic value of these pieces is usually very great since the stones are of high quality and considerable size, but the idea of technical sophistication in setting seems to have been deliberately abandoned. Ironically enough English jewellery designs have only begun to emerge as an influential and widely imitated style with the post-War craft revival, which must suggest that English design can only make a significant contribution stylistically while fighting a series of rearguard actions with industrial and mechanical progress. This was repeatedly demonstrated throughout the nineteenth century. A microcosm of the situation can be seen in the relative success in their chosen aims of Morris and Christopher Dresser. There is no question that the retrograde anti-mechanical ideals of Morris found more favour with his contemporaries than Dresser's revolutionary designs for mass-production. Prince Albert was disappointed of many of his most cherished aims during his lifetime. The failure of his schemes for the improvement of design in industry can hardly be regarded as of comparable importance to his unrealised ambitions for European unity, but it seems probable that he would regard the present situation in commercial and industrial design with a considerable feeling of disappointment.

CHAPTER VIII
Materials and Techniques

Christopher Dresser, whose contribution to the evolution of the applied arts in the second half of the nineteenth century has only comparatively recently been adequately re-evaluated, wrote in 1873: 'If the work be beautiful then it is ridiculous to estimate its value as though the material of which it is composed were of greater worth than the amount of life, thought, and painstaking care expended upon its production.' It is ironical that Dresser, who was one of the very few people to understand that the only way to distribute well designed decorative articles at all widely amongst the less well-off sections of the community was through mass-production, should have been the one to voice the credo of the Arts and Crafts designers so unequivocally and at such a relatively early date. Dresser was, after all, one of the most important figures in the Aesthetic movement and the cult of Japan, on which the Craft Revival movement fed both for inspiration and for a visually and ideologically educated public. *The Studio* recognised Dresser's relevance to the Arts and Crafts movement, an anonymous contributor writing in 1899 (vol. XV pp.104-114) of *The Principles of Decorative Design,* which had appeared in 1873: 'One might quote page after page and not find a line, scarcely a word, that would not be endorsed by the most critical member of the Arts and Crafts Association.'

Dr. Dresser and Ruskin, the latter vigorously deploring both the cult of the diamond and scientific gem-cutting, the former writing the advice to craftsmen which is quoted above, were well in advance of the taste of their time. It was only the growing acceptance of the design ideas put forward by the Craft Revival artists and the Art Nouveau designers in the late nineteenth century which led to a real regard for form and colour as opposed to the simple exploitation of precious materials in the conventional styles evolved almost a century earlier. The following passage appeared in the introduction to the exhibition of Lalique's work held at Agnew's Gallery in London in 1905 (written by Gustave Kahn and translated by Miss Hepworth Dixon): 'Thanks to M. René Lalique, the jeweller's art has been absolutely transformed. Before his advent, what was the jewel but a piece of vain ostentation — a braggart boast, as it were, of the possession of so much wealth? Excellent executants, whose taste was, however, limited by the requirements of industrial art, set the finest diamonds in the most dreary and monotonous of designs. The flower, the knot, the ribbon, the aigrette — do we not know them all? Small wonder that the purely aesthetic element was non-existent in settings which were at once barbarous and naïve...Nor should it be forgotten that M. Lalique has done much to free the world from the all-pervading tyranny of the diamond. Employing the brilliant only when it is necessary to the harmony of his design, he brought into prominence many charming stones which had been forgotten by the world.'

The materials favoured by Lalique, with the exception of horn and frosted glass which he used extensively and made peculiarly his own by employing them with great subtlety, do not strike one as having been especially 'forgotten by the world'. It is rather the use to which he puts his opals, sapphires, rose diamonds, aquamarines and amethysts which is so remarkable, many of the stones being carved or cut in some unconventional fashion, and set into a framework of enamel in a variety of techniques; seen against the fashionable jewellery of the period these materials must have seemed very exotic.

This denial of the accepted categories of value was to be of central importance to the craft jewellers and, in a rather different spirit, to the Art Nouveau designers. This artistic use of materials entirely for effect and without any thought of intrinsic value was matched by a parallel development in purely fashionable jewellery in which the traditional reverence for intrinsic value was as much in evidence as ever, an attitude which led to the fashion for very large, single stones in practically invisible settings, their price simply related to the rarity and cost of the materials. This tended to perpetuate the practice, so deplored by the aesthetic critics like Ruskin, Oscar Wilde and Mrs. Haweis (whose treatise on aesthetic dress, *The Art of Beauty,* appeared in 1878) of imitating valuable jewellery in less expensive materials to provide cheap ornaments instead of evolving a different style, valid in its own right, for this growing section of the trade. That this method of providing cheap jewellery was bound to be self-defeating in the end is proved by the chequered popularity of silver jewellery during the nineteenth century.

The history of the jewellery trade in Birmingham reflects the hazards of the cheap jewellery trade as a whole. In the second half of the nineteenth century, after a series of periods of success with high export figures and a healthy trade in the home market, followed by disastrous periods when the industry was virtually extinct, the trade seemed to be exceptionally buoyant when silver jewellery became very popular after the discovery in 1860 of the rich 'Comstock' lode of silver, in Nevada. The 'sixties and 'seventies were a period of great prosperity for Birmingham, but by 1885 the trade was again on the very brink of disaster owing to a change in fashion which led to the distaste for silver jewellery which often finds expression in writings of this period. The tide of taste only began to change at the turn of the century with the growing popularity of Craft Revival jewellery, for which a way of using silver had been evolved that had nothing to do with cheap imitation of gold work. The use of silver is seen at its best in the buckles and clasps of the period, which can take their place as examples in silversmithing work in the best tradition, rare indeed for silver jewellery.

Predictably enough the Craft Revival jewellers were not interested in, they even positively deplored, the elaborate facet-cutting of precious stones. For the most part the stones used in their jewellery are either simple cabochons, or polished but otherwise in their natural state. In about 1915 Mr. and Mrs. Arthur Gaskin made a necklace from stones picked up on the beach in Suffolk during a family holiday. These were the cornelians, agates and quartz in various colours which abound on the shingle beaches of this country, some areas being renowned for the quality and variety of the gemstones which can

Plate 139. The workshop of Child and Child where silversmiths and jewellers are seen at work. A leather apron hangs beneath the bench to collect the minute fragments of metal which fall during the process of filing and piercing. At the end of the day these findings would be collected together and saved for melt. The majority of techniques employed in the goldsmiths' workshops have changed very little since the Renaissance. (Child Family Collection.)

be found, and which provide an absorbing pastime to collect and polish them. John Ruskin was a tireless campaigner for a return to the use of uncut stones, and his views on this matter were usually respected by the craft jewellers, the only concession to conventional taste being the use (particularly by commercial manufacturers) of oval or drop-shaped amethysts cut in a modified brilliant. The use of diamonds in this type of jewellery was so rare that generally no stock of them was kept, and few of the craft jewellers bothered with a safe for their stones. The stone cabinets of Henry Wilson and John Paul Cooper, square wooden boxes filled with compartment trays which lift out and which still survive with some of their original contents, contain numbers of small cabochon-cut, translucent and opaque stones in different shades of green, blue, purple and red, as well as curious fragments of carved coral, polished crystal, coloured glass and engraved turquoise. To look into these boxes is to understand a little of the creative process which went into the making of jewellery by these two designers, both of whom excelled at the subtle juxtaposition of colours and forms. This subtle use of the fine gradations of colour found in precious stones is an entirely personal thing and cannot be used in commerce, where an element of standardisation is inevitable even in special commissions. It is interesting to notice how great is the difference in this respect between the jewels from designs by artists like Edward Burne-Jones and Charles Ricketts which were made up by commercial jewellers, albeit highly competently, and those conceived and made by one man, with only the help of heavily supervised assistants.

Gold was indisputably the favourite metal of the Victorians, and was used for jewellery during the whole period. Extensive experiments took place with the revival of ancient techniques of gold-working which had fallen into disuse, particularly the techniques of the ancient Roman and Etruscan jewellers which were revealed by the extensive archaeological excavations which took place in the early nineteenth century. By the end of the 1880s it almost seemed as if the intense interest which had been displayed in the mid-nineteenth century by the public and by the metalworkers themselves in both classical jewellery and neo-Gothic and Renaissance revival work, had begun to diminish, and that little new work would be done on the techniques involved — i.e. chasing, filigree and granulation. But the true methods of the Etruscans which had eluded even the Castellani family of goldsmiths and jewellers, those great propagandists for classical techniques whose shop in the via Poli in Rome was an object of pilgrimage during the middle years of the century, continued to fascinate goldsmiths well into the twentieth century. At the turn of the century both the notorious Russian forger Rouchomovsky and Erik Kollin, one of Fabergé's workmasters, were still producing archaeological-style goldwork. Among those who continued to experiment with methods of reproducing the characteristic granulated decoration found on Etruscan goldwork were Emil Lettré of Berlin, Elisabeth Treskow who had a workshop in Essen from 1919-43 and in Cologne from 1948, Johann Wilm who was working with the Deutsche Werkbund in the 'twenties, J. Stettman of the Hague, and William Blackband, a pupil and collaborator in Birmingham of Arthur Gaskin, the head of the Vittoria Street School. Blackband was inspired to begin his researches into granulation techniques by T.B. Wigley, his first teacher at the Vittoria Street School, as early as 1898, when he was only thirteen. Wigley remarked to his class that whoever should rediscover the secret of the Etruscan work would be 'made for life' (see 'A Mystery of the Ancient Goldsmith's Craft Solved', the report subtitled 'The Etruscan Method of Granulation — for long a secret — REDISCOVERED' of a lecture given by Blackband at the Royal Institute on 25 April, 1934, *Illustrated London News*, 28 April, 1934). Blackband claims that his researches were rewarded with success in 1920 — the *Illustrated London News* article shows photographs of his work in 'field-grainwork' (i.e. a patternless covering on the surface of the gold of fine grains), and 'pattern-grainwork' by himself, Castellani and the ancient Etruscan craftsmen — but it is significant that his results were not published until the 'thirties, the period which marks the height of modern activity in this field. Elisabeth Treskow came to London in the early 'thirties for discussions at Goldsmiths' Hall on the subject of granulation techniques; the process of colloidal hard-soldering, which is the technique used for the successful imitation of Etruscan granulation work, was patented by H.P. Littledale in 1933. The successful scientific researches of the twentieth century inevitably led to a reassessment of the contribution of the Castellani family and their many imitators, but whatever the scientific verdict, the fact remains that the Castellanis, as pioneers of the style, had a far wider influence on the taste of their time than the researchers of the 'twenties and 'thirties had in their own. This was probably partly due to the greatly diminished popularity of gold at this period; it was widely used in the form of white gold, which conformed with the fashion for colourless settings for jewellery, being an alloy of gold with silver, nickel and platinum or palladium.

During most of the earlier period covered by this book **silver**, which had such a chequered career during the nineteenth century, was popular with at least a certain section of the public. Although silver jewellery had been out of fashion throughout the 'eighties, it started to creep back into fashion in the late 'nineties with the gradual spread of the taste for Craft Revival jewellery. Although much of the Craft Revival silverwork represents a genuine attempt to find a style which is not merely an imitation in cheaper material of goldwork, it is noticeable that much of the work seems to be carried out with a disregard for either charm or refinement of technique. This was partly involuntary — the craftsmen employed by Ashbee's Guild of Handicraft, for instance, evolved their working methods through a process of trial and error and much of the work is technically clumsy — and partly deliberate, being an ideological rejection of the 'deadening' technical perfection of nineteenth century commercial jewellery so deplored by Ruskin. In his article for *The Studio* entitled 'The Jewellery of Mr. and Mrs. Gaskin', Arthur Wainwright wrote of their early work: 'They did not, and possibly could not, then achieve the mechanical perfection of the trade jeweller. All their work was, of course, handwrought and based upon simple floral forms original to themselves.' At no point in the article does Wainwright suggest that the Gaskins achieved 'mechanical perfection' at a later date, and it is an indication of the extent to which the Vittoria Street Schools were committed to the idea of a fine art training for trade apprentices that a man like Gaskin should have been head of what was, after all, a trade school. Earlier Aymer Valance had written of the Gaskins' work: 'Their home is in a locality where a large amount of very deplorable jewellery is produced; so deplorable that they determined, if possible, to provide an antidote to the prevailing degradation. And the reason why the vast mass of the trade jewellery manufactured in Birmingham is bad is that in style and outline it is utterly devoid of artistic inspiration, while at the same time it is perfect as concerns mere technique.' (See *Modern Design in Jewellery and Fans,* p.4 of the British section.) It was only possible to speak disparagingly of 'mere technique' at a time when technical processes had reached a high degree of sophistication and where the application of the most demanding techniques could be found even in relatively inexpensive trade jewellery, but it is undeniable that the careless application of certain highly subtle metalworking processes to cheap trinkets was hardly advisable, and the wholesale adoption by the Birmingham trade firms of 'Japanese' techniques did result in some truly 'deplorable' jewellery.

The great interest in Japanese art which is evident in all branches of decorative art at the turn of the century dates from the 1860s. Japan had been virtually closed to the western world until the American Commander Perry managed to wrest limited trading rights from the Japanese in the 1850s. By 1862 the Japanese were exhibiting at the International Exhibition in London, and in the same year the architect E.W. Godwin (described by Max Beerbohm as 'the first of the aesthetes') began using Japanese prints to decorate his house. It is a measure of the speed with which the newly discovered style was assimilated into the vocabulary of the mid-nineteenth century decorative designer that 'Japanese' taste jewellery was already being produced by the Birmingham manufacturers in the 1870s. This *Japonaiserie* was largely silverwork decorated with Japanese subject matter in coloured metals. The English assay laws required that the inlaid or applied metalwork should be of a value equal to that of the background, and the silver jewellery is usually decorated, like the goldwork, in different coloured golds, except where this rule has been either ignored or misunderstood, when copper or brass was used to produce the same effect. Different colours of gold and silver are produced by alloying the pure metal with other materials in varied proportions. The addition of copper, with a little silver to improve the working properties, made a pink-red gold. Yellow and green gold are produced in a similar manner. The strength of the contrast in the colours depends on the proportions of the alloying metal, and a considerable range of colours could be produced in this way. True Japanese metalworking techniques are, of course, far more subtle, employing a far greater range of colours and much more unburnished metal; Professor Bisei of Tokyo claimed in 1911 that there were over seventy different alloys for bronze of which about thirty were still in general use by Japanese craftsmen. The complex art of the Japanese metalworker continued to fascinate jewellery designers well into the twentieth century. The lectures and demonstrations given by Professor Unno Yoshimori (Bisei) of the Tokyo School of Fine Art, described in *The Studio* (vol. 52, 1911), and the demonstrations and recipes for metalworking given by Professor T. Kobayashi, also of Tokyo, to the students at the Royal College of Art at the request of Henry Wilson, the head of the metalworking department, inspired a spate of experiments with colouring and inlaying on the part of the Craft Revival jewellers. Henry Wilson added a new section on Japanese methods to the second edition (1912) of his text book, *Silverwork and Jewellery* (first published in 1903), and this may well have added to the new interest in Japanese work, but since 1893 *The Studio* had been discussing Japanese art, with frequent references to both the metal work and the hardstone carvings, which would have inspired the European jeweller.

After the First World War, with the diminution of interest in the Craft Revival movement the use of silver for jewellery declined, much of the later work being rhodium plated to prevent tarnishing, a process which imparts a peculiarly hard and unpleasing texture to the pieces thus treated.

Emerald, rubies and sapphires are regarded, with diamonds, as the 'primary' gemstones. Emerald is a variety of beryl. Flawless stones of good colour are rare and are usually more expensive than diamonds of comparable size. The most highly prized colour is a dark velvety green, and the stone is usually used either in the appropriately named 'emerald' cut or as a round or oval cabochon.

Ruby and sapphire are both varieties of corundum. As with emeralds the flawless stones of fine colour are rare and valuable. The most desirable colour for ruby is a deep red known as 'pigeon's blood', and for sapphires a dark blue, though purple, yellow and white sapphires are also known. Both stones sometimes show 'asterism' — the optical effect whereby light is reflected from the fibrous inclusions which create 'planes' inside the stone, producing a six-pointed star. These star sapphires or rubies are cut *en cabochon,* as are the single ray chrysoberyl 'cat's-eyes'. These stones are found cut in a variety of ways depending on the use to which they are to be put, but these and emeralds display their greatest beauties when the simplest type of cutting is used. The

Russians, whose taste for fine precious stones was legendary, regarded faceting of any kind for these coloured stones as nothing short of sacrilege.

Aquamarine, chrysoberyl, chrysoprase, citrine, peridot, topaz and tourmaline are all pale stones which were very popular at the end of the nineteenth century. The pale blue aquamarine is usually found as a pendoloque or briolette, both drop-shaped stones with facets, as pendants or earrings, or in a large square or oblong emerald cut as the centre stone of a ring or brooch, in combination with diamonds. The other stones which occur in shades of yellow, brown and green of varying intensity are usually found in combination with gold and pearls. The green peridots were particularly fashionable and are often found in Edwardian botanical jewellery set in textured gold decorated with *ombré* enamel. These stones are usually cut in a square or oval with shallow facets at the side and a large 'table' to display the colour.

Moonstones, a variety of feldspar, are almost completely colourless stones which display a faint sheen of blue in certain lights. They became popular at the end of the nineteenth century with other white or colourless materials, with the vogue for colourless jewellery. They were widely used by the Craft Revival jewellers in combination with mother-of-pearl, usually set in silver, and are always cut in a round or oval cabochon.

Amethysts and garnets of a rich dark colour cut *en cabochon* were very popular throughout the Victorian period for neo-Gothic and Renaissance pieces and fell out of favour at the end of the nineteenth century. Where amethysts are used around the turn of the century they are usually the pale-coloured South American stones which are less valuable and far more common than the fine dark purple 'Siberian' stones favoured by the Victorians. The reputation of garnet jewellery suffered during the second half of the nineteenth century from the poor design and workmanship of the Bohemian garnet jewellery which was virtually mass-produced from the small, rather poor-coloured stone found near Trebnitz in what is now Czechoslovakia. The stones were cut into small faceted 'nail-heads' and used massed on to the setting in a restricted range of flower and star shapes, a treatment which does not display the colour of the stone to advantage. The most successful cut for the garnet is the simple cabochon (when cut in this way it is known as a carbuncle) which allows a certain amount of light to pass through the stone.

Coral and turquoise are both opaque stones which were widely used both in the Victorian period and during the later part of the period covered by this book. Turquoise matrix combined with gold became almost a cliché of a certain type of commercial Craft Revival jewellery, being widely used by firms like Liberty's and Murrle, Bennett and Co. Coral is found in combination with other opaque stones like **malachite** and **lapis-lazuli** in jewellery designed by Josef Hoffmann and later Sybil Dunlop and George Hunt. Coral can be used as beads, as small cabochon stones, or in its natural state, *en branche,* and it can be carved into small ornaments. It was regarded as a specific against danger and an amulet of coral was worn by Italian babies from birth, and it is this traditional use which attracted the 'aesthetes'. Coral or turquoise bead necklaces were an almost compulsory accessory to a certain style of flimsy muslin 'artistic' dress. The tradition has survived of godparents giving coral in some form as a christening present to a baby.

Jade has long been valued and collected in the form of small carvings of Chinese origin. It became fashionable in Europe for jewellery soon after the turn of the century, when these Oriental pieces were worn simply bored and threaded on to a silk cord as a pendant. Liberty's imported small Oriental hardstone carvings in a number of different materials as well as jade, such as rose quartz, rock crystal and the traditional ivory netsuke, which were to be worn in this fashion. At the same period Japanese workmen in Paris were turning out horn ornaments of the same kind more or less wholesale. At this early date (i.e. 1904-5) Cartier's began mounting small pieces of jade with engraved decoration in settings of platinum and diamonds, some years before these carvings became popular set with other pale opaque stones in dress clips and brooches. Jade bead necklaces were also widely worn, and depending on the quality of the stones were often very valuable. Jade-set jewellery, of which a large amount survives from the period between the wars, fetches high prices out of all proportion to the interest of the design, and it is necessary to have a wide experience of the qualities of the stone in order to buy wisely in this field.

Opals have, throughout the last century and a half, suffered from a reputation for bringing ill-luck to their owners, which has affected their popularity so adversely that they were hardly used in jewellery at all. After the publication of Walter Scott's novel *Anne of Geierstein* in 1829, in which the body of Lady Hermione is consumed by the evil emanations from the stone, leaving no trace except for a small pile of dust, it was claimed by Harry Emanuel (in *Diamonds and Precious Stones,* published in 1865) that opals were out of favour for thirty years. This claim is belied by the fine display of opal jewellery exhibited in 1851 by Hunt and Roskell, and by the amount of surviving opal jewellery from the mid-nineteenth century. Opals were one of Prince Albert's favourite stones, and he gave a set of opal jewellery to Queen Victoria. This set survives, but without the opals, as Queen Alexandra disliked these stones and they were replaced in 1902 with rubies — perversely against the trend, as by this date opals had become very fashionable, and the delicate opal and diamond pendants which can still be found date from the late nineteenth century and the Edwardian period. A comparatively late development of Liberty's Art Nouveau style was a group of gold pendants and brooches of gold in sinuous forms set with flat-cut opals fitted together in a mosaic effect. These stones remained popular for a number of years; the distinctive opal doublets which combined a layer of opal with a layer of black glas and which were widely used for rings and bar brooches were fashionable in the 'twenties, and can also be found in a more complex banded form, combining diagonals of opal and black glass, the stone again backed with black glass.

Pearls were very fashionable at the turn of the century. Like diamonds, they were hardly ever out of favour during the whole of the Victorian period and had enjoyed a new lease of popularity in the last quarter of the nineteenth century when colourless jewellery was in vogue. The introduction at the very end of the century of the cultured pearl made them widely available, while also disastrously reducing the value of real pearls. The process used to induce the pearl-bearing mussel or oyster to manufacture a pearl by introducing a seed pearl or a piece of mother-of-pearl into the shell was first used successfully by the Japanese Kokichi Mikimoto in 1896. The ready availability of the pearls thus produced brought into fashion the long necklaces of large evenly sized beads of a type that would previously have been far too expensive for any but the most fabulously wealthy owner. It is hard to understand the awe in which the beautiful pearl necklaces owned by the Empress Eugénie and Princesse Mathilde Bonaparte were held, so much has the modern appreciation of pearls been coloured by the availability of Mikimoto's cultured variety.

Both **jet** and **ivory** enjoyed a new popularity in the period between the wars as they were suitable for the jewellery made in the fashionable colour combination of black and white. Both had been widely used for the mourning and memorial jewellery popular throughout the nineteenth century, but the techniques of working and carving these materials had become horribly debased towards the end of the century, and the demand for the ubiquitous crosses entwined with ivy, the bouquets of flowers and the hands holding a spray of leaves of flowers declined sharply in the 'eighties. Both Lalique and Philippe Wolfers have been credited with reviving the use of ivory in jewellery, and there is good reason to support both claims since both men used ivory effectively in their jewellery designs at the turn of the century. Belgian artists had access to the fine ivory from the Congo which was offered to them by the King of the Belgians in an attempt to create a demand for this valuable resource and so benefit the national economy. Richard Garbe, the English sculptor, used ivory frequently in combination with silver or **shagreen** (sharkskin, dried and dyed, usually green, and used as a surface covering) in *objets de virtu* (ornamental plaques, boxes and a tankard by Garbe in these materials still survive), and he was followed in this use of ivory with silver by Onslow Whiting, his co-member of the Guild of Art Workers. Ivory used in combination with gold was used for jewellery by both Josef Hoffman and Dagobert Pêche, a fellow artist also employed by the Wiener Werkstätte. Later Nancy Cunard's famous collection of African ivory bangles, which reached nearly from wrist to shoulder, made both ivory and African native jewellery the height of *chic*.

The interest in surface texture which is apparent in fashionable jewellery and other personal ornaments, like compacts and cigarette boxes, during the 'twenties and 'thirties made materials like shagreen and *coquille d'oeuf,* the crushed eggshell mosaics, popular in both England and France. Both Garbe and J. Paul Cooper, the Craft Revival silversmith and jeweller, had been using shagreen for boxes since about 1903, but the wide use of both these materials came in the 'thirties.

Horn in the form of carved hair ornaments, combs and pendants of Oriental inspiration, became very popular at the turn of the century. Lalique is said to have been the first to use this material, as an alternative to tortoiseshell which had been fashionable for jewellery, particularly in America, throughout the nineteenth century. Horn offers a greater range of colour than tortoiseshell, and when used to display the different tints of brown and cream to good advantage can give an impression of subdued richness. As well as Lalique, both Lucien Gaillard and Vever used horn for combs, often adding enamelled gold and setting pearls or cabochon-cut coloured stones into the design; these are among the best and most uncluttered of Art Nouveau pieces. True to the nature of the material much of the hornwork of this period is Japanese in inspiration. Lucien Gaillard was deeply interested in Japanese techniques and after 1900 he employed a number of Japanese craftsmen in his workshop; other Japanese were working independently in Paris. One firm specialising in horn jewellery was Rosaka et Cie, and much of the work of clearly Japanese origin was signed with the not particularly characteristic names of 'Bonte' and 'Gyp'. These may well be a westernisation of difficult Japanese names.

One of the few English Art Nouveau jewellers to understand this material was Fred Partridge, whose work is unusual in being influenced by contemporary French taste. His combs and hair ornaments are reminiscent of the work of Lalique, Vever and Lucien Gaillard.

The interest shown by the artist-jewellers of the period in unusual materials led to many non-precious metals, stones and substitutes being used for jewellery, not simply in order to reduce the price, as in the Victorian period, but for purposes of experimenting with textures and colours. There is a parallel with the use of paste in the eighteenth century, but generally the experimental work of this later period ignored the conventions of form as well as substance in a way which would have been entirely alien to the craftsmen of the eighteenth century.

Aluminium is a silver-coloured lightweight metal, now associated in most people's minds with saucepans. The material was first discovered in 1827, but a way of processing it for industrial use was not developed until 1854. This new metal seemed to be of a certain interest to the jewellery trade as it was easy to work and enjoyed the great advantage of being untarnishable. In the late 'fifties a small amount of jewellery composed of chased and engraved aluminium and gold was made in France by the great nineteenth century *ciseleur* (metal engraver and chaser) Honoré Séverin Bourdoncle (1823-1893). The combination is not unattractive, quite unlike the more conventional combination of silver and gold or silver-gilt, but the fact that so few pieces have survived suggests that this jewellery did not become popular and the use of the metal was dropped after a very short time. Combining aluminium with other metals posed technical problems which were quite disproportionate to the advantage gained from this metal's resistance to tarnishing. At the end of the century the use of aluminium was revived for making small sculptures, notably by Sir Alfred Gilbert, and its possibilities as a material for jewellery were tested again, this time by the Glasgow decorative artist, Talwin Morris. He specialised in designing buckles in strange combinations of materials, like copper, brass and bronze as well as aluminium, set with coloured glass; a number of these buckles were illustrated (see, for example, *Modern Design in Jewellery and Fans*) and one, of embossed copper set with green glass, is now in the Victoria and Albert Museum.

The American silver manufacturers, Gorham and Company, used the very Japanese-style combination of silver and copper for pieces of decorative metalwork in the 'eighties, and the same combination, often with the addition of brass or bronze, was used for the jewellery made in the design workshop set up under William Codman in the late 'nineties. Later German work in a heavy linear style is sometimes found in a combination of bronze and brass, these metals again being used mainly for buckles and clasps.

The post-war period, with its obsessive interest in the machine style, saw the adoption of further non-precious industrial materials for jewellery making. Both stainless steel and chrome contribute their hard sheeny brightness to the designs of the late 'twenties and 'thirties. Stainless steel is the somewhat misleading name given to the rust-resistant steel containing chromium and nickel which was invented by R. Brearley, working at the Firth Brown Research Laboratory, Sheffield, in 1913. It was widely used in Scandinavia long before it became popular in this country, and the Copenhagen silversmithing firm of Jensen made a number of stainless steel wedding rings, which were popular with anti-materialistic people who despised the idea of intrinsic value in jewellery, a kind of *reductio ad absurdum* of the craft ethic. Since the end of the Second World War stainless steel jewellery has become very fashionable, the best still being made by Jensen's.

Chrome is used in jewellery in the form of chromium plating, which is a thin sheet of chromium deposited electrically on to a base metal to increase resistance to corrosion, and which imparts a hard, bright silvery surface to the object. The quality of chromium plating varies greatly, and when it is too thin it can impart an air of shoddiness to the best designed work. It was widely used in combination with hardstone and crystal beads or plastics in necklaces and bracelets in the 'twenties and 'thirties, and in these inexpensive pieces the quality of the chrome is often rather poor. Chromium-plated brass was used much more successfully by the Bauhaus designer Naum Slutsky, who, as a trained engineer who took up industrial designing, was much more suited by training and temperament to designing jewellery in industrial materials.

The new concept of expendable costume jewellery, imported like the fashion for solitaire diamonds from America and initially greeted in Europe with similar reservations, which was flashy in appearance but without either intrinsic value or careful finish, revived the flagging interest in paste and marcasite, both widely used during the nineteenth century as substitutes for diamonds. Paste stones, both white and coloured, are made from a hard glass with good refractive qualities which can be faceted and polished. The best quality paste is hard to distinguish from real stones, but little modern paste jewellery is of this standard. Marcasite is the name given to iron pyrites cut and polished for use in jewellery. The material is set in dense clusters of faceted 'nail-head' stones and the effect is very similar to the polished steel work of the eighteenth and early nineteenth centuries which was carried out in the same way. The hard steely brilliance of marcasite was very well suited to the geometric style of jewellery fashionable in the 'thirties and it is often found in combination with steel and jet or black glass. Both black and frosted glass were widely used for jewellery in the period between the wars. The colour combination of black with steely grey and textured white was very popular and can be found in both the most valuable jewellery and the very cheap, the designs being carried out in diamond and onyx set in platinum, black and white glass and colourless semi-precious stones set in rhodium-plated silver, or black bakelite with marcasites or pastes set in stainless steel or chrome. A number of different plastics came into use for jewellery at this period, bakelite and celluloid being among the earliest to be used. Celluloid was invented in 1865; its chief defect, apart from a tendency to scratch and distort which is found to a greater or lesser degree in all plastics, is that it is highly inflammable. Bakelite was invented in 1909 by L.H. Baekeland and was widely used in cheap jewellery in the 'twenties and 'thirties. Plastics or synthetic resin substances are particularly suitable for cheap jewellery whose life expectancy is short; they can easily be moulded by heat and pressure, they can be dyed to resemble either translucent or opaque substances and they can be coated with a thin metallic film to resemble gilt or silver metal.

Plastic is most successful when used to imitate substances with a resin-like texture — i.e. amber, tortoiseshell or horn and ivory; it is less satisfactory for translucent materials as it has a low refractive index and cannot take a high polish. It is essentially a costume jewellery material as none of the surfaces have a long life, and is best used as a material in its own right, in combination with metals and stones which also have a limited lifespan like stainless steel and chrome, pastes and frosted glass, to make the very fashionable jewellery for which the taste is too transient to allow of its being made in precious materials.

CHAPTER IX

The Enamelling Revival

It would obviously be an over-simplification to claim that the revival of interest in neglected enamelling techniques, dating from the second half of the nineteenth century, was the technical development of greatest importance to the evolution of a characteristic style both in the Art Nouveau and the Arts and Crafts Movements, to the cult of the Oriental style, but the fact remains that it was probably the extensive use of enamel which made the jewellery of this period so unlike anything produced in the immediately preceding years. The use of enamel decoration for the settings of jewellery had been virtually abandoned in the early years of the eighteenth century, though all the complex techniques of *taille d'épergne, en plein, champlevé, cloisonné,* and painted enamels of all kinds remained in use for the decoration of gold boxes, *étuis* and the small precious accessories for sewing and the toilet which were popular at the time. The use of painted enamel miniatures in jewellery, both in the form of portraits and as small pictures, remained constant throughout the eighteenth century and well into the nineteenth, but the use of enamel as an integral part of the design of a piece of jewellery was regarded as a lost art, and its revival in the 1840s for the enrichment of the newly fashionable neo-Gothic and Renaissance style jewellery was attended by a suitable fanfare of appreciation. The decoration of this type of jewellery is usually carried out in opaque or translucent enamel on gold, as in, for example, the neo-Renaissance work of F.D. Froment-Meurice and the neo-Gothic marriage jewellery designed by A.W.N. Pugin in the late 'forties, examples of both of which were shown at the Great Exhibition in London in 1851.

This 'medieval' and neo-Renaissance jewellery, which was widely copied throughout the nineteenth century and which was still being made in Hungary well into the present century, was followed by the fashion for Egyptian and Japanese style pieces for which the rather similar techniques of champlevé and cloisonné were used. The use of cloisonné was prompted by the appearance on the European art market of Japanese prints and other decorative objects in the late 1850s. A series on the art of Japan which appeared in *The Studio* in 1911-12 includes a long and detailed article on the Japanese techniques of cloisonné enamelling. According to the author, the art of cloisonné was only revived in Japan in 1839, but by 1867 Japanese style cloisonné work was being produced by jewellers and silversmiths in Europe, notably the jeweller Alexis Falize, and the silversmithing firm Christofle in France, who were joined by Elkington's, the large English silversmithing and plating firm. Christofle and Falize showed cloisonné enamel in the Japanese taste at the Exposition Internationale in Paris in 1867. A large group of cloisonné enamel objects, described by a contemporary critic as far surpassing the Chinese or modern Japanese work in quality, and even comparing favourably with the 'exquisite beauty' of the old Japanese work, was shown by Elkington's at the Centennial Exposition in Philadelphia in 1876. The designer of these pieces was Albert Wilms, a Frenchman, who had worked for Christofle in Paris before joining Elkington's in the late 1850s. By the turn of the century the Japanese reached a level of

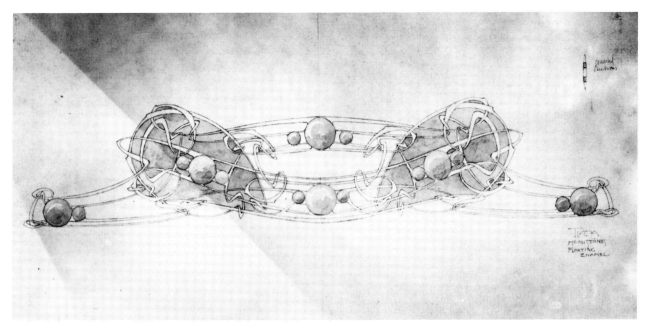

technical sophistication in this branch of enamelling which is truly astonishing, but the designs remained highly stereotyped, and though European enamelling never reached the same standard technically it was always more interesting artistically.

Some of the Japanese-inspired European work is carried out in the very similar technique of champlevé; whereas in cloisonné the enamel colours are separated from one another by metal cloisons, applied thin strips outlining the picture or pattern to be carried out in enamel, in champlevé the compartments designed to take the different colours are formed by hollowing out the surface of the metal in the required shapes. Champlevé was used for work inspired by ancient Byzantine art and for Egyptian style work. Much of the late cheap 'Egyptian' jewellery made after the turn of the century is partly enamelled in this fashion, where the colour is deposited in rather shallow cavities and has often worn away. Where enamel is used as a cheap substitute for coloured stones it is almost always of poor quality, the most interesting work being produced when enamel is used as an integral part of the design.

The interest in traditional styles of goldsmiths' work and jewellery in Russia and Scandinavia at the end of the nineteenth century prompted the revival of the 'Old Russian' style of decoration, which is an elaborate form of cloisonné in which the cloisons are often made of gold wire worked like filigree to produce a beaded edge. In some pieces only part of the applied filigree work is filled with colour, producing the decoration which is regarded as most typically Russian. This interest in traditional styles of metalwork was fostered by the growing influence of the pan-Slavonic movement, the craft movement dedicated to reversing the westernisation of Russian artistic and decorative work which had been forced on the inhabitants of Russia by Peter the Great and greatly encouraged by Catherine the Great, who led the Russian aristocracy to adopt French styles in art and fashion, and to regard native Russian crafts as the nadir of primitive and unsophisticated taste. The pan-Slavonic movement received the greatest encouragement from Tsar Nicholas I (1825-55), and the influence of the Moscow-based decorative artists grew in this climate of Imperial approval, producing during the last quarter of the

Plate 140. A design in pencil and watercolour for a tiara c.1905, by Archibald Knox (1864-1933). The drawing is annotated with the suggestion that moonstones and 'floating' enamel should be used. (The Victoria and Albert Museum.)
Knox was born in the Isle of Man and as a result was greatly interested in his Celtic heritage. This influence can even be detectd in this splendid Art Nouveau tiara. He came to London in 1897 and began designing for Liberty's 'Cymric' and 'Tudric' range of metalwork.
He taught at the Kingston School of Art for a period before the First World War, but was dismissed for his radical ideas. His pupils at the School were later to found the Knox School of Design.

nineteenth century a large group of enamellists working in the 'Old Russian' style. Apart from Carl Fabergé, whose Moscow workshops turned out a large quantity of work in this manner, the best known of these craftsmen is probably Pavel Ovchinnikov. The firm which bears his name was founded in 1851, and received the Imperial Warrant in 1872. Ovchinnikov worked in both cloisonné and champlevé as well as the complex related technique of plique-à-jour, in which the cloisonné work, which has been carried out in translucent enamel, is detached by one method or another from its background, and emerges like a stained glass window. Plique-à-jour, which was widely used in Western Europe at the turn of the century, was first popularised by the Russian enamellists. In origin it is believed to be an Eastern technique, and may have been revived, or reinvented by Ovchinnikov himself.

Other well-known names working in this style in Moscow at the end of the nineteenth century are Ivan Chlebnikov (fl.1869-1918), Foedor Ruckert, Ivan Saltykov (fl.1884-97), Maria Semenova (fl.1896-1904), Gustav Klingert (fl.1865-1916), Anton Kuzmitchev (fl.1886-97), and Vassili Agafanov (fl. c.1900). This 'Old Russian' work was designed for and appealed most strongly to the rich merchant-class families of Moscow and was hardly known outside Russia. Fabergé's work, much of which was in any case in a highly Europeanised revived eighteenth century style, only became widely appreciated in Europe after he had exhibited at the Centennial Exhibition in Paris in 1900, and the productions of his Moscow workshops, which concentrated on Russian-style work, were even then not greatly in demand in Western Europe. There is some evidence of contact with the West, however, in that one piece, a gilded and enamelled tazza very much in the 'Old Russian' taste, made by Kuzmitchev in about 1900, is marked on the base 'Made for Tiffany & Co', and other objects made by this firm were also sold through the New York firm at this date. This trade practice was also followed by Carl Fabergé; an enamelled silver box in the collection of Her Majesty Queen Elizabeth the Queen Mother is similarly engraved.

A similar revival of interest in traditional styles and crafts was also taking place in Scandinavia at this period. The Norwegian firm, David Andersen, specialised in the production of 'Viking' style silverwork decorated with the partially enamelled filigree work called 'skan', and in elaborate plique-à-jour objects designed for them by Gustav Gaudernack. Another Norwegian firm, J. Tostrup, also specialised in the production of plique-à-jour objects at the turn of the century. These were made by the then head of the firm, Torolf Prytz, and are much less traditional in inspiration than Gaudernack's work for Andersen. Looking at the Scandinavian work of this period it is instructive to compare the results of an interest in purely traditional craft revival with the work of the French Art Nouveau designers like Lalique, Eugène Feuillâtre, (who was employed as an enamellist by Lalique and became one of the most accomplished craftsmen of the period in this branch of jewellers' work) and Lucien Gaillard (also an accomplished enamellist who was encouraged to concentrate on jewellery by Lalique himself), who used plique-à-jour widely in their jewellery. Spanning the gap between these styles is the work of André-Fernand Thésmar, who evolved a style based on either Persian or Japanese prototypes (the Japanese-style designs presumably evolved at the time when he was working in cloisonné), and whose pieces (mainly small ornamental bowls) are remarkable for the high quality of the enamel work.

The use of plique-à-jour enamel decoration on jewellery was an easily copied and readily identifiable hallmark of the 'New Art', and as such was widely used by Continental and American commercial jewellers anxious to be identified with the avant-garde. One of the most popular designs using this technique was the dragonfly brooch with a jewelled body and plique-à-jour wings followed closely by butterflies and other insects. These pieces avoid the bizarre appearance of the more experimental women's heads with flowing hair or the 'landscape' pendants produced by Lalique and Fouquet, which are more interesting as pure design but suffer from the defect of not showing to advantage when worn. Much of Lalique's plique-à-jour enamel work, particularly that carried out for his patron, Calouste Gulbenkian, was not seen in terms of wearable jewellery but more as precious miniature sculptures or *objets de virtu*. It is instructive to note how many of the major surviving pieces of Art Nouveau enamel work have been in museums since the year that they were made, and to contrast this fact with the situation in England where the few pieces of Craft Revival jewellery to be found in museums have for the most part been acquired during the last few years. Incidentally, the Victoria and Albert Museum bought French Art Nouveau jewellery at the turn of the century, an act of foresight for which they have reason to be grateful as the prices mount, but the earliest purchase of English Craft Revival work was made in 1921, and the greater part of the collection of this type of jewellery has been assembled since the showing of the Victorian and Edwardian Decorative Art exhibition in 1952. This seems to reflect a basic difference in approach between the Continental designers on the one hand and the craft revivalist on the other. Little English work is decorated with the fragile and impractical plique-à-jour work. The English designers seem to have disdained the technical fireworks of this method (not apparently from any inability to master the admittedly difficult technique but simply from lack of sympathy with the results), preferring to carry out picture enamels *en plein*, or in cloisonné or champlevé work, the subject matter being much influenced by the prophets of the Arts and Crafts Movement, Morris, Ruskin and Burne-Jones.

The widely acknowledged master of the revived 'Limoges' technique of enamelling was Alexander Fisher, though the largest and most ambitious piece carried out in this technique was the 'Herkomer' shield made in 1907 by Hubert von Herkomer. Both Fisher and Herkomer were experimenting with firing techniques designed to produce both a greater range of colours and an effect of pictorial depth which was achieved by firing successive layers of colour on a base of white, sometimes over engraving or repoussé work in a type of

Colour Plate 100. A silver box by Eugène Feuillâtre (1870-1916), the lid decorated with plique-à-jour enamel and set with a large faceted amethyst. (The Hull Grundy Gift to the British Museum.)
Feuillâtre began his career with René Lalique and was responsible for much of the enamel work for that firm before he set up his own studio in 1889.

Colour Plate 101. A brooch and two belt buckles in silver decorated with enamel plaques by Nelson Dawson (1859-1942) and Edith Dawson. (John Jesse.)
Nelson Dawson was a pupil of the enameller Alexander Fisher. In 1901 he founded the Artificers Guild in his Chiswick workshop but in 1903 it passed to Montagu Fordham.

Colour Plate 102.
A hexagonal silver gilt jewel casket by the Handicraft Company, Birmingham 1903, decorated with six enamel plaques and surmounted by a seated female figure also enamelled in the round. The lid bears the following inscription: 'Joy of this world for time will not abide from day to night it changeth as the tide'. The casket was given to Sir David and Lady Stewart for their golden wedding anniversary, 19 July, 1910. (Nicholas Harris.)
The enamel decoration of this box is strongly influenced by the work of Alexander Fisher.

Plate 141. A Freedom Casket by Arthur Gaskin and the staff of the Vittoria Street School for Jewellers and Silversmiths, Birmingham. Made from gold, silver, iron, mother-of-pearl, enamel and niello, it is inscribed thus: 'Presented to the Right Honourable Jesse Collings M.P. with the honorary freedom of the City of Birmingham 18th June 1911. Mercy Charity, Prudence, Hope, Temperance, Justice, Chastity.'
Jesse Collings was a champion of the country poor and well known for the slogan 'three acres and a cow'. The finial of the casket in the form of a milkmaid and a cow refers to this idea.
Gaskin has based his design on a French medieval type and has sought out the various skills of the Vittoria Street School. Bernard Cuzner worked on the repoussé portrait, W.T. Blackband on the wirework and enamel and Charles Thomas did the modelling. The techniques of damascening inlay and niello owe much to ancient jewellery. (By permission of the City of Birmingham.)

refined basse taille, or on burnished foil with inclusions like the paillons which are found in the eighteenth century enamels of Jean Coteau of Geneva. These paillons are also characteristic of the enamelled work by Lalique and Georges Fouquet, the latter being the most sophisticated practitioner of this particularly complex technique.

Fisher was widely influential in England as an enameller through his writing, his classes at the Central School of Arts and Crafts, and his own school, which he set up in his Kensington studio in 1904. One of his best-known pupils was Mrs. Percy Wyndham who became an enthusiastic enamellist under his guidance and carried out a number of pieces in collaboration with him. Mrs. Wyndham's work was included in the 1893 Royal Academy exhibition. Enamelling became an immensely popular aristocratic pursuit, being taken up by Princess Marie Louise, a grand-daughter of Queen Victoria, who was taught by 'a most expert teacher, a certain Mr. William Soper', under whose guidance she successfully copied 'a great many pieces of Fabergé's jewellery', and made a cope clasp which was exhibited in the Royal Academy (see *My Memories of Six Reigns,* by Princess Marie Louise, London 1956). Walberga, Lady Paget also took up enamelling; the following description is taken from a letter written by the painter, Charles Gere, to his sister, from St Fagan's Castle, Cardiff, '. . . in a doorway (was) a strange priestess sort of figure in straight garments and goggles over her eyes, and curious shiny things in her hands. This proved to be Lady Paget in her enamelling costume. She has a little furnace there and does enamel work.' The type of enamelling practised by Fisher and his pupils was particularly suitable as a semi-amateur pursuit as it is relatively easy in the initial stages. Attractive effects can often be obtained almost by accident, and much of the second-rate enamelled work exhibited during the early years of the present century was criticised at the time for relying on just this sort of happy accident rather than on sound technical principles. However, enamelling becomes increasingly difficult as more ambitious effects are attempted. Nelson Dawson learnt enamelling from Fisher and in turn taught his wife Edith this art. A number of Edith Dawson's enamels for jewellery and silverwork remained, unmounted, in the possession of her family after her death, and it is thought that these may have been rejected for one reason or another as being imperfect. Suffice it to say that these tiny jewel-like enamels, many of flowers or insects carried out in minute detail, appear to the uncritical eye of the amateur to be of the highest quality. To maintain the sharpness of detail in the drawing of the original design, and to control the final colours through the successive firings were two of the many problems which beset this type of work, which was also subject to the other hazard inherent in all enamelling techniques, the distortion of the metal backing in the kiln.

Like the Continental plique-à-jour enamel, this Craft Revival style of translucent enamelling was widely copied by commercial firms, who evolved a type of silverwork, often with a spurious 'hand-worked' hammered finish, which was decorated with panels of shaded enamel. Much of Liberty's 'Cymric' silverwork and jewellery is so decorated, and other firms working in a similar style included Charles Horner of Sheffield, William Hutton of Birmingham and Murrle, Bennett & Co., of London. Many of these mass-produced pieces are of very indifferent quality, the metalwork perfunctorily carried out and the enamel carelessly applied, but at its best, when the designs are derived from the work of the few outstanding figures working in this field, such as Archibald Knox (Liberty's) or Kate Harris (William Hutton), it demonstrates the successful application of artistic principles to commercial production in a way which anticipates by at least ten years the efforts of the DIA and the Deutsche Werkbund.

The popularity of enamelled jewellery extended far beyond the confines of either the Arts and Crafts revival or the Art Nouveau movement. It was widely used in commercial production, with the inevitable variation in quality, but at its best it can be as effective as the hand crafted pieces. Shaded or ombré pearly-textured enamel in pastel colours was used to decorate the delicate French and Viennese botanical pieces which were fashionable from about 1890. These are closely related in design and in the unpretentious use of low-value materials to the jewellery of half-pearls and gold which was also popular at this date, and both types were clearly intended for the same middle-class market.

Bibliography

Exhibition catalogues are listed separately at the end of the Bibliography under the town where the exhibition was held.

Anscombe, I. and Gere, C. 1978. *Arts and Crafts in Britain and America*, London.

Arwas, V. 1984. *The Liberty Style*, London.

Barnett, R.D. 1978. 'Lady Layard's Jewellery' in Moorey, P.R.S. and Parr, P.J. (eds), *Archaeology in the Levant: Essays for Kathleen Kenyon*, Warminster, pp.172-9.

Barten, S. 1981. *René Lalique, Schmuck und Objets d'Art*, Munich.

Becker, V. 1980. *Antique and 20th Century Jewellery*, London.

Becker, V. 1985. *Art Nouveau Jewellery*, London.

Blackband, W.T. 1934. 'My rediscovery of the Etruscan Art of Granulation', *The Illustrated London News* (28 April), pp.658-9.

Blackband, W.T., 1950. 'Etruscan Goldwork', *The Jeweller and Metalworker*, London: 15 February, pp.168-70; 15 March, pp.254-6; 13 April, pp.360-4.

Bott, G. 1965. *Kunsthandwerk um 1900*. Kataloge des Hessischen Landesmuseums, Damstadt, no.1.

Bulgari, C.G. 1958. *Argentieri, Gemmari e Orafi d'Italia*, Rome, 1958-74, 4 parts.

Burd, V.A. 1979. *John Ruskin and Rose La Touche*, Oxford.

Burke, Mrs. L. 1856. *The Illustrated Language of Flowers*, London.

Burty, P. 1868. *Les Emaux Cloissonés*, Paris.

Bury, S. 1969. 'Pugin's Marriage Jewellery', *Victoria & Albert Museum Yearbook*, no.1, London, pp.85-96.

Bury, S. 1975. 'Alessandro Castellani and the Revival of Granulation', *Burlington Magazine* (October), pp.664-8.

Bury, S. 1976. 'Rossetti and his jewellery', *Burlington Magazine*, Vol. CXVIII, No. 875. (February).

Bury, S. 1980. 'The Renaissance of the 19th century' in *Princely Magnificence, Court Jewels of the Renaissance 1500-1630*, exhibition catalogue, London, Victoria and Albert Museum.

Bury, S. 1982. *Jewellery Gallery Summary Catalogue*, London, Victoria and Albert Museum.

Cannon-Brookes, P. 1973. *Omar Ramsden 1873-1939*, exhibition catalogue, Birmingham, City Museum and Art Gallery.

Cole, M. 1981. *Whitelands College May Queen Festival*, Whitelands College Monographs, London.

Cook, C. 1925. *The Life and Work of Robert Hancock, Supplement*, privately printed.

Crisp Jones, K. (ed.). 1981. *The Silversmiths of Birmingham and their Marks 1750-1980*, London.

Cunynghame, H. 1906. *European Enamels*, London.

Eidelberg, M. 1981. 'Bracquemond, Delâtre and the discovery of Japanese prints', *Burlington Magazine*, vol. CXXXIII (April), London, pp.221-7.

Evans, J. 1970. *A History of Jewellery*, London, 2nd edn.

Falize, L. 1889. 'L'Exposition Universelle de 1889, Orfèvrerie d'Art Bijoux-Joyaux', *Gazette des Beaux-Arts*. October, Paris, pp.433-59.

Falk, F. 1971. *Schmuck aus dem Schmuckmuseum*, Pforzheim.

Flower, M. 1951. *Victorian Jewellery*, London.

Fontenay, E. 1887. *Les Bijoux Anciens et Modernes*, Paris.

Garside, Anne (ed.) 1979. *Jewelry Ancient to Modern*, exhibition catalogue, Baltimore, Walters Art Gallery.

Gere, C. 1972, *Victorian Jewellery Design*, London.

Gere, C. 1975. *European and American Jewellery 1830-1914*. London.

Gere, C. 1980. 'The Whitelands Cross', *British Museum Society Bulletin* (March), London, p.36.

Gere, C. 1981. 'Rings from 1500 to 1900' in A. Ward *et. al. The Ring from Antiquity to the Twentieth Century*, London.

Gere, C. and Munn, G.C. 1983. 'A rediscovered symbol of Romantic love', *Antique Dealer and Collectors' Guide* (May).

Gomes Ferreira, M.T. 1971. 'René Lalique at the Calouste Gulbenkian Museum, Lisbon', *Connoisseur* (August), London, pp.241-9.

Greenaway, K. 1884. *The Language of Flowers*, London.

Hackenbroch, Y. 1986. *Reinhold Vasters, Goldsmith*, Metropolitan Museum Journal, 19/20, New York.

Hawley, H.H. 1979. 'A Falize Locket', *Bulletin of the Cleveland Museum of Art* (September), Cleveland, Ohio.

Hinks, P. 1975. *Nineteenth Century Jewellery*, London.

Hinks, P. 1983. *Twentieth Century British Jewellery*, London.

Hoffman, J. 1903. *Der Moderne Stil*, Stuttgart.

Hughes, G. 1963. *Modern Jewelry*, London.

Hunt, L. 1837. *Love Letters made of Flowers*, London.

Janson, D.J. 1971. *From Slave to Siren, The Victorian Woman and her Jewelry from Neoclassic to Art Nouveau*, exhibition catalogue, Durham, North Carolina, Duke University Museum of Art.

Klaber, P. 1975. 'Charles Horner's Jewellery', *Antique Collector* (June), London, pp.8-11.

Mordaunt Crook, J. 1981. *William Burges and the High Victorian Dream*, London.

Munn, G. 1975. 'The Giuliano Family', *Connoisseur* (November), London, pp.156-65.

Munn, G. 1977. 'Giacinto Melillo, a Pupil of Castellani', *Connoisseur* (September), London, pp.20-2.

Munn, G. 1979. 'Carlo Doria, a Victorian Enigma', *Connoisseur* (September), London, pp.38-41.

Munn, G. 1983. *Castellani, Giuliano and their influence*. London.

Nadelhoffer, H. 1984, *Cartier, Jewellers Extraordinary*, London.

Penicaud, L. 1902. 'L'Email aux Salons de 1902', *La Revue de la Bijouterie*, Paris, pp.174-7.

Purtell, J. 1972. *The Tiffany Touch*, New York.

Rudoe, J. 1980. *Some Archaeological Revival Jewellery in the Hull Grundy Gift*, British Museum Occasional Paper, no. 10, London.

Rudge, J. 'The Layards, Cortelazzo and Castellani', in *Jewellery Studies* vol. 1, 1983-4, pp.59-83.

Ruskin, J. 1903-12. 'Ruskin's May Queens' in *Collected Works*. Library Edition, ed. Cook and Wedderburn, London, vol. XXX, p.336-46.

Sataloff, J. and Richards, A. 1975. *The Pleasure of Jewelry and Gemstones*, London.

Sataloff, J. 1984, *Art Nouveau Jewelry*, Pennsylvania.

Scarisbrick, D. 1979. 'Classic Gems in an English Masterpiece', *Country Life*, CLXV, London, pp.1796-8.

Scarisbrick, D. 1979. In *Treasures from Chatsworth*, exhibition catalogue, London, Royal Academy

Scarisbrick, D. 1982. 'Charles Ricketts and his designs for jewellery', *Apollo*, Vol. CXVI, No. 247 (September).

Scarisbrick, D. 1986. 'The Devonshire Parure', *Archaeologia*, 108, pp.239-54.

Snowman, A.K. 1962. *The Art of Carl Fabergé*, London.

Tait, H. and Gere, C. 1978. *The Jeweller's Art, An Introduction to the Hull Grundy Gift to the British Museum*, London, British Museum.

Tait, H. (ed.) 1984, *The Art of the Jeweller, a Catalogue of the Hull Grundy Gift to the British Museum* (2 vols.), London.

Truman, C. 1979. 'Reinhold Vasters — the last of the Goldsmiths', *Connoisseur* (March), London, pp.154-61.

Vever, H. 1908-12. *La Bijouterie Francaise au XIXe Siecle*, 3 vols, Paris.

Wichmann, S. 1981. *Japonisme, the Japanese influence in Western Art since 1858*, London.

Wilson, Henry. 1902. *Silverwork and Jewellery*, London.

Exhibition Catalogues

Baltimore, Walters Art Gallery, *Jewelry Ancient to Modern*, ed. Anne Garside, 1979.

Cardiff, National Museum of Wales, *The Strange Genius of William Burges Art — Architect 1827-1881* (and London, Victoria and Albert Museum), 1981.

Dayton, Ohio, Art Institute, *E. Colonna* (ed. M. Eidelburg), 1983.

Hamburg, Museum für Kunst und Gewerbe, *Historismus, Hohe Kunst zwischen Biedermeier und Jugendstil in Hamburg*, ed. J. Jedding, 1977.

London, British Museum. *Jewellery through 7000 Years*, ed. Hugh Tait, 1976 (2nd. edn. revised, 1986).

London, Goldsmiths' Hall. *International Exhibition of modern jewellery, 1890-1961*. October-December 1961.

London, Goldsmiths' Hall, *René Lalique*, (ed. V. Becker), 1987.

London, Royal Academy of Arts. *Alfred Gilbert, Sculptor and Goldsmith*, by Richard Dorment, with contributions from Timothy Idwell, Charlotte Gere, Mark Girouard, and Duncan James, 1986.

London, Victoria and Albert Museum. *Liberty's 1875-1975*, 1975.

London, Victoria and Albert Museum, *Princely Magnificence, Court Jewels of the Renaissance 1500-1630*, ed. A Somers Cocks, 1980.

London, Wartski, *Castellani and Giuliano, Revivalist Jewellers of the Nineteenth Century*, 1984.

Munich, Haus der Kunst. *Weltkulturen and Moderne Kunst*, ed. S. Wichmann, 1972.

New York, Cooper Hewitt, Smithsonian Institution, *Art Nouveau Bing, Paris Style 1900*, (ed. Gabriel Weisberg), 1987.

Paris, Musée des Arts Décoratifs, *Les Fouquets, bijoutiers et joailliers à Paris, 1860-1960*, (ed. M.-N. de Gary), 1983.

Index